LINCOLN'S SECRETARY

A Biography of JOHN G. NICOLAY

JOHN G. NICOLAY, PRESIDENT LINCOLN, JOHN HAY

Taken a few days before the Gettysburg Address.

LINCOLN'S SECRETARY

A Biography of
JOHN G. NICOLAY
by
HELEN NICOLAY

GREENWOOD PRESS, PUBLISHERS
WESTPORT, CONNECTICUT

I had the good fortune *to be one of the delegates from Pike Co. to the Bloomington Convention of 1856, and to hear the inspiring address delivered by Abraham Lincoln at its close, which held the audience in such rapt attention that the reporters dropped their pencils and forgot their work. Never did nobler seed fall upon more fruitful soil than his argument and exhortation upon the minds and hearts of his enthusiastic listeners. The remembrance of that interesting occasion calls up very vividly many other momentous and related events it was my privilege to witness during the stirring years that succeeded.*

In the Representatives' Hall at Springfield I heard him deliver that famous address in which he quoted the Scriptural maxim that a house divided against itself cannot stand, and declared his belief that the Union could not permanently endure half slave and half free.

In the Wigwam at Chicago I heard the roll-call and the thunderous applause that decided and greeted his first nomination for President.

On the East Portico of the Capitol at Washington I heard him read his First Inaugural in which he announced the Union to be perpetual.

▼

On the battlefield of Gettysburg I heard him pronounce his immortal Gettysburg Address.

I saw him sign the Joint Resolution of Congress which authorized the XIII Amendment to the Constitution of the United States.

And once more, on the East Portico, I heard from his lips the sublime words of the Second Inaugural.

FOREWORD

In the year 1860, my father, John George Nicolay, German by birth, American by inclination and adoption, and ardently Republican by conviction, was called suddenly from a round of quiet duties into the very center of our nation's political strife. Abraham Lincoln, newly chosen candidate for President of the United States, turned kindly, deep-set eyes upon him and asked him to become his private secretary.

This was the controlling moment of my father's life. It was a summons to instant duty and a call to service that lasted until his hair grew white and the powers of life ran down. The change from the duties of an hour to those of an epoch was effected without taking him a hundred feet from the room where, for the past three years, he had been acting as clerk to the Secretary of State of Illinois.

I have tried, in the following pages, to set down, using wherever possible his own words, the experiences that especially fitted him, despite great handicaps, to become the biographer of Abraham Lincoln.

CONTENTS

PREPARATION

CONTENTS

X

PREPARATION

1

THE IMMIGRANT BOY

ESSINGEN, MY FATHER'S BIRTHPLACE, IS A hamlet too small to be found on even a large map of Bavaria. Not far from the garrison town of Landau in the Rhenish Palatinate, it was, when my father took me to see it in the summer of 1898, a cluster of tiny gray houses and a tangle of cobblestone streets dominated by a large church. A pleasant village, surrounded by green vineyards and fertile fields, and clamped in the grip of ironbound custom, it was manifestly not a place where a poor man might hope to grow rich or to help his children very far along in the world.

My father's father, John Jacob Nicolai, had, so far as I know, spent his whole life in Essingen up to 1837, when, himself in middle-age, he moved his family to America. He had owned only one *morgenstunde* of land—a tract no larger than could be cultivated in a single morning hour. This was not enough to keep a family of five children in comfort, and he and his eldest sons augmented the family income by practicing the cooper's trade, making the great casks in which the wine of the region was stored.

Frederick Lewis was the eldest son; the second, named for his father, was John Jacob. Next came Catherine, the only daughter, then John, then John George, the youngest, a frail child from the time of his birth. The family name, Nicolai, is common throughout the Continent. What induced my father's branch of the family to substitute a "y" for the final "i" after coming to America, I do not know. I can only guess that they thought the "y" would make it easier for their Midwestern neighbors to approximate the correct pronunciation.

My grandfather seems to have been by nature a gardener, one of those men for whom plants grow gladly, a gift he passed on to my father. My grandmother, Helena Müller, is described as a slight, dark-haired woman with regular features and very penetrating dark eyes. She reverenced religion and loved poetry and music.

The decision to cross the Atlantic was made primarily, but not solely, in the hope of bettering the family fortunes. If we may trust a family legend, they were also in search of liberty. An edict had gone forth decreeing that everyone in Essingen must stand at salute, with head uncovered, no matter what the weather might be, when a member of the reigning house rode by. Frederick Lewis endured this just once, in the pouring rain, then took ship for the New World. The next year, 1837, a lean time when much of Europe went hungry, the rest of the family followed him.

Having disposed of their house and plot of land, they piled such possessions as they could take with them on one of the huge two-wheeled carts of the country and creaked through the gate, whose great stone posts had up to that time marked the limits of John George's known world. Then they set off down the long, dusty road to Le Havre and took passage on a sailing ship bound for New Orleans.

The stay in New Orleans was short, yet long enough to afford my father, who then was five, a poignant sensation. He found himself the center of a group of chattering urchins, of whose talk he could not understand a syllable. He never forgot his feelings at the moment our American speech burst upon his consciousness. The language disability did not last long, however, for my father had an uncommonly keen ear for differences of sound and was always quick at languages.

The family traveled up the Mississippi and Ohio rivers to Cincinnati, already a center for German immigrants. There my grandfather bought a lot and built a little house and within a week of their arrival had young John George enrolled in a school where German and English were taught side by side. In addition to instruction in reading, writing, spelling, and arithmetic, there was a class in American history.

When my grandmother died, and was buried in a little cemetery on a slight rise to the northwest of the town, my grandfather became restless and moved his family successively into Indiana, Missouri, and Illinois. All the regular schooling that came to John George he received in Cincinnati and during their subsequent migration. It amounted in time to about as much as Abraham Lincoln had, but fortunately the schools were somewhat better.

The family trek ended in the Illinois woods, where conditions were very like those that Lincoln experienced in his youth. My father once told a group of young people that his own schooling terminated with three months in "a typical log school house where slates, pencils, pens, paper, and ink were unknown." His schoolmates came from log cabins where frequently a quilt was hung up in place of a door, and where the one small window was glazed with oiled paper.

The mechanical skill with which John Jacob and his sons had carried on the cooper's craft in Essingen did them good service in Illinois. They found a dilapidated gristmill in the southern part of Pike County, rented it, repaired it, and set themselves to grinding the corn and wheat grown by their neighbors into meal and flour. John George, with his keen mind, greater mastery of the new language than his elders', and clear handwriting, was the firm's scribe and interpreter.

The youngest of his family, John George found little companionship at home, and, being physically frail and of different mental caliber from the other lads at the log schoolhouse, he had few friends of his own age. But he was quite happy. With the green woods for a playground, he made friends with the birds and animals there. His quiet movements did not frighten them, and, little by little, they let him in on the intimate secrets of the woodlands. Never a scientific observer, he had throughout his life a sympathetic eye for bird and beast and plant.

In addition to the woods and the gristmill, my father had at that time one other great resource—a book full of wonderful stories that he never tired of reading. This was the family Bible, printed in crabbed German characters, one of the two or three volumes that had made the 4000-mile journey from Essingen. "There is much plausibility," my father once wrote, "in the oft-repeated saying that only three books are necessary to constitute a library —Shakespeare, Blackstone, and the Bible."

Under this definition [he continued] if I did not have a library in my boyhood, I at least had the use of a third of one.... So, when I first felt the impulse to read, this family Bible was my only resource. Like any other healthy child, I did not search it for doctrines of theology, precepts of moral philosophy, or beauties of poetry, but for its stirring, active, realistic pictures of life—its history, which to me had all the charms of romance.

Of its two principal divisions my interest centered wholly

in the Old Testament, and in the Old Testament my favorite field was in what has disappeared from recent editions, the Apocrypha. The Books of the Kings with their record of war, siege, battle, conquest, and captivity, I read over and over with unceasing eagerness; and the Books of the Maccabees were as alluring as later the chronicles of chivalry. Equally was I absorbed in what may be called the romantic episodes: the story of Samson, of David and Goliath, of Boaz and Ruth, and particularly the story, as entertaining as a novelette, related in the Book of Esther.

This period of Bible reading for relaxation lasted about three years. Afterward, among the few books which fell into my hands, were two of Shakespeare's plays, each bound in a single small volume—the first, the *Comedy of Errors*, the second, the tragedy of *Macbeth*. I must confess that I liked the Dromios better than the ghosts and witches. In both dramas I was deeply absorbed in the movement, but still too young to appreciate their literary beauty and power.

Undoubtedly, this early Bible reading "for relaxation" sank deeply, if unconsciously, into his young mind. Its influence may be noted time and again in his style of historical narrative.

His father died when John George was fourteen, and he was put entirely upon his own resources. Perhaps he had sought employment even earlier, for the first scrap of his handwriting that I possess is dated two months before his father's death and reads:

Due Mr Patterson Rader three gallons of rectified Whiskey at this distillery.

John G. Nicolay

He became a clerk in Aaron Reno's store at White Hall, a little town across the river from his former home. His princely salary was four dollars a month, for which he clerked, swept out the store, and kept the books in single entry. Living was not expensive, but at the end of his first year he had managed to save only two silver dollars.

The town's name, White Hall, was not an echo from far-off England, but commemorated the hero of the local version of the Pocahontas legend, Wyatt Hall. Small though the town was, it had some slight literary pretension, since Julia A. Fletcher Carney, author of the poem "Little Drops of Water," was wife of the pastor of its Baptist church. The church was important in my father's life, because it had a Sunday school, and the Sunday school had a library presided over by Mr. Joel Pennington, who was favorably impressed by the diligence of Mr. Reno's clerk in seeking out the best in literature.

We have the testimony of Mr. Reno's daughter that young Nicolay was a good clerk. But when John George was about sixteen, Mr. Reno felt obliged to give his place to a nephew, lately orphaned. I fancy my father was not sorry to leave. His duties did not particularly interest him, and some of them were too heavy for his strength. No boy of spirit likes to admit that he is less strong than his fellows, but both in the store and in the rude athletics of the village his delicate body was a serious handicap. For a time, therefore, he was glad to accept the hospitality of one of his older brothers, who gave him a home until he could find another situation.

2

EDITOR

FROM TIME TO TIME A FAR-FETCHED story appears in Illinois telling how my father got into newspaper work. The editor of a county paper, the story goes, was riding one day along a lonely country road, when he saw a slender lad being cruelly beaten by his stepmother. He rescued the boy, took him into his printing office, and thereby set John G. Nicolay on the road to success. It makes a fine tale, but, since he never had a stepmother, it can hardly be true.

The real story of how my father entered the office of the *Free Press*, the Whig paper published in Pittsfield, Illinois, centers on an advertisement which appeared in that paper on May 11, 1848:

WANTED

An intelligent boy, from 14 to 17 years of age, who can read and write, to learn the Printing Business.

Mr. Pennington and his family had, meanwhile, moved across the Illinois River from Reno to Pittsfield, seat of the newly created county of Pike. One of the Pennington boys read the advertisement, thought of John George, and sent it to him with the message that here was a job after his own heart. John George lost no time in applying. He trudged the long miles to Pittsfield, spent the night on some sacks of wool in the town's "Carding Machine," and was put to work in the printing office the next morning. As he walked up the street that first day in his funny snuff-colored suit, carrying his worldly possessions in a very small bundle, "Squire" Bates's dark-eyed daughter, who later became his wife, saw John George and smiled at him. The attraction was mutual and soon each became an important factor in the other's life. Slender, and scarcely more than five feet tall, Therena Bates was quiet and retiring, but there was spirit in every inch of her small frame. Modestly discounting her good looks, she considered her coal-black hair, straight and long and very abundant, to be her only claim to beauty—a viewpoint amply contradicted by photographs, which show an oval face and expressive, dark eyes.

So it was that my father's real work, his real education, and his real romance all began for him on a May afternoon when he was sixteen. It is an odd coincidence, also, that the name of Abraham Lincoln should have appeared in the same issue of the *Free Press* that set my father on the road which brought the two men together. Not nearly so prominent as the advertisement for a "boy," it was merely an obscure paragraph stating that Stephen T. Logan was to be the candidate of the Whig party to succeed Abraham Lincoln in the United States Congress.

My father's first position on the *Free Press* was nominally that of "printer's devil," which is another name for errand boy and utility man. Actually, a composing stick was thrust at once into his hand, and he found himself setting type. This was long before the days of linotype, and even in a small country weekly like the *Free Press* the total number of characters that had to be set by hand was considerable.

The town of Pittsfield was a New England community set down on the Illinois prairie. Its inhabitants had migrated in a body from Massachusetts some years before, bringing the name of their old home with them. A sprinkling of western and southwestern characters added picturesqueness, but the prevailing tone was of frugal, sterling New England. Mr. Carter, pastor of the Congregational church, was a leading influence. Absolutely lacking in humor, he had rigidly orthodox views, a compelling sense of duty, and most enduring lung power. As often as natural gaiety led the young people into indiscretions of card-playing and dancing, he felt called upon to preach against worldliness, yet his inconvenient sense of justice forced him to admit that even dancing could not be wrong in itself. "But the ten-den-cy is bad!" he declared. After one of his disquieting sermons all the girls would be in tears and the boys muttering mutiny. Everybody respected him but few loved him.

Soon after my father's arrival, a school for singing was started and John George promptly joined it. It had only a short life, its end being, no doubt, hastened by Brother Carter's objection to the "ten-den-cy" of all secular tunes. The school lasted long enough, however, for my father to learn the principles of musical notation, and, when it disbanded, he carried off one of the hymnbooks and taught himself to read music with such effect that he was engaged as organist of Mr. Carter's church at a salary of five dollars a year. The mere money value of this was greatly enhanced by the privilege of practicing whenever he wanted to on the wheezy little music box, and by the opportunity of looking down from the organ loft, on Sunday mornings, on an olive cheek and a knot of blue-black hair.

The young printer's life was at first far from luxurious. He and another *Free Press* employee, David McWilliams, rented a little half-story room over the printing office. They bought bread from Joseph Heck, the baker, and prevailed upon his wife to parch their coffee for them.

Soon John George had the good fortune to be taken into the household of Mr. Z. N. Garbutt, editor and part owner of the paper, where he was mothered by Mrs. Garbutt, a kindly, upright woman who lived with the fear of God and love for humanity in her heart. Long after my father left Pittsfield, to return only for brief visits, he came to her house as if to his own home. He expressed his affection for her and his gratitude in a warm tribute written after her death.

Another stimulating and important influence in his life was an erratic Irish schoolmaster, John Thomson, a graduate and tutor of Dublin University, who had drifted to this far-away spot and stayed to fit young men for college. It was through him that my father met John Hay, an Indiana youth who came to Pittsfield to live with his uncle, Milton Hay, while being prepared to enter Brown University. John Hay and my father quickly formed a friendship which was to deepen with the years and last as long as life itself. For a time, my father dreamed of going to college with this brilliant young friend, but neither his strength nor his purse permitted him to do so. John went East alone, and John George had to be content with a little coaching from John Thomson in mathematics and composition.

The *Free Press* was a good paper, and it grew steadily better during the years my father was connected with it. It had appeared regularly every Thursday morning since the first issue, a record to be proud of. Its four pages set in fine type measured 22 by 32 inches, a size known to the

THE OLD *FREE PRESS* OFFICE

trade as Imperial. The first page was given over to articles of general interest, the second to editorials and news items, which merged gradually into the advertisements and "fillers" and personals that crowded the remaining space. The few cuts used were unforgettable. Foreign news, brought by sailing ship to New York, was flashed from New York to St. Louis by that wonder-working new invention, the telegraph, and from there filtered by slower means throughout the Middle West.

In politics, the *Free Press* was ardently Whig. "Who could not be Whig?" Mr. Garbutt asked with enthusiasm, asserting that the name, originating in Cromwell's time in England, had been made up from the initial letters of the Royalist motto, "We hope in God."

My father remained with the *Free Press* for eight years, filling practically every position in turn. By 1853 he had become a partner. The next year he was sole proprietor. A small, highly glazed visiting card, proclaiming him "Editor, Pike County *Free Press*, Pittsfield, Illinois," has survived to this day the perils of fire and flood and battle.

In a short paper, "Franklin the Printer," which my father read many years later before the Literary Society in Washington, he called the printing office "a poor man's college." He believed that the manual dexterity developed by Benjamin Franklin in so many fields had its origin in the printing office, where, in those early days, makeshifts in type founding and engraving had often to be called into play. Moreover, it was his opinion that Franklin's "liberal and tolerant philosophy dated back to the time when, slowly setting the type for his own pamphlet on the doctrine of Fate, his active thought, playing lightning-like around, over, and under his own arguments . . . showed him that he could construct as good or even a better argument on the other side." The same school provided exactly the same lessons for my father. In an autobiographical fragment, he says:

I am satisfied that in my own case, next to typesetting, I derived more benefit from the effort to write (which in a newspaper office becomes irresistible) than from reading even the best books. Reading another's thought may bring delight or instruction, but formulating one's own, and sending it forth to adventure or do battle in the great world of literature, compels the acquisition of skill, cultivates the habit of prudence, stimulates courage, and imparts strength. To learn to write is like learning to swim; everyone must teach himself. And, as in swimming, perhaps the most important thing to learn is when to stop.

More than once I heard my father regret the lack of those "intellectual tools" that others had acquired at school and at college. I doubt if the readers of his clear prose ever felt this lack in him. His early Bible-reading had colored his style. The woods taught him observation. The printing press trained him, not only in analysis, but in such homely details as spelling and punctuation. I am persuaded that the words he once wrote about Abraham Lincoln's schooling and education apply equally, to his own: that while lazy or indifferent boys often forgot what they learned at one time before they had opportunity at another, "to a boy of his exceptional character these widely separated fragments of instruction were precious steps to self-help, of which he made unremitting use."

Once during the *Free Press* period John George undertook a long journey—a trip to Washington, D.C., to apply for a patent. Machinery had interested him ever since the gristmill days on Bee Creek, and the old "Washington" Press used by the paper had at first seemed very wonderful. But, with time, its slowness irritated him, and

he began to wonder how it could be improved. He worked
on the problem four years, evolving, little by little, a plan,
and then a model, built out of such materials as were at
hand—which were not the materials recommended by ex-
perts. One important part, which should have been made
of metal, was whittled from a pine board. But the crude
model worked.

It seemed worth while to pursue the matter. There was
something heady and adventurous in the idea of owning
a patent; yet his dream did not soar too high. He had no
visions of revolutionizing the printing trade, or of amassing sudden wealth. But he did know that the population
was increasing, and that every small town had its local
paper on whose presses job work was done. For such work,
he believed his invention would be especially useful. Already, with his part-pine model, he had accomplished twice
as much as he could do without it. He believed that, with
a good machine and the help of two men, eight times the
ordinary amount might be done.

In that year of 1852, it took my father ten days to
cover the distance between central Illinois and Washington. Even so, he felt he was traveling at astonishing speed.
"Verily, the old fable of the Seven League Boots has in
our day become a reality!" he wrote. He went first to St.
Louis, which he described as a "modern Babel." He took
refuge on the Cincinnati boat. "For traveling with ease,
comfort and pleasure, nothing can be compared to a good
steamboat," he asserted with conviction. There was only
one drawback. Steamboat travel, especially on our western
rivers, was about as safe as living over a volcano. Shortly
before John George started on his journey, the *Free
Press* published a list of fifty-eight steamboat accidents
that had occurred during the past twelvemonth, resulting
in the death of more than three hundred persons.

In due time the young traveler reached Cincinnati and changed to the boat that was to take him to Pittsburgh. The captain of this craft had made a record coming down the river, but he assured his passengers that on the trip back he was "not trying for speed." Yet it was on his boat that the accident occurred. My father awoke about three in the morning and noticed that the engines seemed to be working under more than ordinary pressure. He was drifting off to sleep again when a great crash, followed by the hiss of escaping steam, startled him into full wakefulness. When, after an eternity, he and other passengers were allowed below, they found the lower deck strewn with pieces of steel and learned that a large connecting rod had gradually loosened and crashed through a cylinder, breaking a pipe that led to the boilers. One man lay unconscious, obviously dying; another, still conscious, had been literally cooked by the escaping steam. After a day's delay, two tugs were sent to the rescue, and, moving three abreast, the injured steamer in the middle, they went on to Pittsburgh. By train, by stagecoach, and by train again, my father then crossed the Alleghenies and in time arrived in Washington.

Like many another traveler he found the city at first disappointing, then fascinating. He wrote lyrical letters about the "silvery fountains" and the "walks smooth as a ballroom floor" in the park surrounding the Capitol, "probably the most beautiful park in the United States." He was impressed by the Capitol's "Rotundo," and also by the freedom with which casual visitors were allowed to roam about the Navy Yard. He found almost the same freedom at the White House. President Fillmore received visitors every Tuesday, and the boy from Illinois shook hands with him a little shyly. By no possible stretch of the imagination could he foresee that in less than a decade he would be writing back to the girl in Illinois that he and John Hay were occupying "a nice large bedroom" and "pleasant offices" in that very mansion—but that the White House furniture was distinctly shabby.

At the moment, his hopes and expectations centered in the Patent Office, which occupied a suite of rooms in the unfinished Department of the Interior. Already, more than 8,000 inventions had been patented; whether, among these dusty models, displayed in glass cases, my father came upon a device for lifting vessels over shoals in western rivers, patented some two years earlier by Congressman A. Lincoln of Illinois, we do not know.

His own patent, No. 9805, is dated November 5, 1852. Evidently he did not stay in Washington until it was actually issued, for on August 18th the *National Intelligencer* added to a kindly notice of the rotary printing press a personal paragraph about its inventor, the first time his name appeared under a Washington date line. He was "quite a youth," a practical printer who, "in his remote residence, had never seen a machine press. We saw him often here, during the time his application was before the Patent Office, and were as much impressed by his modesty and intelligence as with the ingenuity of his invention."

It may be said that patenting inventions was the principal luxury my father allowed himself throughout his life. He obtained five patents: The rotary press in 1852; a shot pouch in 1864; an ingenious window catch in 1870; an exercising machine in 1878; and, in 1891, a folding campstool with a comfortable back, for which his daughter, using it on sketching expeditions, blessed him many times. Besides these patents, a letter preserved among his early correspondence shows that "Harper's"—probably *Harper's Weekly*,—wrote, inquiring about a machine he had contrived for folding paper, saying that the firm had nothing of the kind and might like such help if it was efficient and "not too expensive."

My father derived great pleasure and satisfaction from working on these devices, not one of which ever proved financially profitable. For a short time, he believed this earliest invention of his might mark the beginning of a new career. Changes had come about in the *Free Press* office. Mr. Garbutt had retired because of ill health and died soon after. The paper was being edited by his associate, J. M. Parkes, who asked my father to become his associate, and relations within the *Free Press* office were entirely friendly when, in April 1854, Mr. Parkes announced that John G. Nicolay had severed his connection with the paper in order to devote his full time to furthering his invention. He added his blessing in a concluding line, "We commend both press and inventor." Immediately under this appeared my father's "card," assuring readers that his withdrawal had not been caused by friction or disagreement with Mr. Parkes.

Within six months he was back in the *Free Press* office. He had made arrangements to become the paper's owner and editor, a position he held until the end of Frémont's campaign for president in the autumn of 1856, when my father sold the paper to I. W. and F. M. Cunningham.

Mr. Garbutt, in his editorial days, had given generous space to religious articles, poetry, and fiction. Mr. Parkes's taste ran to long extracts from the English quarterlies. In my father's day, owing partly to natural bias, partly to the country's growing absorption in the slavery issue, more attention was given to national and local politics—sometimes at the cost of delaying news from abroad. When Nicholas I, Czar of Russia, died in 1855, the *Free Press* delayed the announcement one week "for lack of space."

The question of whether or not slavery should be permitted in states yet to be carved out of United States territory had been a matter of growing concern for years. When, in 1854, the Missouri Compromise, which assured freedom to all states lying north of 36° 30′, with the single exception of Missouri, was repealed, and another law was substituted which opened a much larger extent of territory to the possibility of slavery, excitement became intense. The long state of Illinois, extending from Kentucky to the Wisconsin border, had room in it for many opinions on slavery and, as it happened, an unusually able group of political leaders eager to discuss the issue. When they toured the state in a regular tournament of oratory, an important county seat like Pittsfield was not to be passed by. Their speeches were all reported in the *Free Press*, and they were conscientiously applauded or denounced by its new editor, still in his early twenties, who already had more influence in Pittsfield than many men twice his age.

This was the time when Mr. Lincoln, "roused as he had never been roused before," returned to politics, after having for some years taken little apparent interest in national questions. My father used to say that his first sight of the future president was at a political meeting in Pittsfield to which both Lincoln and Trumbull came, neither knowing that the other was expected. Their pleased astonishment and the warmth of their greeting, which was almost an embrace, convinced my father, who had long admired Lincoln as a political leader, that he was also a very human and lovable sort of man. Jon Shastid, Pittsfield's advocate of simple spelling, claimed that it was he who set Nicolay on the road to fame at this time, because, when he met Mr. Lincoln on the street, and the latter asked to be directed to "an honest printer," he took him straight to the *Free Press* office.

My father became more and more interested. He attended every free-soil meeting in the county and addressed some of them himself "at early candle-light," the favorite hour for such gatherings. In 1856, he joined the other anti-Nebraska editors of the state in their call for the convention at Bloomington, at which the Republican party of Illinois formally came into being. He liked to recall the stirring scenes of that convention, where Lincoln made the famous address known to history as his "Lost Speech." The session had been long, and the delegates were tired, but nobody thought of leaving the hall until Lincoln should be heard. He, too, seemed tired when he rose. He began to speak, slowly at first, almost hesitatingly, in his high-pitched tenor voice, but weariness slipped from him like a garment. His voice came under perfect control, and the audience sat spellbound as, towering to his full height, head high and shoulders well back, he swept on to his peroration, calling on all freedom-loving Americans to

> Come as the winds come when forests are rended,
> Come as the waves come when navies are stranded,

and to help the new party put down the great wrong of slavery.

About three weeks later, when the first national convention of the Republican party met to nominate John C. Frémont as its candidate for president, the *Free Press*, forsaking its old Whig traditions, printed the names of the Republican candidates, Frémont and Dayton, on the banner at the head of its editorial column and carried them there throughout the campaign.

SERVICE

3

WIDER HORIZONS

HIS EIGHT YEARS ON THE *FREE PRESS* were good and fruitful years for my father. He had grown from a boy to a man. He had taken part in a great movement and met the greatest man of his time. For him, personally, they were happy years. He was fortunate in love and had a circle of congenial friends and the ever-growing respect of the community. Even his father-in-law-to-be, who differed radically from him in politics, did not think of disputing the belief of the young people that theirs was a match made in Heaven. Toward the end of his life, looking back over his varied career, my father said that the editor of a "live" county newspaper had the most enviable and independent lot in America.

When he finally gave up the *Free Press*, it was not because he was tired of it or felt he had been unsuccessful, but because he questioned whether it could be as helpful to him in the future. He was planning for marriage, and requests for aid came to him from his brothers, who had families and a large share of debts and misfortunes—appeals to which he responded generously all his life.

Besides, he felt the urge to fit himself to take a still larger part in the coming political battle. The campaign

of 1856 had brought him into close touch with prominent
Illinois leaders. He noticed that most of these men, no
matter what their political views, or what positions they
held at the moment, had been trained as lawyers. Des-
perately he had wished to go to college with John Hay,
but that had been impossible, because of lack of funds.
But a lawyer's training did not seem to depend so much
on money as upon the possession of a few books and a great
deal of dogged perseverance. The idea grew upon him.
He confided his ambition to Mr. Gilmer, a respected member of the Pittsfield bar, who told him he was welcome to
use the books in his office. But the permission was given
jestingly, and my father, sensitive at being laughed at,
resolved never to touch one of them. He then asked the
advice of Mr. Grimshaw, another lawyer friend, casually,
in the course of a long ride. Mr. Grimshaw's answer was
that there were "too many lawyers already!" He thought
my father, who had such a strong mechanical bent and
already had one patent to his credit, would do better to
turn his attention to machinery, for which Mr. Grimshaw
saw an immense development in the near future.

This was excellent advice, but to follow it would require
capital and special training quite beyond my father's
reach. Mr. Grimshaw's partner, a retired Campbellite
preacher, was equally discouraging. "Sublety is what a
lawyer needs, George, sublety," he assured him, the inference being that sublety was a quality in which John
George was woefully lacking. But the young man felt it
could be acquired more easily than the wherewithal necessary to set him up as an inventor. His experience with the
rotary printing press had taught him that, even after an
invention is made and patented, many hurdles stand in the
way of success.

So he watched for a chance to sell the *Free Press* and

embark on the new venture without help from anybody. The chance came at the end of the campaign of 1856, when he turned the paper over to its new owners and went to St. Louis, choosing a roundabout route by way of Springfield, in order to spend a night and half a day with Mr. O. M. Hatch, Secretary of State for Illinois, who was an old friend and a connection by marriage of my mother's family. Doubtless his own plans, as well as the affairs of the nation were thoroughly reviewed that night; but if Mr. Hatch cherished the notion of asking the young man to enter his office, he kept his own counsel. Going on to St. Louis, my father established himself in modest lodgings and hunted up a former Pittsfield acquaintance, who was then setting type for a tiny agricultural journal. The editor was a lawyer, who introduced my father to his partner, Norman B. Colman, later Commissioner of Agriculture in Washington. Mr. Colman invited him to use his books, and here he remained until recalled to Springfield a few weeks later by Mr. Hatch's offer of a clerkship in his office. Even then he did not drop entirely out of newspaper work, but acted as correspondent, first in St. Louis and later in Springfield, for the *Missouri Democrat*, the *Illinois Journal*, and the *Chicago Tribune*, signing his articles "Pike" or "Illinois" or "Sangamon." He wrote letters also for the Pittsfield paper, frankly partisan in tone.

Even as early as 1837, when Abraham Lincoln became a resident of Springfield, he noted "a good deal of flourishishing around in carriages" in the new state capital. It had kept this characteristic. Its people were wide-awake and bent on enjoying life to the full. So, in addition to other advantages, this move to the capital of Illinois brought my father important opportunities for social and intellectual development. Several of the young people who were musical made the newcomer especially welcome, for he had a sweet, true, though not strong, tenor voice and had learned to play the flute.

The wealthiest man in Springfield was Nicholas Ridgely, the banker, who had many attractive daughters. Because of his given name and his rather dictatorial manner, the young people nicknamed him the "Emperor." His large house, elegantly furnished in the fashionable Victorian style, was the focal point for the younger set. There music and gaiety reigned, and foreign languages were the fashion. Here my father had an opportunity to brush up on the German he had never forgotten, to enter upon the study of French, and to pick up the few words of Italian that are learned almost of necessity where music is involved. Educationally, therefore, Springfield proved an excellent place in which to build upon foundations already laid by the Cincinnati schoolmaster and the tutor from Dublin.

My father's time was fully occupied, for, in addition to his duties in Mr. Hatch's office and his newspaper letters, he continued his law studies and was admitted to the Illinois bar in January 1859. Also, he became a 2nd lieutenant in a Zouave organization known as the Springfield Grays. He was offered a share in a daily newspaper about to be launched in Springfield, but this he did not accept, in spite of the very flattering light in which it was set before him.

By July 4, 1859 he had won sufficient recognition to be given a place on the program of the city's official celebration. On this occasion he made a speech in German, ending with a German poem of his own composition, which lauded freedom and brotherhood, and emphasized the obligation of loyalty to their new fatherland on the part of Americans of German blood. Most important of all, so far as his own future was concerned, was his work in Mr. Hatch's office, which brought him into daily contact with the men best known among Illinois Republicans. About this, he once wrote:

From the spring of 1857 to 1860 I was Clerk in the office of Hon. O. M. Hatch, Secretary of State of Illinois, who in that capacity occupied a large and well-appointed room in the old Statehouse in Springfield. The State Library, of which the Secretary had charge, was in an adjoining room, also large and commodious, which by common usage was used by all the political parties when assembled at State conventions or during sessions of the legislature, as a political caucus room, the entry being through the Secretary's main office.

This office ... was therefore in effect the state political headquarters and a common rendezvous for prominent Illinois politicians.... Mr Lincoln was of course a frequent visitor, and when he came was always the center of an animated and interested group. It was there, during the years mentioned, that I made his acquaintance. All the election records were kept by the Secretary of State, and I, as Mr Hatch's principal clerk, had frequent occasion to show Mr Lincoln, who was an assiduous student of election tables, the latest returns, or the completed record books.

Politically, he had long been under Mr. Lincoln's spell, but he came to know him personally only in Mr. Hatch's office. Mr. Lincoln, on his part, relied on the quiet efficient young man with his slow smile and often asked his help in finding the election figures, of which he made constant use.

The Republican leaders who met before Mr. Hatch's blazing hickory fire had much to talk about. In the summer of 1858 came the contest between Abraham Lincoln and Stephen A. Douglas for a seat in the United States

Senate. When Mr. Lincoln told his friends that he meant
to challenge his opponent to joint debate, they heartily
approved; but when he showed them the list of questions
he meant to ask, they remonstrated, "If you do that you
can never be Senator!" It was then that he answered:
"Gentlemen, I am killing larger game. If Douglas answers, he can never be President, and the battle of 1860
is worth a hundred of this." Lincoln lost the senatorship,
as they had predicted, but only to become himself President of the United States.

How little he expected such an outcome was revealed in
letters he wrote his friends. To Dr. A. G. Henry he wrote:
"In that day I shall fight in the ranks, but I shall be in
no one's way for any of the places"; and to another friend:
"I am glad I made the late race. It gave me a hearing
on the great and durable question of the age ... and
though I now sink out of view and shall be forgotten, I
believe I have made some marks which will tell for the
cause of civil liberty long after I am gone."

Excitement mounted with the passing months. The
clerk in Mr. Hatch's office had the satisfaction of believing he played a small part in making Mr. Lincoln's views
better known. During the Lincoln-Douglas campaign he
prepared a pamphlet entitled *The Political Record of
Stephen A. Douglas,* which was of more than passing interest, for next year he was asked to send two copies on
to Washington, where, his correspondent told him, it
would probably be used in a forthcoming Senate debate.
Later, when the friends who had advised against the
course Mr. Lincoln took, decided to print and to circulate
the *Lincoln-Douglas Debates* as a campaign document, it
was my father they sent to Ohio to make arrangements
with the publishing firm of Follett Foster & Co. He reported from Columbus that he had been "kindly received,"

that everybody "spoke highly" of Mr. Lincoln, some indeed being "very ardent" in their expressions.

I never heard my father make the claim that he suggested nominating Lincoln for president, but certain warm friends of his in Pittsfield claimed that he did so, on the basis of a widely copied editorial that first appeared on February 9, 1860, in the *Pike County Journal*, Pittsfield's successor to the *Free Press*. Before that time Mr. Lincoln had frequently been mentioned as a possible candidate for vice president. Indeed, as early as mid-April 1859 an enthusiastic editor in Rock Island, Illinois, asked permission to suggest him for the higher office. Mr. Lincoln refused, with the characteristic answer that the idea was flattering, but that he did not think himself fit for the presidency.

His friends thought differently. According to the Pittsfield story, my father, who returned to his old home for brief visits as often as possible, stopped one day at the *Journal* office for a talk with its editor, Daniel B. Bush. Mr. Bush was so impressed by what he told him, that he thrust a pencil into his visitor's hand and bade him write out what he had just said. The result was the following editorial:

FOR PRESIDENT HON. ABRAHAM LINCOLN—Subject to the decision of the National Republican Convention.

We are very confident that we express the almost unanimous sentiment of the Republicans of Pike County in the announcement we make at the head of this article—a sentiment founded not only on the personal attachment to and admiration for Mr Lincoln, but prompted also by a careful estimate of his qualifications both as to his fitness and availability to be chosen as the candidate in the coming campaign.

It is conceded that the states of Pennsylvania, New Jersey, Indiana and Illinois will be the decisive battleground in the

approaching contest, and of them Pennsylvania and Illinois
are most hopeful of Republican success. While Mr Lincoln
would be as acceptable to the Republican voters of Pennsylvania as any man whose name has yet been mentioned, we
know he is beyond comparison the strongest man for the
state of Illinois. We do not state this on mere speculation.
The fact is susceptible of demonstration by figures. Give us
Lincoln as the candidate and we can promise the electoral
vote of Illinois for the Republicans as a sure result. It is due
to the growing interest and power of the West that the next
Republican convention shall give her a candidate on the
Republican ticket, and to no man in the West does the honor
more preeminently belong than to Lincoln. From the introduction of the Nebraska bill to the present time he has
fought the extension of slavery as the champion chosen and
pitted against the apostle of popular sovereignty, and has
wrested triumph after triumph from the Little Giant for
Republicanism in the West.

We will have yet one more battle with the delusion of
Douglasism in the state of Illinois, and with no man's
weapons can we arm ourselves as securely or fight as successfully as with the arguments offensive and defensive with
which Abe Lincoln has furnished us. Whatever may be the
choice of the politicians, the people of Illinois are undoubtedly for Lincoln. They know him honest and capable, a
man of simple habits and plain manners, but possessing a
true heart and one of the noblest intellects in the land. He
maintains the faith of the fathers of the Republic, he believes
in the Declaration of Independence, he yields obedience to
the Constitution and laws of his country. He has the radical-
ism of Jefferson and of Clay, and the conservatism of Washington and Jackson. In his hands the Union would be safe.

I never heard my father tell the story himself; but it
is not impossible, and I like to believe it is true.

A speech by Mr. Lincoln became a matter of importance

throughout the state. By the beginning of 1860 the slavery issue had completely disrupted the old political parties. Before the end of June there were four presidential candidates in the field. Remnants of the old Whig party nominated John Bell of Tennessee. The Democrats split into two factions. Those who held that slavery was right and ought to be extended, nominated John C. Breckenridge of Kentucky. Democrats who refused to consider slavery a moral issue, but held that the choice between freedom and slavery should be made by the voters of each state at the time it entered the Union, chose as their standard-bearer Stephen A. Douglas. The Republican party was the last to hold its national convention. It met in Chicago on May 16th, in a huge temporary building called the Wigwam. Mr. Lincoln was not present, feeling, he humorously told his friend Leonard Swett, "rather too much of a candidate to go, though not quite enough of one to stay at home."

Young Nicolay was there as correspondent for the *Missouri Democrat*. The letters he sent to his paper told of throngs streaming through Chicago streets toward the flag-decked building, and of secret, eager consultations held in hotel bedrooms by friends of the various candidates. Within the packed auditorium, crowds milled about on the floor, while in the galleries were many women, a novel spectacle at a political convention in 1860. Waves of sound rose and fell as well-known delegates were recognized, filing in to take their places. "That's Cassius M. Clay!" "There's Horace Greeley!" Those and other names could be heard amid the applause and hand-clapping that greeted the appearance of each favorite.

On the third day, after all preliminaries had been disposed of and balloting was about to begin, delegates and spectators alike seemed to feel that they were taking part in a memorable historic occasion. When a minister rose and stretched out his hand, inviting all to join in prayer, an almost startling hush fell upon the assembly. My father wrote that, had he closed his eyes, he could have imagined that he and the man of God stood alone in the empty building.

The prayer ended, the multitude of sounds began again. Cheers and waving hats and fluttering handkerchiefs greeted the names of favorites as the heads of state delegations announced their choices. In a clear well-modulated voice William M. Evarts placed William H. Seward in nomination as the candidate of the great state of New York. The audience responded with a wave of enthusiasm. Hurrahs of truly western heartiness greeted Norman B. Judd's announcement that Lincoln was the choice of Illinois. Dayton, Cameron, Chase, Bates, McLean, and Collamer each received a tribute. Then came the suspense of balloting. No choice was made on the first or second ballot, but on the third the trend toward Lincoln was unmistakable.

Again a sudden, almost solemn hush fell upon the great assembly when William M. Evarts rose to announce the change of New York's vote from Seward to Lincoln, and to move that the latter's nomination be made unanimous. Then pandemonium broke loose. A teller shouted a name toward the skylight. From the roof of the Wigwam a cannon boomed, and Chicago's streets were filled with shouting.

That afternoon, when order had been restored, the convention finished its work by nominating Hannibal Hamlin of Maine, a former Democrat, for vice president. As delegates and spectators sped homeward on night trains, they found bonfires already kindled in every town, and a memorable presidential campaign well under way.

4

THE CAMPAIGN OF 1860

IT WAS INDEED A MEMORABLE CAMPAIGN. The growing earnestness of past years, which brought about the formation of the Republican party, had changed the meaning of words like "patriotism" and "justice" from rather misty abstractions to something very different. They now stood for convictions that were both deep and precious. In Springfield, emotions found expression in almost continuous rallies and parades. By day blaring bands led processions through the streets accompanying "floats" filled with white-clad girls who were supposed to represent the several states of the Union. By night bonfires blazed, speeches were made and cheered, and processions of young men wound their way through the same streets, wearing "Wide Awake" uniforms of shiny caps and capes, and carrying blazing torches.

My father returned to Springfield pleased and happy. Mr. Lincoln was to be the standard-bearer of the Republicans. Perhaps my father, while editor of the *Free Press*, had done a little toward bringing this to pass. What more natural than to hope that he might render a still greater service by writing the campaign "Life of the

Candidate" which must be issued at once? He had experience in writing, knew the candidate personally, and believed heart and soul in the principles for which the party stood. But he was to meet bitter disappointment. As he later wrote:

As soon as the Chicago Convention was ended, I was filled with an ambitious desire to write a campaign biography of the Republican candidate for President, and was greatly disappointed and chagrined to learn that that honor had already been promised to a young Ohioan, then little known, but who is now famous in American literature—W. D. Howells, who performed his task much more worthily than I could have done. Only a day or two later, Mr Lincoln appointed me his private secretary without any solicitation on my part, or, so far as I know, of any one else, and I presume simply on account of the acquaintanceship formed as above related. [The personal relations established in Mr. Hatch's office]

This is his bald statement of fact. He was always reserved in writing about himself. But in his own home, with no strangers present, I have heard him tell the story in words that conjured up the whole scene: How, shaken out of his usual reticence, he chokingly expressed to Mr. Hatch his disappointment in not being given the assignment, and how the older man, seeing the depth of his disappointment, laid his hand on his clerk's arm, and said reassuringly:

"Never mind. You are to be private secretary."

He would not have exchanged the memory of that moment for the greatest gift an emperor could bestow. Since his coming to Springfield, his admiration for Mr. Lincoln as a political leader had changed to real affection for him as a man, but never, in his wildest dreams, had he imagined

anything like this! Before he went to bed he sent a note
to the girl in Pittsfield, telling her the great news.

Who promised young Howells the honor of writing Mr.
Lincoln's campaign biography is not clear. Probably it
was some member of the Republican National Committee,
whose headquarters remained in New York. It was inevitable that more than one "Life" of the candidate would
be rushed into print. Foreseeing this, Mr. Lincoln, within
a week of his nomination, wrote out with his own hand
two short biographical sketches, the copying of which was
one of the new secretary's earliest tasks. The longer of
these sketches, covering several foolscap pages, was sent to
Follett Foster & Co. of Columbus, the firm that had published the *Lincoln-Douglas Debates*. Follett Foster & Co.
sent this and other material to William Dean Howells,
who then wrote his *Life of Abraham Lincoln*. It served
its purpose and was speedily forgotten. Cautious Republicans had questioned the wisdom of choosing him for this
task, and warned the candidate that, although the young
man's literary taste was undeniable, he would bear watching, because his anti-slavery views might unduly color the
book. Another copy of Mr. Lincoln's sketch fell into the
hands of John L. Scripps, whose campaign biography
of thirty-two pages was issued as a pamphlet. A third
"Life" was written by W. D. Bartlett, correspondent of
the *New York Independent* and *New York Evening Post*,
who, by adding several Lincoln speeches and sundry newspaper clippings to Mr. Lincoln's terse autobiography,
managed to swell the material to a volume of three hundred and fifty pages.

Agents of other publishing houses came to Springfield
hoping to arrange for an "authorized" life of the candidate. My father had to meet and discourage them—which
tended to keep alive in his mind the memory of his own

disappointment. He offered them all exactly the same biographical information, warning them that it could not be considered exclusive in any sense. But Mr. Lincoln's door was open to all visitors, and he talked with the publishers' agents so kindly that they found it difficult to believe they had not been singled out for special favors. In one instance this led to real annoyance, for Follett Foster & Co., not content with publishing the Howells biography, sent J. Q. Howard to Springfield to visit the candidate and talk with his old friends, after which he wrote a life which the publishers claimed was "authorized" because "the thread of the narrative" had been obtained from such close sources, and because Mr. Lincoln had authorized no other. The ensuing correspondence between private secretary and publishers was decidedly peppery.

Today, it is hard to realize the informality that reigned in Springfield during the summer of 1860. The Republicans maintained no literary or publicity offices there. Telephones and loud-speakers did not exist. Flash bulbs did not flare, and the radio was still undreamed of. The telegraph was such a novelty that not one Morse instrument was to be found in the State House. Indeed, there was only one place in town from which telegraphic messages could be sent, and that was in an inconvenient upstairs office on a side street, off the public square.

Until after the November election my father constituted Mr. Lincoln's entire office force. Throughout the campaign the candidate, having turned over his private practice to his law partner, received visitors daily in the Governor's Room at the State House, which, being used only during sessions of the legislature, was placed at his disposal. It was a room about fifteen by twenty-five feet in size, adequately furnished. My father sent the girl in Pittsfield a woodcut of it that was published in *Frank Leslie's Weekly*, telling her it was "quite accurate" except that it made the room look much too big. A large-patterned and presumably highly-colored Brussels carpet covered the floor. The three huge high windows had inside wooden shutters. A gas chandelier of graceful design hung from the ceiling, but no frivolous glass globes were allowed to impede the light. A square sheet-iron stove might easily have been dispensed with during the hot Illinois summer; but the very business-like water cooler was doubtless popular, though furnished with only one stout tumbler.

The *Frank Leslie* picture shows Mr. Lincoln standing in the middle of the room, talking with a visitor. His secretary is seated at a desk in the corner, and numerous other figures are added to show the diversity of the candidate's guests. One evidently represents the artist's idea of an Abolitionist—a middle-aged gentleman in broad-cloth, wearing spectacles and the unmistakable expression of a fanatic. Another, seated as though he meant to remain all day, might serve as a cartoon of Uncle Sam, with his high hat and striped pantaloons. A third figure, shadowy but prophetic, wears a coat of military cut. Mr. Lincoln's pioneer friends, who were always warmly welcomed, are not shown, nor are the artists who tried to catch likenesses of the candidate as he moved about. The woodcut shows a banjo clock and several framed pictures on the wall, and a section of stout chain hanging across one corner of the room. This roused the curiosity of Therena Bates, who asked about it in one of her letters. My father answered:

The chain . . . has no particular significance. It is whit-tled out of wood and is a very perfect model of a common log-chain. It was sent to Mr Lincoln by some man in Wis-consin who wrote that being a cripple and unable to leave his bed, he had the rail brought in from the fence, and amused himself by whittling it out.

Other gifts arrived, until the Governor's Room took on the aspect of a museum, so many axes and wedges and log-chains were sent the candidate. He used them in his explanations and anecdotes of pioneer days, making them serve the double purpose of amusing his visitors and keeping the conversation away from dangerous political reefs. For, despite the friendly atmosphere immediately around him, and the huzzahs and torchlight processions in the streets, anxiety and even enmity grew visibly as the weeks rolled by. With the South making ugly threats, it behooved the candidate to walk warily, to keep silent on party questions that might lead to controversy, and to remain even more silent on problems of national politics. He received so many letters asking questions and giving contradictory advice that, in self-defense, he composed a form for his secretary to follow in answering them:

Dear Sir: Your letter to Mr Lincoln of ———— by which you seek to obtain his opinions on certain political points has been received by him. He has received others of a similar character; but he also has a greater number of the exactly opposite character. The latter class beseech him to write nothing whatever upon any point of political doctrine. They say his positions were well known when he was nominated, and that he must not now embarrass the canvass by undertaking to shift or modify them. He regrets that he cannot oblige all, but you perceive it is impossible for him to do so.

Yours &c

J. G. Nicolay.

So the candidate continued to exchange pleasantries with casual visitors, while watching the ever-growing menace behind the circle of friendly faces. He made no impromptu speeches, beyond a word of greeting to passing street parades, and wrote no public letters. Even the con-

fidential letters in which he gave advice on campaign
matters did not exceed a dozen in number.

Every morning about ten o'clock he came to the Governor's Room, bringing the mail he had received at home.
It seems impossible that a presidential candidate of such
unusual appearance could go anywhere unrecognized, but
as late as October 16th my father wrote:

> Mr Lincoln, coming to his office this morning, was accosted
> by a stranger inquiring the way to the same place. Mr
> Lincoln offered to show him the way and, arriving there,
> very much electrified the stranger by turning 'round and
> saying "I am Lincoln."

His personal appearance seemed to worry the candidate
much less than it did some of his followers. Yet it must be
confessed that the coarse woodcut sold on the streets of
Chicago the day he was nominated confirmed the impression that he was remarkably ill-favored. Tradition has it
that a special photograph was taken for the occasion,
the photographer doing his best to make him look the way
he thought a presidential candidate ought to look. At the
last minute, however, Mr. Lincoln, either impatient or
forgetful, ran his long fingers through his hair, creating
a disorder that was further intensified in the woodcut.
A letter my father wrote to Therena Bates tells what one
Pennsylvania Republican decided to do about it. It also
shows, better than reams of comment, the state of "art"
in the Middle West at that time.

> Did you ever see a real pretty miniature? I do not mean
> either an ambrotype, a daguerreotype or photograph, but
> a regular miniature painted on ivory. Well, a Philadelphia
> artist (Brown, his name is), has just been painting one of
> Mr Lincoln, which is both very pretty and very truthful—
> decidedly the best picture of him that I have seen. It is about

twice as large as a common quarter-size daguerreotype or ambrotype, but so well executed that when magnified to life size one cannot discover any defects or brush marks on it at all. It gives something of an idea of what a *painter*—I mean a real artist, can do. It has been painted for Judge Read of Philadelphia, who has become so disgusted with the horrible caricatures of Mr Lincoln which he has seen that he went to the expense of sending this artist all the way out here to paint this picture, which will probably cost him some $300., the price of the painting alone being $175. I had a long talk with the artist today... He says that the impression prevails East that Mr Lincoln is very ugly, an impression which the published pictures of him of course all confirm. Read however had an idea that it could hardly be so—but was bound to have a good looking picture, and therefore instructed the artist to make it good looking whether the original would justify it or not. The artist says he came with a good deal of foreboding that he would have difficulty in making a picture under these conditions. He says he was very happy when on seeing him he found that he was not at all such a man as had been represented, but that instead of making a picture he would only have to paint a portrait to satisfy Judge Read. He will go back home as agreeably disappointed in Mr Lincoln's manners, refinement and general characteristics, as in his personal appearance.

A bit of after-history concerning this portrait is not out of place. In August 1860, when the miniature was painted, Mr. Lincoln's face was smooth-shaven, but before he became President he let his beard grow; whereupon, William Sartain, a skillful New York engraver, copied the portrait in black and white, adding a beard to bring it up to date. So we have this Brown miniature both "before and after taking."

Mr. Lincoln might jest and indulge in reminiscences with his visitors, but he showed no lack of decision in

ABRAHAM LINCOLN.

FROM A PHOTOGRAPH BY HESLER

The above was circulated in Chicago on the day of Lincoln's first nomination for President

THE CHICAGO WOODCUT

With notation in John G. Nicolay's handwriting.

meeting issues as they developed. Occasionally, the private secretary was sent away on errands during the campaign. In July, he went to Terre Haute, Indiana, to interview Richard W. Thompson, who was believed to have influence with the Know-Nothing vote. The instructions he carried with him were terse and to the point:

> Ascertain what he wants.
> On what subjects he would converse with me.
> And the particulars if he will give them.
> Is an interview indispensable?
> Tell him my motto is "Fairness to all",
> But commit me to nothing.

By October, the feeling of anxiety among Republicans had become personal as well as political. My father wrote:

Among the many things said in a general way to Mr Lincoln by his visitors, there is nearly always an expressed hope that he will not be so unfortunate as were Harrison and Taylor, to be killed off by the cares of the presidency, or as is sometimes hinted, by foul means. It is astonishing how the popular sympathy for Mr Lincoln draws fearful forebodings from these two examples, which may after all have been only a natural coincidence. Not only do visitors mention the matter, a great many letters have been written to Mr Lincoln on the subject.

One day Dr. Albert Hall, a Springfield minister who was waiting to speak to Mr. Lincoln, saw two young country boys peer anxiously in at the door. Seeing the candidate, the elder, evidently relieved, said to his brother, "He's here. Come on in." When Mr. Lincoln spoke to them, they told him their father had sent them to town to find out if a rumor that he had been poisoned, current near their home, was true. "Dad says you must look out and eat nothing except what your old woman cooks for you," said one of them earnestly, "and Mother says so too!"

My father's duties were to attend to the mail and to receive visitors. At first, letters came at the rate of about fifty a day. Unversed in the technique of handling such volume, my father was a little distressed at the thought of having to attend to it. Later on, fifty letters seemed nothing to him. After the election, when the mail had greatly increased, he asked John Hay, who fortunately was living in Springfield, to help him.

In spite of his many activities—for he was still pursuing the varied lines of study and pleasure he had entered upon in Springfield—he found time occasionally to jot down notes that might be useful if he ever should write a Lincoln biography. This was an idea that haunted him. On October 25th he wrote:

This morning Gen. Welch of New York called on Mr Lincoln. The conversation having turned on Gov. Chase, and the fact of his being in the Senate instead of the presidency, Mr L. said—"And I declare to you this morning General— that for personal considerations I would rather have a full term in the Senate—a place in which I would feel more consciously able to discharge the duties required, and where there was more chance to make a reputation and less chance of losing it—than four years in the presidency.

On the day before election my father wrote hurriedly:

Sanford called to see—if the alarms of many persons might not by some means be relieved—"The alarms from the South are seriously affecting our work—am myself largely interested—yet no orders from the South [North?]—. Reassure the men honestly alarmed."
Lincoln—"There are no such men ... Have thought much about it ... It is the trick by which the South breaks down

every man.—I would go to Washington without the support of men who supported me and were my friends before the election. I would be as powerless as a block of buckeye wood."

(The man still insisted.)

L. "The honest men (you are talking of honest men) will look at our platform and what I have said—There they will find everything I could now say or which they would ask me to say—All I could say now would be repetition. Having told them all ten times already, would they believe the eleventh declaration?

"Let us be practical.—There are many general terms afloat such as 'conservatism'—'enforcement of the irrepressible conflict at the point of the bayonet'—'Hostility to the South' &c.—all of which mean nothing without definition ... What then could I say to allay their fears, if they will not define what particular act or acts they fear from me or my friends?"

(Gentleman hands him letters)

—"Recognize them as a set of liars and knaves who signed that statement about Seward last year."

(Gentleman insists there are other names on the list.)

[Mr L. who had talked quite good-naturedly before, evidently betrayed a little feeling at this part of the conversation.] (After reading the letter)

"Well, after reading it it is about what I expected to find it. (Laughing) It annoyed me a little to hear that gang of men called respectable. Their conduct a year ago was a disgrace to any civilized man."

(The gentleman suggested that the South was making armed preparations &c.)

L. "The North does not fear invasion from the Slave States, and we of the North certainly have no desire and never had, to invade the South. I am rather pleased at the idea that the South is making some 'preparation.' They have talked about a Black Republican victory until the—"

Gen. "Have we backed this time?"

L. "That is what I am pressed to do now. If I shall begin to yield to these threats—if I begin dallying with them, the men who have elected me, if I shall be elected, would give me up before my inauguration—and the South seeing it, would deliberately kick me out ... If my friends should desire me to repeat anything I have before said, I should have no objection to do so. If they required me to say something I had not yet said I should either do so *or get out of the way.* If I should be elected my first duty to the country would be to stand by the men who elected me."

Small wonder that even Mr. Lincoln's great patience gave way after three months of such a campaign, with the threat of political trouble growing darker every hour. On November 6th my father wrote:

It is election day—and Hon. A. Lincoln has just been over to vote. The Court House steps (in which building the polls were held) were thronged with people who welcomed him with immense shouting and followed him in dense numbers along the hall and up the stairs into the courtroom, which was also crowded. Here the applause became deafening, and from the time he entered the room until he cast his vote and again left it, there was wild huzzahing, waving of hats, and all sorts of demonstrations of applause—rendering all other noises insignificant and futile.

A newspaper tells us that, hemmed in as the candidate was, he could only make acknowledgment by lifting his hat and smiling as he left the hall, "and when he smiles heartily it is something good to see."

The next letter to Pittsfield told Therena that election day did not end for the secretary until half past four on the morning of November 7th, and that even then he could not sleep for the noise and the rejoicing.

We have heard enough to make it certain that Mr Lincoln is elected President, and we of course all feel happy over it.

He will get large majorities in all the Free States except New Jersey, whose electoral vote we can abundantly spare. We shall carry this State by from ten to fifteen thousand majority. Of course our state ticket will be elected. . . . We had a pretty lively time on election day. At night we lighted up the Representatives' Hall, and it was filled nearly all night by a crowd shouting, yelling, singing, dancing, and indulging in all sorts of demonstrations of happiness as the news came in. Across the street in an ice-cream parlor kept by a Republican, were a large number of Republican ladies who had a table spread with coffee, sandwiches, cake, oysters and other refreshments for their husbands and friends. It was "Happy times" there also.

On the 11th he wrote:

I can scarcely realize that, after having fought this slavery question valiantly for six years past, and suffered so many defeats, I am at last rejoicing in a triumph which only two years ago we hardly dared dream about. I remember very distinctly how, in 1854, soon after I had bought the *Free Press* office, I went to Barry with others and heard Mr Atkinson the preacher make the first anti-Nebraska speech that was made in Pike County in that campaign. Though I was fighting then as something more than a private, I should have thought it a wild dream to imagine that six years after I should find victory so near the Commander-in-Chief.

5

PROBLEMS OF A PRESIDENT-ELECT

THE CAMPAIGN HAD BEEN STRENUOUS. My father, writing to invite Therena and a party of Pittsfield friends to come over for Springfield's official celebration, told her the people looked almost too tired to indulge in a "grand hurrah." He did not believe they would do it "were it not...a formality which, in this case, cannot well be avoided. ... From this [time] on the inauguration will be the next important event. ... I can see plenty of work ahead."

There was also plenty of anxiety, especially for the President-elect. Less than a week after the election, General Winfield Scott, head of the United States Army, sent Mr. Lincoln a copy of a paper he had previously forwarded to the Secretary of War and several other influential men, but which the Buchanan administration chose to ignore. My father put away among his notes a summary of its contents:

The document signed by the General was "Views suggested by the imminent danger [Oct. 29, 1860] of a disruption of the Union by the secession of one or more Southern States." The "Views" went on to say—

Concede the right to secede, and it is instantly balanced by the correlative right of the federal government to re-establish by force its former continuity of territory.

The Union once broken, there would be no hope of re-uniting it except by the sword, which would involve sanguinary results.

A smaller evil would be, allow the formation of new confederacies—probably four.

The natural boundaries would probably be

1st. The Potomac River and Chesapeake Bay to the Atlantic.

2d. From Maryland along the crest of the Alleghanies to some point on the coast of Florida.

3d. The line from the head of the Potomac to the West or Northwest.

4th. The crest of the Rocky Mountains.

Will not the South be less secure and have less rights under the new order of things, than the old?

The excitement is caused by the prospect of a Republican election. My sympathies are with the Bell and Everett ticket. I cannot believe any constitutional violence or breach of law is to be apprehended from Mr Lincoln's administration.

There is some danger of an early act of rashness—the seizure of one or more of the forts on the Southern coast, which have either small or no garrisons.

With a faithful Army and Navy and a moderate but firm Executive for the next twelve months, secession may be averted.

Exports should be as free as at present and duties on imports collected outside of cities.

The "Views" eschew the idea of invading a seceding State.

The document was accompanied by a copy of a note to the Secretary of War saying orders ought to be given to commanders of the Barrancas, Forts Moultrie and Monroe, to be on guard against surprise, &c.

Mr Lincoln replied in a very brief note, merely thanking

the General for this renewed manifestation of patriotism as a citizen and a soldier.

That was all Mr. Lincoln could do! No matter how he might wish to interfere, he was only President-elect and would have no legal power until after March 4th, which was still four months away. Meanwhile, he had no lack of advice. Visitors increased. So did the mail. My father, used now to the flow of letters, wrote Therena that a large part of them fell into two classes: " . . . those merely congratulatory, and those asking for office, neither of which I answer. The majority of letters I have sent off for a week past have been those containing Mr. Lincoln's autograph."

With visitors it was different. On November 15th he wrote:

Judge Buck of Kentucky, quite an old man, a relative of Mrs L. who is on a visit here, had a long talk with Mr Lincoln this morning. He strongly urged upon him the duty of saving the country by making up his Cabinet of "conservative men"—one or more of them from the South, and who should not be Republicans, saying that by such a course Kentucky would stay in Union. But that if obnoxious men like Seward, Cassius M. Clay, &c. were put in the Cabinet, and a sectional administration organized, the people of Ky. would feel themselves driven to go with S.C. Judge B., while he disclaimed any desire to have Mr L. abate any principle, yet made a very strong appeal to him to make his administration conservative in the way he pointed out.

Mr Lincoln listened to him attentively and only replied briefly.

He asked the Judge to tell him in what speech Mr Seward had ever spoken menacingly of the South, and said that so far as he knew, not one single prominent public Republican had justly made himself obnoxious to the South by anything

he had said or done, and that they had only become so because the Southern politicians had so persistently bespat-
tered every Northern man by their misrepresentations to rob
them of what strength they might otherwise have.

He told the Judge that the substance of his [Judge
Buck's] plan was that the Republicans should now again
surrender the Government into the hands of the men they
had just conquered, and that the cause should take to its
bosom the enemy who had always fought it, and who would
still continue to fight and oppose it.

He told him he should however give his views a serious and
respectful consideration.

The composition of Mr. Lincoln's cabinet was of great
concern to politicans, who fancied that by studying its
membership they could forecast the new President's policy.
The truth is that on the very night of election when he
sat alone with the operators in the little telegraph office
in Springfield, reading returns until convinced of Republican victory, he had determined on his cabinet's general
outlines. He believed thoroughly in representative government and the power of public opinion and knew that
he should need the help of all factions within the Republican party. Four of the men who had contested the nomination with him in Chicago were leaders of large groups.
He would therefore take these four—Seward, Chase, Cameron of Pennsylvania, and Bates of Missouri— into his
circle of closest advisers. But since making plans and
carrying them into effect are very different matters, he
felt there was no need prematurely to take the public into
his confidence.

So he continued to receive visitors and much unsolicited
advice. On December 11th two gentlemen from Indiana
came to present the claims of Caleb B. Smith to a seat in
the cabinet and, incidentally, to belittle those of Schuyler

Colfax for such an appointment, saying he was "too in-experienced," "a man of detail" whose reputation had "been manufactured by newspaper scribblers."

Mr Lincoln replied that being determined to act with caution and not to embarrass himself with promises, he could only say that he saw no insuperable objections to Indiana having a man in the Cabinet, nor to Smith being the man.

On the next day it was Frank P. Blair, Jr., who came, "in the main," to learn Mr. Lincoln's views as to the duty of the government in case of attempted secession, but also to urge the claims of Edward Bates, of Missouri. He rep-resented Mr. Bates as being strongly against secession, indeed, as denying the right or possibility of breaking up the government "under any pretext." My father's notes state that "Blair went away very much pleased with the President's views."

Mr. Bates was the only member of his future cabinet to visit the President-elect. Wishing to talk with him, Mr. Lincoln with his customary directness sent word by Mr. Blair that he meant to call upon Mr. Bates on the follow-ing Saturday. To the rather formal Mr. Bates this seemed most irregular and unfitting. He sent back word that, instead, he would come to Springfield. On December 15th my father wrote:

When I went to breakfast this morning I found the name of Mr Bates on the hotel register. He soon after came into the dining-room and seated himself at the head of the table near which I was sitting, and where I had ample opportunity of studying his appearance. He is not of impressive exterior; his hair is gray and his beard white, and his face shows all the marks of age quite strongly.

He came to Mr Lincoln's room at about 9 A.M., entering with very profuse civilities and apologies for having come before Mr L's hour. . . . (His flow of words in conversation is very genial and easy—seeming at first to verge upon extreme politeness, but soon becoming very attractive. Afterwards, in serious conversation with Mr L., Mr B. became quite earnest and spoke his thoughts in clear concise language, indicating a very comprehensive and definite intellectual grasp of ideas, and a great facility of expression.) Leaving him in the room with the morning paper to look over, I went to notify Mr L. of his presence, who soon returned with me.

Their meeting (they had an acquaintanceship of eight years' standing) was very cordial; and the ordinary salutations being over, Mr L. entered at once upon the important subject-matter of the interview.

Without further prelude Mr L. went on to tell him that . . . since the day of the Chicago nomination it had been his purpose, in the case of success, unless something should meantime make it necessary to change his decision, to tender him (B.) one of the places in his Cabinet. Nothing having occurred to make a change of purpose necessary (he had waited thus long to be enabled to act with caution) . . . he now offered him the appointment.

He said in doing this he did not desire to burden him with one of the drudgery offices. Some of his (B's) friends had asked for him the State Department. He could not now offer him this, for the reason that he should offer that place to Mr Seward—in view of his ability, his integrity, and his commanding influence and fitness for the place. He did this as a matter of duty to the party, and to Mr Seward's many and strong friends, while at the same time it accorded perfectly with his own personal inclinations—notwithstanding some opposition on the part of sincere and warm friends. He had not yet communicated with Mr Seward, and did not know whether he would accept the appointment. . . . He would probably know in a few days. He therefore could not now offer him (B.) the State Department, but would offer him what he supposed would be most congenial, and for which he was certainly every way qualified, *viz.* the Attorney-Generalship.

Mr Bates replied by saying that until a very few days ago he had received no word, or hint even, that any of his friends had made any such application in his behalf. He expressed himself highly gratified at the confidence which Mr L. manifested in him by the offer just made. He alluded to the fact that years ago he had declined a similar offer made by Mr Fillmore. Were the country in the same condition ... no inducement would tempt him to assume the duties of such a position. But the case was different. The country was in trouble and danger, and he felt it his duty to sacrifice his personal inclination and, if he could, to contribute his labor and influence to the restoration of peace in, and the preservation of, his country.

Mr Lincoln expressed himself highly gratified at his determination. By way of preparing himself for the questions which the new administration was likely to encounter he desired him between this time and the inauguration to examine very thoroughly, and make himself familiar with the Constitution and the laws relating to the question of secession, so as to be prepared to give a definite opinion upon the various aspects of the question.

On one other point he desired him also to make some examination. Under the present administration the mails in the South had been violated with impunity, and with the sanction of the Government. Under the new Government he feared some trouble from this question. It was well understood by intelligent men that the perfect and unrestrained freedom of speech and the press which exists at the North was practically incompatible with the existing institutions at the South, and he feared that radical Republicans at the North might claim at the hands of the new Administration the enforcement of the right, and endeavor to make the mail the means of thrusting upon the South matter which even their conservative and well-meaning men might deem inimical and dangerous.

Mr Bates said he would carefully look into both these questions. On the latter he had, without special investigation, always easily arrived at the opinion that the U.S. mails ought of right to be sacred and inviolable. Certainly the present practice, which permitted petty postmasters to examine and burn everything they pleased, would not be tolerated or countenanced by the most despotic governments. At the same time he foresaw the practical difficulty of enforcing the law at every cross-road.

Much further conversation was had, both during the morning and in the afternoon, when Mr L. called on him again at the hotel. Their views were very fully and frankly exchanged.

Mr Bates's conversation shows him to be inflexibly opposed to secession, and strongly in favor of maintaining the government by force if necessary. He forcibly illustrates his temper by saying that he is a man of peace, and will defer fighting as long as possible; but that, if forced to do so against his will, he has made it a rule *never to fire blank cartridges.*

During the afternoon interview Mr L. showed Mr B. a private letter he had just written to Hon. John A. Gilmer of N.C. (an M.C.) who had through Mr Corwin solicited his opinions on a number of questions.

Mr L's letter said that he was averse to writing such a letter as Mr C. desired, and only wrote *in private*, as he did, to avoid having his silence misconstrued. He could not shift or change the ground upon which he was elected. A new letter or declaration was sought that his enemies might represent him as repenting of and apologizing for having been elected. His old record would serve every patriotic purpose in showing the South he was not dangerous. He had no thought of recommending the abolition of slavery in the D.C. or the abolition of the inter-state slave trade. Even were he to make the recommendation Congress would not follow it. He felt precisely the same about the employment of slaves in arsenals, dock-yards, &c. In using the patronage in slave states where there were few or no Republicans, he should not enquire of the politics of the appointees, or whether they owned slaves or not. He would recommend the people of the several localities if they would permit it. On the territorial question he was inflexible. If any State laws conflict with the Constitution he would be glad to have them repealed. But as a citizen of Ill. or Pres. of the U.S. he could not recommend the repeal of a Vermont or South Carolina statute, &c.

Not all Mr. Lincoln's callers were courteous, or even well-mannered. His secretary wrote Therena about the visit of "a regular genuine secessionist, with a blue cockade on his hat." Why he came was a mystery, for he "sat on the sofa, looking rather foolish, saying nothing and turning his hat over and over in his hand, as if he didn't exactly know whether it would seem cowardly to appear to be trying to hide the cockade, or whether it would be impudent to be appearing to try to display it." Across the room sat a stout Yankee farmer, whose manners were even worse, for he persistently tried to goad the Southerner into a fight. It was Mr. Lincoln who interposed, jesting good-humoredly with the southerner, and finally sending him off with a copy of the *Lincoln-Douglas Debates* under his arm. As a rule however, visitors were courteous and intelligent, and discussions were serious.

On November 15th my father made this note:

Two gentlemen were in today, and the conversation turning upon the existing troubles in the South . . . Mr Lincoln said to them, "My own impression is at present (leaving myself room to modify the opinion if, upon a further investigation, I should see fit to do so) that this government possesses both the authority and the power to maintain its own integrity. That, however, is not the ugly point of this matter. The ugly point is the necessity of keeping the government together by force, as ours ought to be a government of fraternity.

A month later:

From conversations and expressions at different times during the last three weeks the following are substantially his opinions about secession:

The very existence and organization of a general and national government implies the legal power, right and duty of maintaining its own integrity. This, if not expressed, is at least implied in the Constitution.

The right of a State to secede is not an open or debatable question. It was fully discussed in Jackson's time, and denied not only by him, but by a vote of —— to —— in Congress.

It is the duty of a President to execute the laws and maintain the existing government. He cannot entertain any proposition for dissolution or dismemberment. He was not elected for any such purpose.

As a matter of theoretical speculation it is probably true that if the people (with whom the whole question rests) should become tired of the present government, they may change it in the manner prescribed by the Constitution.

When Mr Lincoln came into the office this morning, after the usual salutations, he asked me what the news was. I asked him if he had seen the morning dispatches. He replied "No." "Then," said I, "there is an important rumor you have not seen. The *Times* correspondent telegraphs that Buchanan has sent instructions to Maj. Anderson to surrender Fort Moultrie if it is attacked.

"If that is true, they ought to hang him!" he said with warmth.

After some further conversation, he remarked, "Among the letters you saw me mail yesterday was one to Washburne (of Ill.) who had written me that he had just had a long conversation with Gen. Scott, and that the General felt considerably outraged that the President would not act as he wished him to in reënforcing the forts, &c. I wrote to Washburne to tell General Scott confidentially that I wished him to be prepared, immediately after my inauguration, to make arrangements at once to hold the forts, or, if they had been taken, to take them back again."

Afterwards he repeated the substance of the above in another conversation with Wm. H. Herndon, adding at the close with some emphasis, "There can be no doubt that in *any* event that is good ground to live and die by."

Under date of December 11th my father made this note:

Mr Lincoln today received a letter from Hon. Wm. Kellogg M.C.—the Member from Illinois—who has been placed on the Committee of 33 raised by Boteler's motion to consider the secession portion of the President's message, asking advice as to his action in the Committee.

Mr Lincoln answered advising him to entertain no proposition for a compromise to the *expansion* of slavery—That if this were done, the work achieved by the late election would all have to be done over again. That Douglas would again try to resuscitate his "Popular Sovereignty". That the issue had better be met now than later.

Mr L. also intimated that he, Kellogg, knew that he believed the Fugitive Slave law of the Constitution ought to be enforced.

Next month, when a loyal commander of the Pennsylvania militia wrote assuring the President-elect that the men under him could be relied upon to respond to any demand for military duty that he might make of them, Mr. Lincoln directed my father to reply:

Mr Lincoln desires me to answer that while he does not now deem it necessary to avail himself of the services you so kindly offer him, he is nevertheless gratified to have the assurance from yourself that the militia of the State of Pennsylvania is loyal to the Constitution and the Union, and stands ready to rally to their support.

Early in the new year, writing to Therena that he had little news to send her, he explained that, of course,

...I mean news that interests you and which I am at liberty to impart.... I necessarily hear something new every day that would be of infinite interest sometimes to one and sometimes to another, but about which my duty is to say nothing. I am gratified to be able to tell you that I have renewed evidence that Mr Lincoln reposes entire confidence in me, which I deem a sufficient guaranty that my present confidential relation to him will be continued, though not a word has been said by either of us since the election.

In political matters there is no important change.... The Secessionists are still rampant.... The people of the Free States and their representatives in Congress are all a unit in their determination not to budge an inch from the position they have occupied during the whole campaign.... Mr Lincoln, while he is not unmindful of the troubles which are at hand, and while he sincerely wishes they were not existing, is nevertheless not in the least intimidated or frightened by them.

Personally, my father did not think the threatened secession would take place. Giving his reasons at length, he stressed the consideration of money. It was easy enough for a State to *resolve* itself out of the Union. But no State or nation could exist without government. If the Cotton States broke from the Union, they would have to establish another government. The cost would be great. Where was all this money to come from? "Why, the South does not even pay her own postage!" She might gain a little from free trade with Europe, but only a little. As for the slave trade which it was proposed to reestablish, that was a forlorn hope: "The great European nations are much more anti-slavery than we people of the North!"

If this grand American experiment of free government is to be a failure, it will be quite as well we should know it now as at any future time. If the caprice of one or half a dozen States is to be stronger than our Constitution, then, in God's name, the sooner we make the discovery the better. With either event I shall be content, for we can cut off the traitor-breeding Cotton States and still have the most magnificent and successful empire on this globe!

The wildest rumors were flying about.

Neither of the reports which you have heard is true, [he wrote Therena,] Lovejoy has not been shot, and Buchanan has not resigned. The latter event would be hailed by the people of the North as the greatest blessing which could just now take place. . . . Truly the country is in great danger—but it is from the traitors and imbeciles who are at the head of national affairs, and not from the beggarly mutinous crew down South.

The Illinois legislature was to meet early in January, after which the Governor's Room in the State House would be needed for its customary uses. Mr. Lincoln took a room in the Johnson Building, across the street from the hotel frequented by Republicans. Here, his secretary was to have both working and sleeping quarters. Mr. Lincoln, who intended to receive most of his visitors at home, would come in occasionally. It was a good room, my father thought—"A very comfortable place if I can keep the crowd out." He hoped to be fed at the hotel as before, but increasing crowds rendered this precarious. Physical discomforts, however, passed unnoticed in the onrush of events. Leaden skies added to the gloom, as we learn from

a long letter to Therena summarizing the crowded, dis-
tressing days during which one southern state after
another seceded, and Major Anderson, despairing of receiving the desired permission, "took the responsibility"
of moving his little command from Fort Moultrie to
Sumter. The letter continued:

The weather has been so rainy and foggy for two or three
days past that the telegraph wouldn't work well, and we
have very little news of what is going on elsewhere in the
world. We scarcely know therefore whether Springfield is in
the Union yet or out of it, or what the secessionists are
doing.

On January 27th he wrote Therena that "yesterday"
Mr. Lincoln "determined definitely" to leave Springfield
for Washington on February 11th, and he outlined the
proposed itinerary. Since it was unwise to put fantastic
notions into a girl's head, he did not tell her about a
secession plot said to have been discovered, whose aim
was to get possession of Washington, turn it into the
capital of a southern confederacy, and prevent the inauguration of the new President. Nor did he even mention
letters he had received from Mr. A. W. Flanders of
Burlington, Iowa, who wanted to make a shirt of mail
for Mr. Lincoln to wear on the journey. Mr. Flanders
claimed he had once occupied the chair of chemistry "in
one of the Philadelphia colleges," and, because of his connections with metalworkers "and makers of apparatus
generally," he felt sure he could have such a garment
made secretly, without anybody's knowing for whom it was
intended. He recommended one "plated with gold, so that
perspiration shall not affect it. It could be covered with
silk and worn over an ordinary undershirt. Several letters

added interesting details. He recommended chain armor as being the most flexible.

If Mr Lincoln wishes to be protected in this way he had better get an undershirt made to fit him exactly, as a coat fits when buttoned up, to reach from the neck to the hip bones, and also as low behind and in front as would not interfere with sitting down. Let this be measured and cut out by a tailor from woolen flannel, and ascertained to be an exact fit by buttoning. This should be washed and should fit well about the armholes, reaching midway to the elbow. This I can have stuffed with cotton and then make the coat of mail to fit exactly over it. If he concludes to have this done there is not much time to lose. You can send it to me by mail or express. . . . It will probably take about ten or twelve days to make the one here after the pattern is received. . . . I am told that Napoleon III is constantly protected in this way, and that his life was thus saved from small pieces of the Orsini shells which killed his horses and several persons. I shall be very happy to get this done for Mr Lincoln if he will accept of it, and really hope he will not go to Washington without it.

None of my father's answers to Mr. Flanders' letters have been preserved. We only know that in spite of the impressive setting forth of advantages and precedents, Mr. Lincoln left Springfield without the protection of a gold-plated coat of mail.

6

THE JOURNEY TO
WASHINGTON

THE DEPARTURE TOOK PLACE ON A DIS-
mal morning when low-hanging clouds dropped rain
and snow alternatingly. Despite the weather, nearly a
thousand people had gathered about the dingy little
railroad station to bid Mr. Lincoln good-by. The older ones
were sad and apprehensive. The boys, on the contrary,
were full of excitement, for were not three of their own gen-
eration—Tad and Willie Lincoln and their elder brother
Robert, who had returned from college to make the trip—
going on that presidential train!

Mr. Lincoln stood in the waiting room, shaking
hands with old friends and neighbors. Some, overcome
by emotion, merely pressed his hand in silence and passed
on. A bell clanged the preliminary signal for departure.
He entered his car, and it seemed to some of his friends
that the small amount of morning light lessened visibly
as he passed from view.

After the conductor's hand was already on the bell rope,
he reappeared on the back platform to make his little
speech of farewell—probably the saddest, most eloquent
speech that ever fell from the lips of a successful can-

didate. As the wheels began slowly to turn, the bystanders cheered, and in that cheer the boys shouted loudest of all. Their clear young voices were probably the last sound to reach Mr. Lincoln's ears as he was borne away from Springfield forever.

He was reminded that the press would want to print his farewell words. Resignedly, he sat down to write them out. My father took the pencil from his hand. The copy made on the train is thus partly in his handwriting, partly in the President's own.

The family party consisted of Mr. and Mrs. Lincoln, with their three sons, Lockwood Todd, and Dr. W. S. Wallace. Accompanying them all the way were my father and John Hay, Mr. Lincoln's two old friends, David Davis and Norman B. Judd, Colonel E. V. Sumner, Major David Hunter, Captains George W. Hazard and John Pope, Ward H. Lamon, J. W. Burgess of Wisconsin, George C. Latham, and the brilliant young colonel of Volunteers, E. E. Ellsworth, who was to lose his life so tragically soon after. A number of Springfield friends went with them as far as Indianapolis where the first night was spent, and at almost every stop on the way delegations came aboard to offer their good wishes. Some, to whom the experience was new, seemed terribly afraid of forgetting their lines, but Mr. Lincoln soon put them at their ease. Some were unknown to fame. Others would have been recognized anywhere. None of them created more interest than Horace Greeley when he climbed aboard at Girard, Pennsylvania, wearing his famous white hat, and carrying his "well-known red and blue blankets." "He got off the train again at Erie."

From Indianapolis my father wrote to Therena:

It is now eight o'clock at night and we have been one day on the journey to Washington. We had a rather pleasant ride over the railroad from Springfield here; saw crowds of people at every station—found the streets of this city full on our arrival. If it were during a campaign it would be called 50,000 at least—through which with difficulty we made our way to the Bates House...where I am writing this. The house is perfectly jammed full of people. Three or four ladies and as many gentlemen have even invaded the room assigned to Mr Lincoln, while outside the door I hear the crowd pushing and grumbling and shouting in almost frantic endeavors to get to another parlor at the door of which Mr Lincoln stands shaking hands with the multitude. It is a severe ordeal for us, and increased about ten-fold for him.

Perhaps my father had not yet heard of the greatest ordeal the President-elect faced that day—the loss of his inaugural address. Mr. Lincoln had written it in Springfield, withdrawing himself some hours each day from his ordinary receptions to go to a quiet room on the second floor of a store occupied by his brother-in-law, where he could think and write undisturbed. After it was finished, he placed it in the hands of William H. Bailhache, one of the editors of the *Illinois State Journal*, who locked himself with a single compositor into the composing room of his newspaper. Here, in Mr. Bailhache's presence, the inaugural was set up, proof taken and read, and after a dozen copies had been printed the types were immediately distributed. All this was done in such secrecy that not even the most alert newspaper reporter, seeing Mr. Lincoln daily in his usual haunts, had an idea of what was going on.

For the journey, however, Mr. Lincoln had merely placed the document in a little old-fashioned black oil-cloth handbag and given it in charge of his eldest son, telling him to "Take care of it" but not telling him what it contained. Robert, aged eighteen, was probably the happiest and most carefree member of the party. During the campaign he had come into considerable notice as the "Prince of Rails," and a group of Indianapolis youths of his own age waited to seize upon him and do the honors after their own capricious fashion.

The crowd at the station had been so poorly controlled that only about half the party reached the carriages provided for them. The rest, including Robert, had to make their way to the hotel as best they could, on foot, and with luggage in hand. It was then that the boys had pounced upon Robert and carried him off. He had reached the hotel long before his father, who was being driven ceremoniously through the streets. No sooner had Mr. Lincoln arrived and worked his way through packed corridors to his room than he was called to address the crowd from a balcony outside.

When at last he had time to think about his little black bag, Robert had disappeared. There was considerable delay before he could be found and brought back to answer his father's anxious questions. He replied with bored and injured virtue that, arriving in the confusion, with no room assigned to him, he had handed the bag to the hotel clerk—"after the usual manner of travelers."

"And what did the clerk do with it?"

"It is on the floor behind the counter." Robert, still bored, thought a great fuss was being made about nothing.

Visions of his inaugural, printed with flaming headlines a fortnight ahead of time in all the morning newspapers, floated before the President-elect. Without a word he threw open the door and made his way through the crowded halls to the lobby. A single stride of his long legs took him over the counter that divided the clerk's desk from the rest of the room. Then he fell upon the small mountain of luggage that lay behind it, while bystanders craned their necks and the clerk stood horrified. There were many black bags in the pile. Taking a little key from his pocket, Mr. Lincoln began unlocking such as the key would open. The first half dozen yielded a wide assortment of undesired articles. Then he came upon his own—inviolate. He carried the bag back to his room, handed it once more to his son, told him this time what it contained, and added, "Now, you keep it!"

"You bet I did!" Robert once assured the writer. Then he continued, reminiscently, "Father did not scold. He never alluded to it again."

Newspapers outdid themselves in descriptions of the train on which Mr. Lincoln traveled. It rushed through the landscape at thirty miles an hour. The engines that drew it from place to place were richly decorated and given patriotic names like "Union" and "Constitution." One, which burned coal, was equipped with a new device called a "smoke consumer." Especial attention had been given to safety, and until the train reached the eastern city of Buffalo, a high official of the Western Telegraph Company traveled on it in charge of an apparatus that would have made it possible to connect with telegraph wires between stations, in case of accident. There were three different passenger cars; one for the press, one for local escorts; and a new and very elegant one for Mr. Lincoln's own party. This was equipped with "the latest system of ventilation," draped in deep blue with silver stars, and had the national colors, hanging "in beautiful festoons from the ceiling." Its floor was "covered with rich tapestry," while divans and sofas and luxurious armchairs "were disposed in different parts of the car as would be the furniture in a tastefully arranged drawingroom."

White handkerchiefs fluttered from the crowds that gathered to see this magnificent train go by, and when an ice-gorge obstructed its passage across the Hudson, necessitating a long detour, skaters greeted the President-elect with cheers and banners. One fervid account summed up the impressions of the whole journey, which lasted nearly two weeks, in four words: "Crowds, cannon and cheers."

Years after, my father wrote, "It is hard for one who has not had the chance of personal observation to realize the mingled excitement, elation and fatigue which Mr Lincoln and his suite underwent for nearly two weeks during this memorable trip." Every time the train stopped the crowd outside shouted for a speech. After a while Mr. Lincoln learned to sit quietly in his car until notified by the conductor that the train was about to start. Then he would appear on the back platform to bow, with no time left for speaking. But it was manifestly hard for him to do this—his impulse was always to meet people fully half way and talk to them. As often as possible, evening receptions were arranged in cities where the party was to spend the night. After all the necessary official ceremonies this added to the strain. My father wrote from Cleveland:

I expected after we got fairly started that I would find time at least to mail you a paper once in a while, but it turns out that I don't get time to buy, let alone to mail them. The morning we left Indianapolis I went to the office and got half a dozen already put up in wrappers. They are yet in my carpet-bag, undirected. . . .

Mr Lincoln has received an immense reception at every place yet visited—so large that it has been a serious task for us of his escort to prevent his being killed with kindness.

In some cities police protection was far from adequate, but real disorder occurred only three or four times during the journey. "In most places," my father reported, "the preparations were reasonably satisfactory, and in a few of them as perfect, orderly and quiet as is possible on occasions where the interest is centered, and where crowds are so large."

At Columbus, Mr. Lincoln's friends learned how necessary it was to be on the alert every minute. The magnificent new Ohio State House was just finished, and the Committee of Arrangements proudly planned an informal reception to be held after morning ceremonies before the legislature. The guests were to stand in the State House at a point where two great corridors crossed each other. People were to enter by one door, pass through the building in a straight line, and make their exit through the door opposite. But not enough police were detailed to guard the other doors. Before anyone knew what was taking place, the other doors had been forced, and crowds were bearing down on Mr. Lincoln from three sides with a force that threatened actually to crush him and those about him. Colonel Lamon, of Mr. Lincoln's suite, a man of extraordinary size and strength, was able to place himself in front of Mr. Lincoln and, by great exertion, to keep the crowd back until Mr. Lincoln could be hurried to a place of comparative safety behind a pilaster. Though this protruded only a few inches, it was enough to ease the pressure until the influx could be checked.

At Cleveland, arrangements were very nearly perfect; but at Buffalo they broke down completely. My father wrote:

The Committee not only did nothing, but didn't seem to care. . . . We took the matter into our own hands, and finally arranged pretty much everything. I don't know when I have done so much work as yesterday. The best criterion I can give you of my condition is the appearance of this letter—I feel just as it looks.

When they were nearing Pittsburgh a freight wreck delayed their special train until very late. The night was stormy, and they expected the station to be deserted. Instead, they found crowds pushing and yelling in a semi-obscurity that seemed intensified by the few feeble gas jets. A small cavalry escort and carriages for the presidential party had been stationed too near the tracks. When the train came rushing out of the darkness with headlight glaring, bells ringing, steam escaping, and whistles blowing, the horses took fright and almost stampeded. "We finally got Mr Lincoln into a carriage," my father wrote, "but having accomplished that, it looked for a while as if we would never get the carriage out of the crowd. . . . I hope we shall not get into another such rush." Major Hunter had his arm so badly injured that it was feared he could not continue the journey.

The party was scheduled to leave next morning at five. At that hour everything was vacancy and gloom. Snow covered the ground. Clanging bells and the hissing of steam sounded through the empty station. The only human beings to be seen were the muffled figures of trainmen going about their tasks. This was the only time during the journey when shouting crowds were absent.

Although Mr. Lincoln had refused to wear a shirt of mail, the danger of an attack upon him was not imaginary. On February 21st, he heard from two trustworthy sources that there was likely to be trouble—perhaps even an attack—at Baltimore, where, at that time, railroad cars were drawn by horses slowly through the streets from one depot to another. William H. Seward, who was to be Secretary of State, sent his son to Philadelphia with urgent messages from his father and General Scott. Another warning came from Allen Pinkerton, a Chicago detective employed by the Philadelphia, Wilmington, and Delaware Railroad.

He and Mr. Seward both urged the President-elect to change his plans and to pass through Baltimore on a night train, several hours ahead of his announced schedule.

Norman B. Judd, perhaps the most active and influential member of Mr. Lincoln's suite, urged him to go on to Washington that very night. Mr. Lincoln said that would be impossible, since he had promised to raise a flag before Independence Hall early the following morning, and after that to go to Harrisburg to visit the Pennsylvania legislature. He had no further engagements. Other members of his suite were called into conference, and, after listening to all they had to say Mr. Lincoln decided to heed the warning. He told them he felt no personal fear of assassination, but that this was no longer a personal matter. It had become a public question involving the orderly transmission of authority in the United States Government, which he, as an individual, had no right to put in jeopardy.

The plans were altered—but as little as possible. The flag raising took place at sunrise, immediately after a reception in Independence Hall. The morning was cold. My father, who stood close to Mr. Lincoln, remembered that the latter removed his hat and stood bareheaded during the short prelude of speechmaking and prayer. Then, the time having come to raise the flag, Mr. Lincoln threw aside his overcoat and went at the task as if he were still an efficient backwoodsman. My father remembered, too, how grandly the breeze caught the unfolding flag as it ran upward and spread it to display all its stars. A myth grew up to the effect that the President-elect had performed the rite in his shirt sleeves. This my father strongly denied. "He simply took off his hat at the beginning of the speech-making, and his overcoat when it came time to pull."

The flag raising over, Mr. Lincoln kept his appointment in Harrisburg, then returned to Philadelphia. With Colonel Lamon as his only companion, he took a night train that brought him into Washington early next morning, where he was met by Mr. Seward and Representative Washburne of Illinois. News of his safe arrival being flashed over the country by telegraph, there was no longer danger of attack. The rest of the party, following the original schedule reached the capital late that afternoon.

For this change in his program Mr. Lincoln was accused of "sneaking into Washington in disguise," wearing a long cloak and a Scotch cap—a costume which would certainly have called instant attention to his tall figure.

My father's first letter from Washington began:

We all arrived here safely last evening about five o'clock, Mr Lincoln having preceded us the night before. I assure you it was a real pleasure to get to our journey's end, with the prospect of a little rest now and then. During the last week of our trip, in the great whirlpools of New York and Philadelphia, not a moment was our own.... One of the papers I sent you from New York I went to the printing office and bought and had wrapped up after two o'clock A.M. last Thursday.

Of course I need not try to detail the incidents of the trip. These you have no doubt sufficiently gathered from the newspapers.

For the present we are quartered at Willard's Hotel. The original program was to go to a private house which had been rented for the purpose.* This plan having been changed,

---

* A note on pages 46-47 of *Lincoln and the Patronage* by Harry J. Carmon and Reinhard H. Luthin tells us this was "Mr. Smoot's house, on Franklin Row," engaged by the Illinois delegation. The plan was changed by Thurlow Weed, who said it would never do to allow Mr. Lincoln to go to a private house, and be under the influence of State control.

and no rooms having been reserved, all the party except Mr
Lincoln have but sorry accommodations. Well, next week we
hope to be in the White House where perhaps it may be
better.

You need have no present fears about our entire safety
here. There is not the least apprehension about trouble at
the inauguration, or at any other time. That cloud has blown
over.

On the morning of March 4th, he went to Mr. Lincoln's
room at the Willard and made, at his direction, a few
minor changes in the wording of the inaugural address.
Then he accompanied the President-elect to the Capitol.

My father's next letter must have given Therena a real
thrill, for it was the first one she received dated from the
Executive Mansion. "We had a gratifying and glorious
inauguration yesterday," he told her. "A fine display,
and everything went off as nicely as it could possibly be
devised." At that point he had to lay the letter aside, and
two days passed before he found time to finish it.

The morning of March 4th had not dawned propi-
tiously, but the clouds soon broke away. Street sweepers
had been plying their brooms most of the night before
along the route of the parade, so that Washington's un-
paved streets, usually either a sea of mud or filled with
clouds of yellow dust, were fairly clean.

The town was therefore at its best when President
Buchanan called for Mr. Lincoln at his hotel, and the
two rode side by side through brilliant sunshine to the
Capitol in the inaugural parade. But under this pleasant
surface there was distinct tension. Because of threats made
that the new president would not be allowed to take office,
General Scott had posted sharpshooters on commanding
roofs along the line of march, and in the windows of the
Capitol itself; and the battery on the brow of the hill,

which was to thunder forth the presidential salute had orders to fire a more deadly volley if need arose.

The crowd which, according to the newspapers, was "larger by half than on any similar occasion," was composed chiefly of men. Although it was generally well-mannered, enough young toughs had joined it (coming, it was said, from Baltimore) to stage a demonstration of their preference for Buchanan's policies over those of the Republicans. This small riot had been promptly quelled, but those responsible for keeping order were very much on the alert.

Unusual noises were regarded with suspicion. A strange low clatter recurring at intervals of about three seconds caused real concern until traced to its innocent source. This proved to be only a company of New Hampshire men who marched in the parade wearing the heavy boots with "pegged" soles, common in their northern climate. The warmer weather of Washington had caused the wooden pegs to shrink, and as they marched in rhythm all the pegs complained in unison.

The cautious *National Intelligencer* pronounced the parade "in some respects" the most imposing the city had ever seen. Almost twenty military organizations took part, along with "numerous dragoons on foot." A final touch of splendor was provided by the local Republican Association, whose float, drawn by six white horses, was filled with laurel-wreathed little girls to represent the States of the Union. These had with them, according to one newspaper account, *two* Goddesses of Liberty.

A temporary platform large enough to seat three hundred officials and people of importance had been built out from the central entrance to the Capitol. The rest of the onlookers gathered around it in the eastern plaza. According to custom, the Vice-President-elect first took the oath of office in the Senate Chamber, then the notables filed out into the sunshine to take their seats on the platform.

In the central group were President Buchanan and Mr. Lincoln, the Chief Justice who was to administer the oath, his clerk who carried the Bible, and several others, noticeable among them being Stephen A. Douglas, one of the defeated presidential candidates, who had also been Lincoln's antagonist two years before in their contest for a seat in the Senate. But until his death he was most loyal to the new administration.

After the inaugural address was finished and the applause had died down, Roger A. Taney, Chief Justice of the United States Supreme Court, arose. Even in his voluminous robes of office he looked very old and small and shrunken beside the tall man who stood facing him, gaunt and strong. The clerk stepped forward and opened his Bible. Mr. Lincoln placed his hand upon it and slowly and distinctly repeated after the Chief Justice the words that changed him from Abraham Lincoln the plain citizen who had as many rights as had millions of his fellow Americans (and no more), to Abraham Lincoln, highest officer in the land, on whose shoulders rested the power, the responsibility, and the heartbreak of administering this great trust.

The battery on the brow of the hill thundered its salute. Three great cheers broke from the people in the East Plaza. Friends on the platform crowded up to offer congratulations. Soon Mr. Buchanan and President Lincoln disappeared into the Capitol, then re-entered their carriage and drove to the White House where the ex-President took leave of his successor upon the threshold, wishing him happiness and a successful administration.

In the Executive Office, General Scott welcomed the President, and his new duties commenced at once. Some were trivial, some exacting and perplexing, but all were in a President's day's work. The first official communication handed Mr. Lincoln after he entered the White House was a letter from Major Anderson, reporting that provisions for his little force in Fort Sumter would be exhausted before relief could reach him.

A great and momentous decision had to be made. Yet he must show himself that night at the inaugural ball. Several hundred strangers and sightseers were already clamoring at his door to wish him well; and word came that the gorgeously decorated float that figured in the parade had just drawn up before the White House, and all the little girls were climbing down, hoping to be kissed by the new president.

On the evening of March 7th, my father, seizing a spare moment, resumed his interrupted letter to Therena:

I wrote as far as the above on the day after the inauguration when I had to lay it aside ... and until now have been unable to find a moment to take it up again. ... I know that you would cheerfully grant me absolution if you could but half appreciate how my time is taken up. ... Mr Lincoln is inaugurated and has got the government started. For the present, as I wrote you, you need not have apprehensions of danger to him or those about him. I consider myself quite as safe here as I used to be in the *Free Press* office years ago.

Since I commenced writing this I have again been called away to appease visitors who are importuning to see Mr Lincoln, so don't be surprised if I break off anywhere and fold this up and mail it to you, for I am going to send you something tonight if it is only an empty envelope.

The first official act of Mr Lincoln after the inauguration was to sign my appointment as Private Secretary. ... As the work is now it will be a very severe tax on both my physical and mental energies, although so far I have felt remarkably well. By and by, in two or three months, when the appointments have all been made, I think the labor will be more sufferable. John Hay and I are both staying here in the White House. We have very pleasant offices and a nice large bedroom, though all of them sadly need new furniture and carpets. That too we expect to have remedied after a while.

We all stayed at Willard's Hotel the week before inauguration. There was of course a great crowd there, and so many ladies in the parlors as to make it seem like having a party every night. Since my arrival I have been to one party, one wedding, and the inaugural ball, which by the way, was really a very successful and brilliant affair. Today the *Corps Diplomatique* made their formal call upon the President, and tomorrow night the first public reception takes place.

He reported that this first public reception was pronounced "the most successful ever known here." For more than two hours people streamed rapidly through the doors, "and many climbed in at the windows."

It was withal more "tonish" than such things usually are. Of course in such a crowd crinoline suffered, and at least fifty men have been swearing worse than "our Army in Flanders" ever since . . . over the loss of new hats and valuable overcoats. But for particulars I must refer you to the *Star* I mailed you this morning.

At that time the second floor of the White House was shared by the President's family and the office force, the family occupying the western half, the offices the eastern half of the building. My father's office must have been next to that of the President, since most, if not all, of Mr. Lincoln's visitors seem to have passed through it on their way to call upon him, and William O. Stoddard hints in his reminiscences that sometimes it offered a convenient line of retreat for the President when he sought the more private parts of the Mansion. John Hay's office was near by, and various assistants and clerks, added to the force as the war developed, were fitted in as space permitted. Soon after his arrival my father wrote:

As the existing laws do not provide for an assistant for me, I have had John Hay appointed to a clerkship in the Department of the Interior and detailed for special service here at the White House, so that he gives me the benefit of his whole time.

My father appears to have been entirely responsible for John Hay's presence in Washington. In Springfield, when the time of departure for Washington neared, he asked his chief if John might go with them. An odd expression crossed Mr. Lincoln's face, turning all its ruggedness into lines of perplexity, as he answered: "But I can't take all Illinois with me!"

He did, however, decide he could take John Hay, and nobody ever regretted the decision, even though—as is recorded—Mr. Hay's family disapproved at the time because, they said, such a move would "necessarily interfere with his law-studies."

7

THE PRIVATE SECRETARIES

LIFE IN WASHINGTON SOON SETTLED DOWN for my father and John Hay into a threefold existence: political, personal, and social. On the social side he and John Hay seem to have been expected to act as liaison officers between the new administration and a highly critical local society, which was inclined to write its name with a very big *S*. During the previous administration, its atmosphere had been distinctly southern, and it prided itself on a *savoir faire* that had been sufficient to guide Washington without mishap through the ordeal of a visit from His Royal Highness, the Prince of Wales. Broad-minded members of this group might admit that Mr. Lincoln meant well—possibly that, according to his lights, he even had political sagacity—but they were sure that these people from the West were socially out of the question.

Mr. Lincoln, however, had lived in Washington as a Member of Congress. His wife never found it difficult to accustom herself to the ways of fashion. His official household was gently coached by the State Department (the private secretary not being above asking advice). So, all things considered, the new administration got on very well

socially, to the disappointment of its critics. At first even
the manner of dancing in Washington seemed strange to
the young man who had danced with the best of them in
Springfield. After explaining the differences to Therena,
he wrote, "It may be fun to dance in this way, but according to a 'barbarian's' view, there is very little sense or
reason in it."

There is an amusing list in my father's handwriting, of
what gentlemen should wear on occasions of ceremony:

Coat;
  Black dress
  Blue   "   bright buttons.
Pants;
  Black—white in summer.
Vest;
  Black.
Shirt;
  (Here the paper was left virgin white.)
Gloves;
  White or straw kids.
Boots;
  Boots or shoes.
Cravat;
  White.

The President conformed in dress to the prevailing
mode, as he had done all his life. He was always neat, and
his coats were made by a good tailor. But he never lost
the loose-jointed gait of the frontiersman, and his garments seemed to hang upon him rather than to be worn.
When he donned the "white or straw kids" demanded by
fashion for evening receptions, his large hands seemed
doubly conspicuous—great white shapes against the black-
ness of his attire. Mrs. Lincoln, standing beside him, short
and plump and very dressy in her hoops and laces and

pearls, made his height all the more apparent. The old Washington set came to pay its respects—with reservations, thinking them an odd-looking couple.

One of my father's important duties was to supervise arrangements for official functions. The list of diplomats, with their respective ranks, was prepared by the State Department. This was especially useful, since it was supplemented with helpful details: A titled foreigner should never be addressed as "Sir." If a diplomat should come to the White House in the evening to make a friendly call, it would be well for the President to "go down." The President and his family might dine early when alone, but the hour for state dinners was seven o'clock. The Lincolns soon improved on this, sending out invitations for seven-thirty.

The detail that bored my father most of all was the seating of guests at state dinners, where "unbreakable" rules of precedence loomed large, yet occasionally had to be side-stepped because of personal or political feuds. Worst of all, some last-minute illness or caprice might cause an expected guest to send a "regret," which of course upset the whole apple cart, and the work had to be done over again. This was a hard assignment for a young man who had come to America in an emigrant ship and had grown up in the woods and in a country printing office. How painstakingly he solved such problems is shown by his neat diagrams of the banquet table, the ladies' names in decorative red ink, the gentlemen's in black— accompanied by lists of the guests originally invited, and of those who finally came.

In fulfilling duties of this kind, my father was conscious at times of friction behind the scenes. I should like to quote at this point his account of an episode that occurred a year later, prefacing it with the explanation that among the helpful hints sent over from the State Department was this: "*Parties if given, must be entirely informal or accidental.*" Tiring in the course of a year of this restriction, Mrs. Lincoln sent out invitations in February 1862 for a party which was by no means "accidental." After it was over, Washington newspapers printed columns about the beautiful costumes worn by the ladies and the gracious manners of everybody present, ending with enthusiastic descriptions of the sugar ornaments on the supper table. My father's confidential report to Therena was less complimentary:

Half the city is jubilant at being invited, while the other half is furious at being left out in the cold. It was a very respectable if not brilliant success. Many of the invited guests did not come, so the rooms were not at all overcrowded.... Those who were here (some of them having sought and almost begged their invitations) will be forever happy in the recollection.... Suffice it to say that the East Room ... looked very beautiful, that the supper was magnificent, and that when it was over, by way of an interesting little finale, a couple of the servants, much moved by wrath and wine, had a jolly little knock-down in the kitchen, damaging in its effects to sundry heads and champagne bottles.

This last is strictly *entre nous.*

In time, of course, the young private secretary found some delightful people among the local residents. He enjoyed going for social relaxation to an unpretentious home about which he wrote at length to Therena:

On Tuesday night I attended a little party at Mrs Eames's. Mr Eames was formerly connected with the *Washington Union*, for many years the organ of Democratic administrations here, though now, like other things, passed away. Afterwards he went as Minister to Venezuela. Both he and his wife are very intelligent, amiable and hospitable; and by reason of their position and long residence here as well as abroad, know almost everybody and consequently draw around them the most interesting class of people that visit Washington. Although they have but a small house, and live in a very moderate style, their parlor is really a sort of focal point in Washington society, where one meets the best people that come here. By the "best" I do not mean mere fashionable society people, but rather the brains of society—politicians, diplomats, authors and artists, and occasionally, too, persons whose social and political position merely, and not their brains, entitle them to consideration, such as titled foreigners, pretty women, &c. Politically it is a sort of neutral ground where men of all shades of opinion—Republicans, Fossil Whigs, with even an occasional spice of a Secessionist, come together quietly and socially. Usually we go there on Sunday evenings, say from eight to eleven, without any formality whatever, merely "drop in," coming and going entirely at pleasure and talking to whom and about what everyone pleases. A variety of people of course bring with them a variety of languages, and so, while the key-note is almost always English, the conversation runs into variations of French, German and Spanish. Mr and Mrs Eames speak all of them but the German.

The party on Tuesday evening was given to Lady Georgiana Fane, daughter of the Earl of Westminster I believe, a very rich, reasonably intelligent, horribly ugly English old maid, who is traveling in the United States. . . . The guests talked and acted just as the same number of any other well-informed people would do. I find it an agreeable place to visit, and the best place in the city to meet distinguished people.

After another evening there he wrote:

I had the pleasure of meeting Charlotte Cushman, the great actress, and a Miss Stebbins who is a sculptress. . . . They sail from New York for Rome on the 17th. Charlotte Cushman is, I think, the most masculine woman I ever saw, though evidently a woman of very great intellect. She is getting old and ugly.

But society's annoyances and amusements merely cast a thin deceptive veil over the Washington scene. People attended the theater, gave parties and received and returned calls, just as they performed many other acts of daily living—partly from habit, partly because such acts are instinctively recognized as steadying influences in times of stress. The real interest lay, not in who had or had not been invited to Mrs. Lincoln's grand party, but in who could most quickly reach the President to ask help or to give advice.

The comparative leisure to which the President's secretary at first looked forward—a time when he could at least attend to the President's mail without being constantly interrupted by requests to "see Mr. Lincoln for only five minutes"—never came. When war descended upon the country the crowds besieging the White House did not lessen; they merely changed character, men in civilian dress giving way to a larger proportion of officers in uniform, and to tearful women, sometimes with babies in their arms, who came to plead for soldiers in trouble. John Hay has told us that these crowds had a character all their own, a mixture of enthusiasm, deep emotion, and greed—strange indeed, but not entirely ignoble. Almost every tale these people brought was worth listening to; but after a time their mere numbers seemed to rob them of individuality, and they merged into a great cataract of emotion that poured over the President.

At first he had refused to limit his office hours in any way, saying, "They do not want much, and they get very little.... I know how I would feel in their place." So, the visiting began before breakfast and ended late at night.

Soon, even Mr. Lincoln saw that something must be done to curb this demand upon his time, and he agreed to limit the official visiting period to five hours—from ten in the morning till three in the afternoon. Later on, he cut the hours to three—from ten until one. His secretary found this "a great improvement," though the kindly president was constantly breaking his own rule to oblige importunate visitors. He was so sympathetic, and disliked so sincerely to say "No," but had to say it so often, that one is tempted to believe the story that credits him with exclaiming, when told that he had a slight case of varioloid, "At last I have something I can give everybody!"

He had not the defense of conventional phrases behind which a man less frank might have taken refuge. Even his greetings were honest. For example, he never said "I am delighted to see you," unless that was really the truth. Instead it would be "How do you do?" or "What can I do for you?"

He was never able to bring himself to conform strictly to official usage. Indeed, he was hopeless where mere established etiquette was concerned, and he continued to do things in a way peculiarly his own, spontaneous and unconventional. His casual manners endeared him to his admirers but alternately shocked and distressed the more conventional. A general, impressed with his own rank, did not like to be called downstairs from his desk, even by the President of the United States, to be introduced to a captain, just because Mr. Lincoln chanced to discover that they came from the same state. But in spite of such heedlessness of established custom, the President had a keen sense of official courtesy, and a quietly assured manner which showed that he fully realized the dignity of his office. "He will not be bullied—even by his friends," John Hay wrote.

At that time the law provided for only one private secretary, a duty now officially assigned to three, and actually performed by many more. John Hay's help had been secured, as we have seen, by a subterfuge. Attending to the mail, which was theoretically the primary duty of these young men, was only the beginning. A daily digest of the news had to be prepared and laid before the President who was too busy to do more than glance at the telegraphic reports in the local papers.

Then there were endless visitors to be seen and persuaded, whenever possible, that an interview with the President was unnecessary. After that, times and seasons had to be arranged for the irreducible minimum of interviews. Pompous senators, who in previous administrations had been accustomed to stride unchallenged through well-filled anterooms and enter the Presence, were inclined to resent it when these "mere boys from the West" presumed to block their way to the "new man."

These "mere boys" did look very young, and not at all formidable, but those who tried to oppose them found that the President's secretaries usually carried their point. My father, who was then twenty-nine, was more than five feet ten inches tall, but thin almost to emaciation. Never in his life did he weigh more than a hundred and twenty-five pounds. His eyes were blue, his hair a dark brown, which changed in time to snowy white. His peculiarly sensitive mouth was partly hidden by the mustache and small beard he wore from early manhood. People who knew him in wartime commented on his "slow smile." He smiled frequently, but seldom laughed aloud. His quiet movements were a secret he had learned when, as a boy, he had made friends with the wild things of the forest. His mind was as agile as his movements were gentle. One who knew him superficially, as all Washington soon came to know him,

(left)

JOHN G. NICOLAY

(right)

JOHN HAY
From the collection
of Frederick Hill
Meserve

THE PRIVATE SECRETARIES
(1861-65)

described him as calm and unemotional, with the "gift of hearing the other fellow talk." Also, he was known as a man who was quick to take a hint, and (a most valuable quality in a private secretary) who "never said anything worth quoting."

John Hay, whose gaiety and smooth rosy cheeks and wonderful brown eyes made him look even younger than his twenty-three years, seemed at once more boyish and more sophisticated than my father. He would have felt at home in any drawing room, just as my father would have been at home in any forest. He might have drawn to himself more criticism in Washington had he not been born with peculiar charm of manner. It was said that he "laughed through the war." Be that as it may, John Hay never laughed *at* it; and his lighthearted social tact added a welcome element to life in the White House. His admiration increased daily for the tall, sad, yet humorous man on whom the war burden was settling so cruelly. Even the President's rare bursts of annoyed impatience made him appear only more lovably human.

"Now go away!" he exclaimed to a visitor who clung to him persistently repeating over and over again, a futile request. "Go away! I cannot attend to all these details. I could as easily bail out the Potomac with a teaspoon!"

He called John Hay "John," and regarded him almost as a son. The President's attitude toward my father is summed up in the latter's statement: "There was never any red tape between us." He addressed him by his last name, as he did most of his friends—even those he had known since boyhood. Informal though he was, there were certain conventions the President rarely failed to observe; this was one of them, and it commanded formality in return. Robert Lincoln once told the writer that even his mother habitually addressed the President as "Mr Lincoln." Contrary to popular belief, he was not commonly called "Abe" after he was grown. "Old Abe" and "Father Abraham" were expressions of affection coined and used by his fellow countrymen when speaking of, but not to, Mr. Lincoln.

Letters came to the White House by the bushel. Some, usually the unimportant ones, were marvels of copperplate curliness. Others were nearly illegible scrawls. All of them had to be sifted and sorted by the secretaries. Silly and abusive letters were assigned to their obvious destination, the wastebasket. Letters carelessly or through ignorance misdirected were referred to the various departments to which they should have been sent in the first place. A few, comparatively speaking, but still more than he could read, were placed on Mr. Lincoln's desk.

After he had been in Washington several months, my father came upon a letter from David Davis, forwarding a complaint from "Mr Phelps, the oldest member of Congress, and as strong a Union man as lives." Mr. Phelps stated that an opinion was "quite prevalent" that these presuming youngsters deliberately prevented letters from reaching the President. My father saw to it that this particular missive reached Mr. Lincoln with all speed, and wrote Mr. Davis:

Literally considered this is true. [Then he went on to point out why, nevertheless, the charge was erroneous and untrue.] A moment's reflection will convince you that the President has not time to read all the letters he receives, and also that [among any] hundred miscellaneous letters there will be a large proportion which are obviously of no interest or importance. These the President would not read if he could. ...So far as I know your own letters have always received a special attention not only from the secretaries, but from the President himself.

Since this was the first complaint of the kind received from a person of standing, my father asked, as a matter of justice alike to the President and to himself, that similar direct grievances be communicated to them at once. He ended with these words: "I have shown this letter to the President, and have his permission to send it." Having thus expressed himself on paper, he marked it "not sent," and laid it away—as Mr. Lincoln sometimes did, after having relieved his feelings in the same way.

When the mass of correspondence finally grew too great for the two secretaries to handle, extra help was secured, as John Hay's had been, by whipping the devil around the stump—a clerk being ostensibly appointed to one of the departments, then assigned to "duty at the White House." William O. Stoddard, perhaps the earliest of these, was originally a clerk in the Department of the Interior, authorized to sign land patents for the President. But since few land patents were signed during the war years, he was told to report at the White House where land patents could be signed just as well. He was given a desk in Mr. Hay's office, and among other duties took over the care of Mrs. Lincoln's mail. She liked "Stod" better than she liked either my father or John Hay, and appears to have called upon him for all kinds of services, which they were only too glad to delegate to him.

When, after some months, Mr. Stoddard was incapacitated by illness, my father asked that Edward D. Neale of Minnesota be appointed in his place, and that Charles H. Philbrick of Illinois, an old-time friend, be made a second-class clerk in the Department of the Interior and assigned to duty at the White House. This accounts for the number of individuals whose families claim, quite innocently, that they were "Private secretary to President Lincoln." Legally and officially my father was the only one. John

Hay was known as his assistant. The others did clerical work and filled in as occasion demanded. When both my father and John Hay were absent, it was "Stod" who carried messages from the President to Congress, messages he described as "paper latch-keys, opening every door." In his book of reminiscences he characterized my father as "the impassable Mr Nicolay," who "has a fine faculty of explaining to some men the view he takes of any untimely persistency." On another page he remarked, "People who do not like him—because they cannot use him, perhaps— say he is sour and crusty. Good thing that he is. The President showed his good judgment when he put Mr Nicolay just where he is."

As the war went on, the President's face grew haggard and careworn. He slept badly. He was just as kind and listened with the same sympathetic patience to the requests and petitions of his visitors, but his hearty laugh was heard less often. Sometimes, wandering about the Executive Mansion, when he should have been in bed even if not asleep, he would see a light in the bedroom shared by his secretaries, and enter, book in hand, to enjoy with them some odd conceit with which he sought to gain momentary relief from thoughts that oppressed him. The strange appearance of his tall spare figure in his night clothes seemed to John Hay funnier than the jest he came to read to them. After chatting a few moments, he would go out again. Turning to each other, the young men would speak affectionately of him as "The Ancient," or "The Tycoon"—or, if they were especially moved, as "The American."

The household staff all loved him. William O. Stoddard expressed his feeling by saying that no matter who called upon Mr. Lincoln, "the visitor seemed to diminish in size in contrast with him."

8

WASHINGTON ISOLATED

M Y FATHER TOOK CARE TO BE OPTIMIS-
tic in his letters to Therena. Five weeks after the
inauguration he wrote:

All the excitement we have here now is over the prospect
of a war with the South which the newspapers insist is near
at hand. I myself do not see the prospect in so gloomy a
light. . . . I do not think that either the authorities or any
number of the people of either section want a civil war.

On April 11th, the day Major Anderson refused the
Confederate demand to surrender, he wrote:

Don't get alarmed at the "rumors of wars" . . . There is
some idle gossip about the danger of a demonstration being
made by the Secessionists against the Capital, but I do not
regard it as being at all probable. The Southerners will, I
think, need all their forces in their own country."

Then he went on to tell of various measures already
taken to safeguard the city. A company of volunteers had
been mustered into active service; another would be added
if necessary. Guards were set nightly about the public
buildings. "John Hay and I were challenged by a sentinel

last night as we were returning from down town to the White House."

At midnight on April 14th he wrote that that morning he had copied the President's proclamation calling for volunteers.

I shall not write much. The news you will of course read before you could possibly see it in this letter.—That Fort Fisher has been taken by the southern rebels—That the President has called out 75,000 men to put down the rebellion, and that Congress is to be convened in July. All these things will make stirring times. I can hardly realize that they are so, even as I write.

On April 19th the Massachusetts Sixth, hurrying to the defense of Washington, was attacked as it passed through Baltimore. Late that night he wrote Therena:

Before this reaches you, if indeed it reaches you at all very soon, you will have read that we are having rather stirring times here. The President's proclamation has been responded to unanimously by the people of the North; and their enthusiasm has stirred the secession feeling and fanaticism of Virginia, and fanned its rebellion into flames. [He followed this with a summary of events at Harper's Ferry and at Norfolk.] At Baltimore today a collision occurred between the troops (a Massachusetts regiment) coming here to defend the city, and the Secessionists, in which several were killed on both sides. It is, I believe, the first bloodshed in this civil war and, singularly enough, is the anniversary of the first bloodshed in the Revolution.

We are expecting more troops here by way of Baltimore, but are also fearful that the Secessionists may ... cut off all communication. We have rumors that 1500 men are gathered and under arms at Alexandria seven miles below here, supposed to have hostile intentions against this city; and an additional report that a vessel was late this evening seen

THERENA BATES NICOLAY

Taken from a broken daguerreotype.

landing men on the Maryland side of the river. All these things indicate that if we are to be attacked at all soon, it will happen tonight. On the other hand we have some four or five thousand men under arms in the city, and a very vigilant watch out at all the possible directions of approach. All the public buildings are strongly guarded; the Secretary of War will remain all night in his Department, and General Scott is within convenient reach. I do not think any force could be brought against the city tonight which our men could not easily repel. . . . Unless they are obstructed somewhere on the way, we think there will be enough troops here by tomorrow evening to render the city very safe. . . . The organization of the militia and the late arrival of troops have been making things quite warlike for a few days past; but we have been much more impressed with the conditions surrounding us by the arrival of Miss Dix, who came to offer herself and an army of nurses to the Government gratuitously for hospital service.

John also was much impressed by the arrival of Miss Dix. "She makes the most munificent and generous offers," he wrote in his diary.

The approaching troops were "obstructed," and it was not until April 25th, almost a week later, that the city felt itself entirely safe. Both young men kept hurried notes during these days of crisis. My father, in fact, made two sets of notes. The more laconic read:

Attempt of Union troops to pass through Baltimore.
Dispatch from Gov. Hicks at 2½ o'clock about collision.
Special train and messenger—"Send no troops."
Comm. arrived at one o'clock at night. (Went to Cameron)
Comm. had interview with President in the morning.
President & Gen. Scott promised to try to send troops around Balto.
Saturday Pres. telegraphed to Gov. Hicks & Mayor Brown to come.

Gov. Hicks had gone to Annapolis—could not. Mayor asked by dispatch whether he should come alone. I woke the Pres. at 1 A.M. Saturday night and by his direction telegraphed "Come."

Interview. Complaint of Mayor. Pres. shows dispatch in justification.

They start home—receive dispatch.

Return post-haste to President.

Have another interview with Pres.

He orders troops back from Cocekeysville.

Gen. Scott and Sec. War dissent.

Harper's Ferry Armory evacuated and burned.

Gosport Navy Yard and vessels destroyed.

A dreary and anxious Sunday.

Committee of "Christians."

Monday—resignations.

Rumors of demonstrations against Capital.

Intercepted dispatches—No communication.

Seward writes letter to Governor Hicks.

Tuesday—great public anxiety.

Talk of proclaiming martial law.

Suspension of business.

Wednesday do. Return of *Pawnee* with marines from Gosport.

Insecurity of city—Navy Yard—Conversation with Captain Dahlgren.

Militia of District unreliable.

Thursday—Arrival of 7th Regiment.

Great public relief.

Governor Hicks convenes legislature.

Proposition to disperse or arrest.

Pres. *vs.* Writes to Scott giving his reasons, but empowering him &c.

Change of feeling in Balto. Officers take their offices.

Offers to permit the reestablishment of travel and communication.

Saturday—Dispatch from Md. Legislature that Comm.
Public-Safety Bill has passed to second reading in the
Senate &c.
Comm. from Legislature.—Bob McLean—speech—submissive.
Sunday.—Seward letters about negroes.
Tuesday—Comm. from Governors of Pa. O. Ind. Ill. Mich.
Wis.

The fuller notes elaborate certain points. They tell us
that the regiment attacked in Baltimore was the Sixth
Massachusetts Volunteer Militia. As it marched through
the streets from one railroad station to the other, it was
set upon by a mob, and fired on the mob in return. A telegram from Governor Hicks and Mayor Brown to apprize
the President of this closed with the request, "Send no
more troops through Baltimore."

About 1 o'clock that night a committee arrived from
Baltimore desiring an interview with the President. The messenger waked me, and instead of waking the President I went
to the War Department where the Secretary of War was
staying to be prepared for emergencies. The mission of the
Committee was if possible to induce the Government to send
no more troops through Baltimore. I woke the Sec. War, who
was not disposed to listen to such a proposition, and went to
sleep again. I learned however from the Chief Clerk that
there were no troops (to their knowledge) on the way which
would reach Baltimore before eight next morning, when they
could see the President with their proposal. This satisfied
them for the time being and they went away.

Next morning by eight they were with the President, or
rather met him at the foot of the stairs as he was going down
to speak to General Scott who was in his carriage at the
door. [General Scott suffered from gout, and the President
was trying to save him all possible pain.] They mentioned

their errand to both, and General Scott promptly suggested "Send them around Baltimore." The President agreed to the suggestion "if in a military point of view" it were practicable, and gave the Committee a note saying that it was his wish, in order to avoid further present difficulty. With this they went home apparently satisfied.

Saturday April 20th the President telegraphed Governor Hicks and Mayor Brown to come to Washington for consultation about affairs. At about midnight a dispatch came from Mayor Brown saying Governor Hicks had gone to Annapolis, and asking if he should come alone. I dispatched for the President, "Come."

Sunday morning the 21st he came with several other gentlemen, one of them being one of the Committee which had come the night before. The first committee had asked only that troops might not be permitted to come through Baltimore, and had gone home seemingly perfectly satisfied with having them come around the city. But a day had made a wonderful transformation. The day before the President had said to them half playfully, "If I grant you this, you will come tomorrow demanding that no troops shall pass around." His words were literally verified. The second Committee assumed as a fact that the people of Baltimore and Maryland were highly incensed at what they believed to be preparations for the invasion and subjugation of the South, and were up in arms, and were resolved to the sacrifice of their lives to permit no more troops to come through their State. President replied that the capital being in the center of Maryland and being in danger, the troops must come to defend it, and must of necessity come through Maryland, there being no other route. He referred again to General Scott's suggestion to bring troops 'round by the Relay route.

The "Committee of 'Christians'" mentioned in the more hurried notes was made up of earnest peace-loving church members, who came to ask the President to recognize the independence of the Southern States.

Washington took on the aspect of a city under siege. The supplies of flour and grain in the Georgetown mills were seized. Business was suspended, stores were closed and locked, the streets remained empty save for hurrying patrols. At the first news of burned railroad bridges and attacks on troops, all transient dwellers in Washington wanted to go home—and the desire was not lessened by a rumor that every able-bodied male might be impressed for the town's defense. On Monday the 22nd several hundred clerks in the government departments gave way to their southern sympathies and resigned their offices. Certain military and naval officers did likewise. One was Commodore Franklin Buchanan, who turned over the Washington Navy Yard with its ships and stores and priceless machinery to Commander Dahlgren and departed, leaving him with scarcely enough marines to keep watch against possible incendiaries. Another was Captain John R. Magruder, who commanded a battery upon which General Scott had placed much reliance for the defense of the city. No case of desertion gave the President greater pain. "Only three days ago," he said, "Magruder came voluntarily to me in this room, and with his own lips, and in my presence, repeated over and over again, his asseverations and protestations of loyalty."

The President had his emotions well under control. In the presence of others he gave little sign of the anxiety he was enduring, but on the 23rd, one of the days of darkest gloom, after the business of the day was over and he thought himself alone, one of the White House staff, passing the open door of the Executive Office, saw him pacing the floor, then pause and look wistfully out of the window in the direction from which help was expected, and heard him exclaim: "Why don't they come? Why don't they come!" Next day, when they still had not come, and he was talking to the wounded men of the Sixth Massachusetts, he spoke with an irony that only the intensest feeling could wring from him: "I begin to believe that there is no North. The Seventh Regiment is a myth. Rhode Island is another. You are the only real thing."

Among my father's notes I find this: "Mails suspended. The telegraph cut. Lane's improvised Frontier Guards perform squad drill in the East Room and bivouac on the velvet carpet among stacks of new muskets and freshly opened ammunition boxes." John Hay wrote in his diary:

April 18. The White House is turned into a barrack. Jim Lane marshalled his Kansas warriors today at Willard's, and placed them at the disposal of Major Hunter, who turned them tonight into the East Room. It is a splendid company worthy such an armory. Besides the Western Jayhawkers it comprises some of the best material of the East. . . . Jim Lane walked proudly up and down the ranks with a new sword the Major had given him. The Major made me his aide, and I labored under some uncertainty as to whether I should speak to privates or not. . . . All day the notes of preparation have been heard at the public buildings and the armories. Everybody seems to be expecting a brother or "young man" in the coming regiments.

April 19. About midnight we made a tour of the house. Hunter and the Italian exile Viveldi were quietly asleep on the floor of the East Room, and a young and careless guard loafed around the furnace fires in the basement; good looking and energetic young fellows, too good to be food for gunpowder—if anything is.

After help arrived, he wrote:

I went up with Nicolay, P. and W. to see the Massachusetts troops quartered in the Capitol. The scene was very novel. The contrast was very painful between the gray-haired dignity that filled the Senate Chamber when I saw it last, and the present throng of bright looking Yankee boys, the most of them bearing the signs of New England rusticity in voice and manner, scattered over desks, chairs and galleries, some loafing, many writing letters slowly with plow-hardened hands, or with rapid-glancing clerkly fingers, while Grew stood patient by the desk and franked for everybody.... Ellsworth telegraphs that his regiment has been raised, accepted, and that he wants them sent to Fort Hamilton for preliminary drill.... Much is hoped from the gallant colonel's Bloodtubs. They would be worth their weight in Virginia currency in Fort McHenry tonight!

Those who saw the arrival of the Massachusetts Seventh on April 25th never forgot it. A great crowd had gathered, and when the regiment marched up wide Pennsylvania Avenue toward the White House in well-formed ranks with music playing and banners waving the oppression that had hung over the city was swept away as by an invigorating breeze. Cheer upon cheer rang out, windows were thrown up, house doors were flung open, and people poured out into the streets to welcome them.

My father explained a week's silence to Therena by telling her that had he written sooner, his letter would have traveled no farther than the nearest letter box, or into the hands of the "Baltimore Barbarians."

Our intercourse with the outside world was cut off. We heard frequently from Baltimore and different parts of Maryland ... uniformly the report was that all heretofore Union men had at once turned secessionists. ... Here we were in this city, in charge of all the public buildings, property and archives, with only about 2000 *reliable* men to defend it. True, we had some 3000 men in addition of the District Militia under arms. But with the city perfectly demoralized with secession feeling, no one could *know* whom of the residents to trust. We were not certain but that at the first moment when Fate would seem to preponderate against us, we would have to look down the muzzles of our own guns. ...We were not only surrounded by the enemy, but in the midst of traitors.

Not that we were at any time in serious danger. With the reliable force at our disposal we could have held the city against largely superior numbers. But had the rebels suddenly precipitated five or six thousand men upon us, which it seemed possible for them to do, it would have given us an infinite deal of trouble.

Then there was another danger. As Sunday, Monday and Tuesday successively passed by without bringing the expected reinforcements, the suspense and uncertainty among the city population grew to such a pitch that a very small untoward circumstance or accident would have stirred up a riot or panic. Fortunately everything went on quietly and smoothly until the arrival of the Seventh Regiment from New York, adding a third to our defensive force and also bringing us the certain information that several additional regiments were at, and this side of, Annapolis. This at once put an end to the suspense ... and men went to talking, laughing, trading and working as before, and since yesterday morning at ten o'clock you couldn't discover from anything but the everywhereness of uniforms and muskets that we are in the midst of revolution and civil war.

9

THE FIRST GREAT BATTLE

AFTER THOSE HECTIC DAYS IN APRIL 1861
life in Washington became more normal, but it was
not the life of peace. The crowds in the White House anterooms changed their character. Forts soon girdled the
city, and one of Society's favorite diversions was to drive
out to visit them. Another was to attend band concerts.
Sometimes the music had an artillery accompaniment. One
of my father's letters tells about a grand concert at the
Navy Yard, attended by the President and Mrs. Lincoln.
He wrote that, after the program, "We went on board one
of the ships and witnessed a little cannon practise, a
Dahlgren gun being fired at a target placed about as far
away as the nearest Confederate battery had been erected
to bombard Fort Sumter."

On another day he wrote:

We have music here in the President's grounds every
Wednesday and Saturday evening, when the grounds are
open to everybody.Yesterday at about half past five there
was quite a large crowd here promenading in the grounds,
when all at once a very brisk firing of musketry was heard
on the other side of the river. There was almost instantaneous
excitement in the crowd, and everybody rushed down to the

99

edge of the grounds where they could see across the river. Several of us went on top of the house, and with a spy-glass could see that it was no battle, but only a detachment from one of the regiments over there, engaged in practise at loading and firing at will. They kept it up for about half an hour, and we had a chance to hear what a small battle or skirmish sounds like at a distance.

Secretary Welles thought he saw in these outdoor concerts an opportunity to foster war enthusiasm, and ordered the Marine Band to play a larger number of patriotic airs. Music meant a great deal to my father, whose ideas on the subject, however, had more to do with melody and harmony than with the throb of drums. An entry in the diary of the Secretary of the Navy tells us that Mr. Nicolay protested, but that he answered sternly that this was "no time to educate the people in sentimental ditties," and that his order would stand.

My father wrote Therena that he had little war news to impart. Both sides were pushing forward war preparations, and he reminded her, for his comfort as well as hers, that the resources of the North were certainly twice as great as those of the revolted states.

The White House continued to be a very busy place, but it was never, during the Lincoln administration, a gay one. Yet probably no President laughed more often than he did. Carl Schurz once likened Mr. Lincoln's hearty laughter to that of the hero of *Sartor Resartus*—"a laugh of the whole man from head to heel." "If it were not for this vent I should die," he told a scandalized congressman who came to talk of serious things and found him laughing at a jest. Then, seeing that the man was hurt by his apparent levity, Mr. Lincoln lapsed quickly into the patient gravity with which he listened to serious pleas and appeals.

A man of many moods but absolute singleness of purpose, he was so unconscious of self that not only his mind but his physical frame responded to the emotion of the moment. When he learned, early in the war that his old friend Colonel E. D. Baker had been killed at Ball's Bluff, he left headquarters, utterly unheeding the orderly's salute, both hands pressed to his heart, his features convulsed with grief.

Certain peculiarities were likely due in part to his great height. Not all chairs are made for men as tall as he. Those who saw him, when he went to the War Department late at night to read the last military dispatches, sitting on the very edge of his chair, with one knee almost touching the floor, failed to realize that such a position was quite natural when compounded of eagerness, utter unconsciousness of self, and the measurements of a chair originally built for a man shorter than himself.

A note my father put away in an envelope marked "Special Lincoln Mem." is dated July 3, 1861, and reads:

This evening the President, in conversation with Mr Browning to whom he had just read his message, not yet completed, said, "Browning, of all the trials I have had since I came here, none begins to compare with those I had between the inauguration and the fall of Sumter. They were so great that could I have anticipated them I could not believe it possible to survive them."

And he said to General Schenck:

If to be the head of Hell is as hard as what I have to undergo here, I could find it in my heart to pity Satan himself.

Yet members of his cabinet accused Mr. Lincoln of levity! Fortunately his joy was as spontaneous as his grief. 'I myself will telegraph the news to General Meade!" he cried, seizing his hat, when, in July 1863, Secretary Welles brought him news that Vicksburg had fallen. Then he stopped, his face beaming, caught Mr. Welles's hand, and almost embracing him said, "I cannot tell you my joy over the result. It is great, Mr. Welles, it is great!"

When he laughed heartily his whole body seemed filled with mirth. An old Springfield friend, with deep insight, called laughter "the President's life-preserver." He found in it what many men seek in alcohol—something to make him forget care for a moment and thus bring him renewed strength to bear his burden. Yet such was his self-control that he could make his face a mask when he chose to do so, and it was not often that casual visitors realized the depths of his feelings. He considered it a duty of his high office to keep up the courage and spirits of his countrymen during the dark days of war. For this he had need of all his endurance and all his self-control.

At best his sleep was light and capricious, and many were the wakeful nights he passed. "I believe I feel trouble in the air before it comes," he once said, entering the room of his secretaries to bring news he had just received of a military disaster.

No, the White House was not a gay place in those days, despite the President's laugh and his quaintly humorous sayings, or John Hay's youthful cheerfulness, or the official functions, or even the pranks and doings of the two little Lincoln boys who brought an undercurrent of normal life into its rooms and corridors.

Before the end of May 1861 the great East Room was the scene of a stately military funeral held for young Colonel Ellsworth who had come to Washington with the presidential party only two months before. He was one of those phenomenal youths who flash through history now and again—a combination of genius, energy, and self-confidence that had won the admiration of thousands. He had been interested in soldiers from childhood, and the goal of his early ambition had been West Point. Poverty and misfortune having closed that door to him, early manhood found him in Chicago without friends or money— almost without food. But he managed to get together a volunteer company of about sixty Chicago youths, mostly clerks and business employees, and to clothe them in gaudy Zouave jackets and loose trousers that appealed alike to his opulent color sense and to his disapproval of the restricting uniforms then worn in the Army. Training them to high efficiency in a drill of his own devising, he boldly took them on a tour to show our Eastern cities "the best trained company in America." New York gave him three days of enthusiastic acclaim. West Point could find only one fault with his Chicago Zouaves—that they did not follow the "regular" drill laid down in military textbooks—which was just what he intended to improve upon. He and his men returned to Chicago bearing many trophies, but his methods were too revolutionary to be countenanced by those who could have profited by them. In 1860 he was in Springfield, earning a bare pittance in lawyers' offices. Mr. Lincoln took him to Washington and after the inauguration made him a second lieutenant.

With the beginning of actual war, Ellsworth felt he could do better work outside of the Army, resigned his commission, and went to New York where he raised a regiment of 1100 men among the city's firemen, choosing these men because they were used to a rough life and already knew the value of discipline. He brought them to Washington where he continued their training in a camp outside the city. It was to this regiment that John Hay referred in his diary as "the gallant colonel's Bloodtubs."

When Alexandria, Virginia, was entered by Union troops at daylight on May 21st, Ellsworth marched at the head of his men. The town made no resistance, the rebels having prudently retired. But a Confederate flag still floated defiantly over Alexandria's leading hotel. Ellsworth was seized with a whim to take it down with his own hands and did so, but was shot dead by the hotel proprietor as he descended the stairs with the flag in his arms.

After the funeral, my father, who was one of the pallbearers, wrote to Therena:

I had thought myself to have grown quite indifferent and callous and hard-hearted, until I heard of the sad fate of Colonel Ellsworth, who, as you will already have read, was assassinated at the taking of Alexandria by our troops last Friday morning. But since that time I have been quite unable to keep the tears out of my eyes whenever I have thought or heard or read about it. . . . I had known and seen him almost daily for more than six months past, and although our intimacy was never in any way confidential as to personal matters, I had learned to value him very highly. He was very young—only twenty-four I think—very talented and very poor—a combination of the qualities upon which sadness and misfortune seem to prey. He had by constant exertion already made himself famous, and that against obstacles that would have been insuperable to any other. Since my acquaintance with him my position has enabled me to assist him in his plans and aspirations until I felt almost a direct personal pride and interest in his success. Knowing his ability and his determined energy I knew that he would win a brilliant success if life were spared to him. So that to me his death seems almost a fatality, and though I know the whole nation will mourn for him, yet I am grieved also to feel that they do not half appreciate his worth or their loss.

One day in May a committee representing the governors of six northern states—Pennsylvania, Ohio, Indiana,

Illinois, Wisconsin, and Michigan—came to assure the President of their loyalty and their desire to help crush the rebellion, but also to "demand" that "a positive and resolute policy" be pursued by his administration:

> They did not excuse or justify the impatience existing in some quarters . . . but their States did desire some assurance that the Government was in earnest and would go forward . . . without parleyings or compromise.
>
> A question had arisen as to how these States should protect their borders. If, for instance, Kentucky should secede, as was feared, Cincinnati would be insecure without the possession of Covington Heights across the river. Yet if they took these, the whole State would be in arms at the pretended invasion. The General Government had not indicated what it would do in this case. Ohio desired to know whether, in such a case, local or federal authority should act.

Mr. Lincoln's answer assured them that federal authority would be upheld. The admiration of his secretaries for the way in which the President met his problems grew daily. Years after, my father wrote that it was "impossible to portray by any adequate words, the labor, the thought, the responsibility, the strain of intellect and the anguish of soul he endured" during those early months of war.

Amid such happenings it was inevitable that my father's wish to write a biography of this man should revive and grow from hope to resolve. It also changed in scope. An ephemeral thing like a campaign sketch would no longer suffice. It must be a substantial history telling the story of Mr. Lincoln's life and also of his administration. Perhaps it might even reach the length of two volumes. He talked the matter over with Hay, and the two agreed to write it together. They told the President of their plan. He not only approved, but promised them his personal help.

After that they set about collecting material more systematically; but the press of daily duties interfered with the recording of daily events, and many pages of their notebooks remained forever blank. From time to time, however, they prepared notes intended only for their own eyes, though of necessity these became less frequent as the war gained momentum.

During this hectic time, they naturally had few holidays. But on May 31, 1861, my father wrote enthusiastically to Therena about his "second horseback ride since coming to Washington." In company with John Hay and Robert Lincoln, he crossed the Long Bridge into Virginia where soldiers were busy throwing up defenses to guard the bridge, then rode up the long hill to Arlington House, "old family mansion of the Custis family, the relatives and descendants of Washington." It occupied, he thought, one of the most beautiful situations imaginable—"just opposite the city on a high sloping hill that rises from the Potomac." At that time the estate, in custody of the government, was being kept and cared for just as the Lees had left it. He described the house and furniture, which, he told Therena, brought back "the good old 'First Family' days of Virginia when plantation grandeur atoned somewhat for their assumption of family pride."

In the garden we found an old negro at work, who was born at Mt Vernon before General Washington's death. We asked him many questions—delighted him with introducing Bob the President's son, in whom the old darkey expressed a lively interest—and further pleased him with a gift of small change. Altogether I don't know when I have passed so satisfactory and pleasant an afternoon.

Soon my father had an opportunity to make a short trip to Illinois. Back in Washington before the 4th of July, he wrote that the President, engaged in writing his message to Congress, refused to receive calls either of friendship or business, except from members of the cabinet or high officials.

This has relieved me very much of both annoyance and labor, but I expect that from tomorrow and during the session of Congress I shall again have my hands full. . . . Don't fear that I will fail to take proper care of myself here. . . . There is much more probability that my situation here will have the tendency to make me lose my temper rather than my health.

After the national holiday he wrote her:

The interest of the week just past of course centers around the "Fourth" and the special session which was to begin that day. . . . On the morning of the "Fourth" there was a rather fine review by the President and others. . . . One very pretty incident varied the monotony of the marching of the troops.

Among the regiments is one called the "Garibaldi Guards," made up entirely of foreigners, many of whom have served in European wars. There are, let me say by way of somewhat describing the regiment, men of six or eight different nationalities in it, who speak as many different languages. It is said . . . that the Colonel gives his commands in French, that being the universal language, and understood by the captains of all the companies, who repeat them respectively in German, Spanish, Italian, French, Hungarian &c &c to their men.

In preparing for the review each man had stuck a small sprig of box or evergreen into his hat, and as the successive ranks passed the platform on which stood the President and other officers, they took them out and threw them towards him, so that while the regiment was passing, a perfect shower of leaves and flowers was falling on the platform and the street, which latter was almost covered with them. It was unexpected, and therefore strikingly novel and poetical. Day before yesterday the "Garibaldians" were sent across the river, and, having an idea that there was a fight ahead, they went over the Long Bridge with their loaves of bread stuck on the points of their bayonets, and singing the Marseillaise.

The impression grew that an important battle must soon be fought near Manassas, but few of the loyal inhabitants of Washington doubted its outcome. Spirits were high during the next fortnight, and good news continued to come from the front. When General McDowell's army advanced toward the enemy, the rebels retreated "most precipitately," leaving behind a variety of things, including a freshly cooked breakfast to which one of the Confederate officers had been about to sit down. On July 10th my father wrote:

"The war remains about the same. We are in almost hourly expectation of news of a battle from General McClellan's division in western Virginia. Preparations are being made by General McDowell I think for a forward movement from opposite here towards Manassas Junction.... When the movement is made we do not expect defeat.

On July 14th he reported that they were "all in a high state of gratification" over continued good news from General McClellan's army, and that he had promised himself "a ride across the river to see our camps and fortifications." On the 16th, after mentioning the abandoned breakfast, he added, "Where the enemy will stop and give battle, or whether they will do so at all we do not of course know, and are therefore anxiously awaiting news every moment."

At noon on the 21st:

I think General McDowell's object is to get to the **rear of** the enemy's position before he will offer a general battle.

Actions are, however, almost always controlled more or less by accidents which cannot be foreseen. . . . Even while I write this, dispatches come which indicate that a considerable part of the force is engaged, so that we may know by tonight whether we are to be successful in this fight. . . . Of course everybody is in great suspense. General Scott talked confidently this morning of success, and very calmly and quietly went to church at eleven o'clock.

3½ P.M. . . . During say two hours the President has been receiving dispatches at intervals of fifteen minutes from Fairfax Station, in which the operator reports the fluctuations of the firing as he hears it, at the distance of three or four miles from the scene of action. For half an hour the President has been somewhat uneasy as these reports seemed to indicate that our forces were retiring.

After getting his dinner he went over to see General Scott whom he found asleep. He woke the General and presented his view of the case to him. But the General told him these reports were worth nothing as indications either way—that the changes in the currents of wind, the echoes, &c &c., made it impossible for a distant listener to determine the course of a battle. The General still expressed his confidence in a successful result, and composed himself for another nap when the President left.

From about four to six dispatches continued to come in saying the battle had extended along nearly the whole line—that there had been considerable loss on both sides, but that the secession lines had been driven back two or three miles (Some of the dispatches said to the Junction.) One of General Scott's aides came in and reported substantially that General McDowell would immediately attack and capture the Junction, perhaps yet tonight, but certainly by tomorrow morning.

At six o'clock, the President having in the meanwhile gone out to ride, Mr Seward came into the President's room with a terribly frightened and excited look, and said to John and me, who were sitting there:

"Where is the President?"

"Gone to ride," we replied.

"Have you any late news?" said he.

I began reading Hansen's dispatch to him.

Said he, "Tell no one. That is not so. The battle is lost. The telegraph says that McDowell is in full retreat, and calls on General Scott to save the capital," &c. "Find the President, and tell him to come immediately to General Scott's."

In about an hour the President came in. We told him, and he started off immediately. John and I continued to sit at the windows and could now distinctly hear heavy cannonading on the other side of the river. It is now eight o'clock, but the President has not yet returned, and we have heard nothing further.

Monday morning, July 23d. Thus go the fortunes of war. Our worst fears are confirmed. The victory which seemed in our grasp at four o'clock yesterday afternoon is changed to an overwhelming defeat—a total and disgraceful rout of our men. The whole army is in retreat, and will come back as far as the lines of fortifications on the other side of the river. These have all the time been kept properly garrisoned and are strong enough to make the city perfectly secure.

Retreating troops not only came as far as the fortifications on the Virginia side of the Potomac, they flowed across the Long Bridge into Washington itself, creating near-panic as they came. The citizens loyal to the North quickly rallied. In a movement entirely spontaneous and unprompted, they opened their doors to offer food and refreshment to the hungry and dejected soldiers.

Some senators and members of Congress, prompted by curiosity and sure of victory, had followed the army to witness the sights and sounds of battle. These hurried to the White House where Mr. Lincoln remained awake all night, listening to their stories.

In his next letter my father wrote Therena that the defeat was no worse than he had already reported.

Our forces retreated, as I wrote you, but so far we have not heard that they have been pursued even an inch by the enemy. I have no doubt that we had fairly won the battle, and that had the stampede not occurred among our troops, the enemy and not we would have retreated.

This is a conclusion borne out by a later admission of General Johnston that "the Confederate army was more disorganized by victory than that of the United States by defeat," and by the rueful summary attributed to Mr. Lincoln—"Ah, I see. We whipped the enemy and then ran away from him."

"But the fat is all in the fire now," my father's letter continued, "and we shall have to crow small until we can retrieve the disgrace somehow." Then he ended on a note of determination: "Preparations for the war will be continued with increased vigor by the Government."

10

THE WEARINESS OF WAITING

THE BATTLE OF BULL RUN MAY BE SAID
to have ended the first period of the Civil War. The
three months since the fall of Sumter had been a time of
emotional stress and overconfidence on both sides. After
Bull Run overconfidence changed to grim determination
to wage war to the utmost.

This made necessary a total reorganization of the Union
forces—almost the creation of an entirely new military
establishment, for the regular army had been pitifully
small when Lincoln become President. Of a total of only
17,113 men, 14,000 were in distant parts of the country,
guarding the long frontiers or protecting settlers from
hostile Indians. The 75,000 who had eagerly answered
President Lincoln's first call for troops were enlisted for
only three months, and this term had almost expired when
the battle of Bull Run was fought. These volunteers were
at once mustered out. Whole regiments, as well as single
recruits, immediately re-enlisted "for three years or the
war," and did inestimable service in speedily training the
new recruits. Congress enlarged both the Army and the
Navy, and Washington became the center for organiza-

tion of all these forces—a Federal city, surrounded by camps and yellow earthworks.

Since the President's signature had to be on every new appointment or advance in military rank, this necessitated an endless amount of writing on Mr. Lincoln's part. My father has said that the President would sit down at his desk day after day before a pile of such documents six or eight inches high and go at the monotonous task "with the patient industry of a laborer sawing wood." It truly was heavy labor, for all the commissions were made out on heavy parchment which was very oily and hard to write upon.

For months my father hopefully believed that the war would be short—though he confessed to Therena that he did not see very plainly how and where the end would come. "So far," he wrote, "the necessity still exists for more men, more preparations, and more time in which to make them." The great extent of the line dividing North from South made it necessary to hold so many men for garrison duty as to cut down materially the number available for combat operations. As time went on, he reminded her of a prediction he had made when Washington was cut off from the rest of the world, that the day might come when her home in Pittsfield, only twenty miles from the Missouri border, would be in greater danger of capture than Washington itself. He did not think the citizens of Pittsfield would be disturbed, or Washington captured. "Both are possible," he wrote, "but not at all probable."

But the war did not end quickly. It dragged on for four long years. On Mr. Lincoln, because of his civil obligations as President, and his military status as Commander-in-Chief, rested the final responsibility. Toward him was directed some of the praise for success, and all of the

blame for failures. Early in August 1863 John Hay
wrote my father, exulting and marveling:

He is managing this war, the draft, foreign relations, and
planning a reconstruction of the Union all at once. I never
knew with what tyrannous authority he rules the Cabinet,
till now. The most important things he decides, and there is
no cavil. I am growing more and more firmly convinced that
the good of the country absolutely demands that he should
be kept where he is till this thing is over. There is no man in
the country so wise, so gentle and so good. I believe the hand
of the Lord placed him where he is.

Yet the President was powerless to control the vagaries
of the weather on which so much depends in war, or any
one of a thousand other unpredictable but controlling
events. The two young men who stood near him watched
him grow visibly older under the strain. The shocking
change can be seen even today by placing side by side two
photographs of the President, one taken in 1860, the other
a few days before he died. The first shows a man in vigorous middle age; the other a man on whose face care has
engraved deep lines and suffering placed its unmistakable
seal.

The days of the two young men were filled with duties,
many of which seemed fruitless and even puerile in view
of the national crisis. But the duties had to be performed:
people had to be met; questions to be answered; interviews
with the President to be arranged or discouraged; letters
opened and answered; errands disposed of; and always
there was the element of uncertainty—the strain of looking
for and expecting important news.

During the four war years my father wrote twice a
week to Therena. Fully two-thirds of these letters begin
or end with, "We have not yet heard," or "We are await-

ing with anxiety," or some similar expression of suspense. He gave her what war news he could and rounded out his letters with accounts of unimportant happenings that would keep her in touch with his daily life: the parties he attended; a wonderful microscope he had seen; how Hermann the Magician had come to the White House and performed his tricks in slow motion for the amusement of the President; the reaction of certain young ladies and their parents and pastors to his invitation to attend the opera, a form of amusement still distrusted in some quarters on moral grounds.

If he had nothing else to write about he would compose a letter about the winged insects fluttering among the gaslights over his desk. Even if unspoken, there was frequently a hint of ill health in his missives, for Washington was no health resort. In summer, odors likened by John Hay to "ten thousand dead cats" floated through the south windows of the White House from the still unreclaimed Potomac Flats; the city's sewage system was primitive and in winter the streets were clogged with slush or icy mud. "It seems to take two men to keep one well secretary in the office," my father wrote.

When he or John fell ill, one did the work of both, and sent messages in cryptic slang to the absent one. Whatever the wording, the meaning was always the same: "This is a God-forsaken hole. Keep out of it as long as you can. We get on quite as well without you." But pointed messages did not always arise from the state of their health. After Stanton became Secretary of War, John Hay wrote to my father who was away on business:

Dear Nico: Don't, in a spasm of good nature, send any more people with letters to me requesting favors from Stanton. I would rather make a tour of a smallpox hospital.

My father and Therena were both studying French. Occasionally, he would send her a whole letter in French. More often he added a French paragraph to his more fluent English. Always the war remained the all-engrossing topic.

There is a sort of sameness in everything that surrounds us here [he wrote] that makes it almost impossible to get oneself interested in anything but that which somehow pertains to the war or the troubles of the country. The subject is of intense interest, but when one is situated as I am, where they themselves cannot do anything whatever to advance or retard it, the contemplation of it grows irksome at times. [In another letter] This everlasting frittering away of hours and days is one of the many disagreeable features of life here. [And again] With all my self-taught calmness and self-possession I sometimes get so fidgety and nervous that I am strongly tempted to do one of two things; either to go off somewhere into the Northwest back-woods where I couldn't hear of war and revolution for a year or two, or else to get into the most active and hottest part of the fight, wherever that might be. This being where I can overlook the whole war and never be in it—always threatened with danger and never meeting it—constantly worked to death yet doing (accomplishing) nothing, I assure you grows exceedingly irksome, and I sometimes think even my philosophy will not save me. It is a feeling of duty and not one of inclination that keeps me here. The man who lives in a cabin at the head of some hollow, with corn-bread enough to keep him from starving, and quinine enough to keep off the ague, has quieter nerves and more present satisfaction than I have.

And he realized that, if these were his feelings, how much more acute those of the President must be.

Fortunately, his sense of humor enabled him to find amusement now and again, even in opening the mail. The President had time to read only about one in a hundred of the letters coming to the White House, but we may be quite sure my father placed before him one from that ardent Republican Phineas T. Barnum, who wrote to tell him that Secessionists had become so scarce in New York that he could not find one to exhibit in his Museum. As for my father's own mail, letters came addressed directly to him, as the quickest way of gaining the President's attention, and not a few of the writers claimed personal acquaintance as an excuse for asking favors. The prize letter came from a lady in a small Iowa town, carefully written in a spidery feminine hand, on notepaper surrounded by a patriotic red and blue border. The writer admitted that she had met him only once, years before, when she visited Pittsfield as a mere child. Nevertheless she appealed to him

As an acquaintance in whose opinion I have the utmost confidence, to write me a few lines in regard to the Rebellion now so disturbing to our nation. . . . Do you think England will recognize the Southern Confederacy? Or that our "Loyal Land" will have any trouble with her? Is Lord Lyons a remarkably smart man? How long do you think this unnatural war will continue? &c.

These questions may seem quite foolish to you—but we live in the *Far West* and are unable to learn of the progress of the war as often or as correctly as we wish, and if you will send us what you think of it, you will enlighten and delight us very much.

It is dizzying to reflect how widely an answer to this, written by the President's private secretary, would have been copied in the newspapers.

Crowds continued to make their way to the White House. Mr. Lincoln's secretaries estimated that, in spite of all they could do to reduce the number of his visitors, three quarters of the President's waking hours were spent in meeting people. In addition to those who came by appointment and others who managed by hook or by crook to gain an interview, people thronged to the public receptions he held, usually at noon on days when the Cabinet was not in session. The doors would be opened, and all who wished to do so might enter. For an hour men and women of all classes, from all parts of the country, would pass before him. Not a few brought children with them, and to children the tall President was very kind.

His friends urged him to spare himself the fatigue of this endless greeting and handshaking, reminding him that he would never see a large proportion of these visitors again, and that many came to ask favors he could not grant. But he replied that he could not do without these "public opinion baths" because they kept him in touch with the "plain people" who had elected him. Indeed, during the course of such a reception, there was scarcely a subject of popular interest that was not touched upon and briefly discussed.

Every morning, when my father or John Hay carried their digest of daily news to him, they marveled to find him already so well-informed. The secret lay in these same public receptions. Every visitor added unconsciously an element of enthusiasm or prejudice to the words he spoke. Since Mr. Lincoln had not left behind him his wide knowledge of human nature when he entered the White House, he found even the prejudices illuminating.

Busy though he was, he had leisure and sympathy for each person. He hated to say "No," yet, having to say it so often, he strove to keep the conversation on a plane where the "No," if it must be spoken, would hurt as little as possible. Practically every account of an interview with him, long or short, speaks of his kind, friendly manner, or of his telling an aptly humorous story. More than one of his visitors has said that the outstanding quality of his manner was benevolence, a wish to do somebody some good, if that were possible. Yet he was not at all averse to lively repartee. Perhaps the wittiest "No," he ever spoke was his answer, late in the war, to a man who asked for a pass to go to Richmond. "I would gladly give you a pass," the President assured him, "if it would do any good. But in the last two years I have given passes to 250,000 men— and not one of them has managed to get there yet!"

Another of the President's time-consuming duties was routine desk work, which nobody could do for him. After the first large expansion of the Army, commissions that piled up for him to sign become less numerous, but only to be replaced by reports on court-martial sentences which came to him for final decision. These reached a total of nearly 30,000 a year. Though comparatively few were for capital offences, such cases came to him by the hundreds, and each one that was brought to his notice became the object of his personal care and solicitude. John Hay's diary tells of a July day when six hours were spent in this work. He noted the eagerness with which the President caught at any possible excuse for saving a condemned soldier's life. He was merciless only in cases where meanness or cruelty was shown by the culprit. He was especially averse to punishing cases of cowardice with death, saying it "would frighten the poor devils too terribly to kill them." He called these his "leg cases." "Let him fight, instead of shooting him," he indorsed on the report about a man who had deserted and then re-enlisted.

Secretary Stanton and others protested that Mr. Lincoln was ruining the Army by too much clemency. The President agreed that the reasons they gave for strictly enforcing the law were good—in theory—but said that he "did not think he could do it." He "did not believe it would make a man any better to shoot him," and that he was not at all sure how he would act himself, if shots were whistling by and great oblong shells shrieking in his ears. On another occasion he said that if a man had more than one life a little hanging "would not hurt this one," but that since the soldier could not be brought to life again, he thought he would pardon him. Some of the reasons he gave for granting pardons were whimsical enough, but there was a sound principle underlying his actions. He tried to probe for motives, and if a man's general record was good, he accepted that as presumptive evidence that he meant to do right, even though his "cowardly legs" got the better of his will power.

The President was personally brave. He demonstrated this courage beyond question when Fort Stevens near Washington was under fire. Mr. Lincoln was at the fort and, anxious to see everything, could scarcely be persuaded to leave the exposed position in which his tall figure, topped by a high silk hat, made him a conspicuous target.

The danger of assassination disturbed those about him much more than it did himself. This was another case in which he accepted theories put forth as good, but could not bring himself to act in accordance with them. Since he had never wished to injure anybody, he could not make himself believe anyone wished to do him bodily harm.

Once he was actually fired upon as he rode out to spend a summer night at the Soldiers' Home. He thought his horse had merely taken fright at the accidental discharge of a gun, until somebody showed him the bullet hole through his hat. Even then he refused to believe the shot had been meant for him, and he especially asked that no mention be made of it in "the press."

As to the possibility of danger in or near the White

House, he dismissed it by saying that a certain amount of risk was unavoidable unless he shut himself up in an iron box, from which he could not exercise the functions of President. "Why put up the bars" he asked, "when the fence is down all around?" The White House grounds were guarded, and because Mrs. Lincoln worried when he went over to the War Department at night, unarmed and alone, as he was wont to do, he carried a stout stick—when he happened to remember it. Later, when it was decided that he should have the protection of a cavalry escort on his afternoon drives, he submitted; but he did so unwillingly, saying the jingle of sabers and spurs made so much noise that he and Mrs. Lincoln could not hear their own voices, and that the men of his escort seemed so young and so unused to firearms that he feared injury from their carelessly handled weapons, far more than from the bullet of an assassin.

Inside the White House, Edward Moran was on duty at the front door, as he had been since he was appointed to the post, years before, by President Zachary Taylor. Moran was a host in himself—a short, thin, humorous Irishman, to be trusted equally with state secrets, or with the diplomatic management of the President's unpredictable young son Tad. Upstairs, in the corridor just outside the door to my father's office, Edward, a trustworthy colored man, stood to admit visitors, after carefully looking them over. Those who had appointments with the President underwent further inspection as they crossed to enter Mr. Lincoln's private office. Sometimes, in spite of all this care, questionable characters did get as far as the private secretary. One day my father wrote Therena:

That you may be reassured in the prospect of a speedy crushing out of the rebellion I must inform you of a new agency about to take part in the contest.

The other morning my doorkeeper brought in a plain looking but also very rational looking young man, ordinarily dressed, appearing perhaps more than anything else to be a farmer. I asked him to be seated ... when he at once without circumlocution and in a very matter-of-fact and businesslike way stated the object of his call.

"I am here," said he, "about the business of this war. ... I am commissioned from On High to take the matter in hand and end it. I have consulted with the Governor of York State, and he has promised to raise as many men of the militia of that State as I need. But as I didn't want to proceed without authority, I came here to see General Halleck. I have had an interview with him and he told me that he could not give me any men or assistance, that nobody but the President had any authority to act in the case. I have therefore come to see the President to obtain his consent to begin the work. Although no power is competent to stop or impede my progress, yet I desire to act with the approval of the authorities. I shall take only 2000 men, and shall go down South and get Jeff Davis and the other leaders of the rebellion and bring them here to be put in the lunatic asylum—because they are plainly crazy, and it is of no use to be fighting with crazy men."

In reply I assured him that the President was so engaged that it would be impossible for him to gain the desired interview—that the President would give him no men nor authority of any kind—and that whatever he did in the matter he must do on his own responsibility. He appeared to be satisfied that I properly represented the President, and went away saying that he should write at once to the Governor of York State to raise and organize his force for him, and proceed with his work.

All this transpired with as much gravity and method as if it had been a little conference about any matter of routine business, and an observer would have thought that I was as crazy as the man himself from the perfectly serious and natural manner in which both he and I talked the matter over.... I find the best way to dispose of such people is to discuss and decide their mad projects as deliberately and seriously as any other matter of business.

One of the notes he made about current affairs and put away among his private papers in the fall of 1861 was a long and detailed account of the trouble that had developed with General John C. Frémont, the Republican candidate for president in 1856, whose brilliant early career in California had earned him the name of "The Pathfinder." When war darkened the horizon, Frémont had seemed to promise great hope for the future. He had been made Federal commander of the Western Department, with headquarters at St. Louis. For a time all went well. Then complaints began to be made of General Frémont's reckless expenditures and of his equally reckless tendency to issue orders at variance with those of the administration. In August he issued a proclamation declaring free all slaves belonging to rebel masters in the State of Missouri and directed that their masters, if caught with arms in their hands, should be shot.

This greatly troubled the President and General Scott, who foresaw that the proclamation, as worded, would have a most discouraging effect on the Union men in Kentucky, who up to that time had managed to keep their state loyal. Mr. Lincoln wrote General Frémont a kindly private letter, pointing out his objections, and asking that he "as of your own motion" modify his proclamation to conform to an Act of Congress passed a short time before. Frémont answered that he preferred such an order should come from the President, who thereupon issued it.

This, however, was only part of a complicated Missouri quarrel in which Frémont was accused of gross mismanagement, of unfitness for duty, of surrounding himself with favorites, and of denying himself to others, no matter what their rank or business might be. To make an investigation, the president sent to St. Louis the Quartermaster General of the Army, and a member of his own Cabinet, Postmaster General Montgomery Blair, of the influential Missouri family which had much to do with giving Frémont this office. Within a week Mr. Blair telegraphed that Frémont ought to be removed; but the President refused to do this until they returned and reported to him in person. In October my father, who was in Illinois for a few days, wrote privately to the President from Springfield:

I have taken some pains to learn the feeling here as to Frémont. The universal opinion is that he has entirely failed *and that he ought to be removed*—that any change will be for the better. I am told that since the surrender of Mulligan no one has ventured even to defend him except Governor Koerner who was here for a day or two. So far as Illinois is concerned, there will not be the least risk or danger in his unconditional removal at this time.

He enclosed this report in a private letter to John Hay. Its closing paragraph read:

Frémont is "played out." The d——d fool has completely frittered away the finest opportunity a man of small eminence ever had to make his name immortal.

For some reason known only to the postal authorities this letter, though franked with my father's name, was designated a "dead letter" and did not reach its destination until the following January.

On Thanksgiving Day my father's emotional barometer was very low. Turning to that sovereign remedy for the blues, helping someone else, he wrote Therena that their warm personal friend, Dr. John Hodgen of St. Louis, was in Washington seeking an appointment as Brigade Surgeon, so that he might keep the superintendence of a military hospital in St. Louis. My father thought he might "help him through" the usual red tape.

The outlook that autumn was certainly not cheerful. A memorandum my father made and sealed in an envelope about the time he went west, indorsing it "Conversation with the President, October 2d" is revealing.

Political.

Frémont ready to rebel

Chase despairing.

Cameron utterly ignorant and regardless of the course of things

Cameron

Selfish and openly discourteous to the President

Obnoxious to the country

Incapable of either organizing details or conceiving and advising general plans.

Financial.

Credit gone at St Louis

" Cincinnati

" Springfield

Insurance claims left for Congress to audit.

Overdraft today, Oct. 2, 1861—12,000,000

Chase says the new loan will be exhausted in 11 days.

Military.

Kentucky successfully invaded

Missouri virtually seized

October here, and instead of having a force ready to descend the Mississippi, the probability is that the Army of the West will be compelled to defend St Louis.

Testimony of Chase
        Bates
        The Blairs
        Meigs
        Glover
        Gurley
        Browning
        Thomas, that everything in the West, military
        & financial, is in hopeless confusion.

Small wonder that he wrote Therena "pretty much everything seems to be going wrong."

In December, the forceful removal from the British mail steamer *Trent*, by Captain Charles Wilkes of our Navy, of two Rebel Commissioners, James M. Mason and John Slidell, after they had evaded the blockade and were on their way to England, plunged the administration into a new perplexity. On December 16th my father wrote:

The only excitement of the day is the late news from England, which looks a little squally, and is therefore making all the weak knees that are in the country shake. So far however, I do not see anything that is sufficient cause for alarm. England has, throughout our whole trouble, acted in a contemptibly mean and selfish spirit, and we need therefore not wonder in the least if we hear her bluster over a suppositious blunder on our part This is purely a question of international law, to be settled by diplomacy, and I think when they come to hear our argument they will begin to draw less hasty conclusions than now. A pretty full examination establishes the clear legality of the act of Commodore Wilkes.

A few days later he added:

Our English difficulties have assumed a tolerably serious shape. Still, I do not think the prospect of a war with

Great Britain is at all imminent. There is, in my opinion, still ample time in which to arrive at an understanding by means of calm talk. War would be quite a serious thing for England as well as for us, and the advantages she might hope to gain by one are, after all, very temporary. She might break our blockade and obtain cotton for her manufactories; cripple our navy and render us a less dangerous rival on the seas; she might possibly burn or destroy some of our seaport towns. All these would be serious injuries for us, but we could recover from them and retaliate by similar injuries on Canada. The worst phase of such a contest would be that it would retard the solution of our war with the South. The final result would still be inevitable, *viz*: that the people of the free Northern States are to be the substantial masters— the dominating power—within the present limits of the Union, possibly of the continent.

Brought to the actual test, the latent resources of this country will be found to be very great. The nation's strength in the matter of *intelligence*—I mean its diffusion—and in *improvement* will be found to play a very important part, should a really great struggle be upon us. We have, during our fifty years of peace, learned to *learn* everything rapidly. See for example the result of seven months' study in war. In this time we have learned more about it than we had done before in the whole fifty years. If necessity compels us to study it for five or ten years longer, I feel confident we shall not stand at the foot of the class.

In all the national resources we are quite strong. Financial ruin would come; but that would not lessen the number of bushels of corn, the number of horses, or fighting men. Such a probability or even a possibility is of course not an agreeable anticipation; but should it come, I for one will accept the fact and still have faith that our national strength is equal to the task.

His Christmas letter to Therena was distinctly in minor key. After the season's greetings, which he maintained should be spoken in heartiness, instead of being frozen in ink, he continued:

If at this time you are wishing me "the same blessing" let me say I am very thankful for the wish, because it is all I have of the reality. John and I are moping the day away in our offices like two great owls in their holes, and expect in an hour or two to go down to Willard's and get our daily bread just as we do on each of the other three hundred and sixty-four days of the year, without anything special to remind us that there are ever any such things as Christmas dinners with social sauce and other hilarious condiments, calculated to make one forget the drudgeries and "un-holy" days of life.

11

MONITOR AND MERRIMAC

O N JANUARY 16, 1862, MR. LINCOLN AP-
pointed Edwin M. Stanton Secretary of War in
place of Simon Cameron, who was sent as Minister to
Russia. "So far as the Secretaryship is concerned I think
the change a very important and needed one," my father
wrote. "I do not know Mr. Stanton personally, but he is
represented as being an able and efficient man, and I certainly shall look for very great reforms in the War Department. So far, the Department has substantially taken
care of itself."

Mr. Stanton had been Mr. Buchanan's Attorney General from December 1860 to March 1861. Shortly
after becoming Lincoln's Secretary of War he told his
new associates about a Cabinet meeting held during the
previous administration, when Fort Sumter was under
discussion. At that time J. B. Floyd was still Buchanan's
Secretary of War as he had been for the past three years.
When Stanton told the Lincoln Cabinet this story, Floyd
had become a Confederate general and had escaped from
Fort Donelson just before its surrender. My father's note
follows:

"What a pity Floyd escaped," someone had exclaimed. "I am sorry he got away," answered the Secretary of War. "I want to catch and hang him." Continuing, Stanton said, "The last time I saw Floyd was in this room lying on the sofa which then stood between the windows yonder. I remember it well—It was on the night of the 19th of last December. We had had high words and almost come to blows in our discussion over Fort Sumter. Thompson was here— Thompson was a plausible talker, and as a last resort, having been driven from every other argument, advocated the evacuation of the fort on the plea of generosity. South Carolina was but a small State with a sparse white population—We were a great and powerful people and a strong vigorous government—We could afford to say to South Carolina, 'See, we will withdraw our garrison as an evidence that we mean you no harm!' I said to him, 'Mr. President (Buchanan), the proposal to be generous implies that the Government is strong, and that we, as the public servants, have the confidence of the people. I think that is a mistake. No administration has ever suffered the loss of public confidence and support as this has done. Only the other day it was announced that a million of dollars had been stolen from Mr. Thompson's Department. The bonds were found to have been taken from the vault where they should have been kept, and the notes of Mr Floyd substituted for them. Now, all I have to say is that no administration, much less this one, can afford to lose a million of money and a fort in the same week.' Floyd lay there and never opened his mouth. The next morning he sent in his resignation and never came into the room again."

Great anxiety was felt at that time about the fate of General Burnside's expedition to Roanoke Island. My father condensed the news, when it came, into two short sentences: "A great storm encountered, a vessel wrecked, and a colonel drowned. The result doesn't sum up well at all."

Military affairs in the West became critical, and he wrote:

We have been waiting here in the greatest anxiety ... to hear the result of the battle at Fort Donelson. Yesterday morning we received dispatches detailing how Admiral Foote with his six gunboats attacked the fort on Friday, but also how his boats were disabled and he forced to withdraw just when victory was in his grasp. Last night we had ... a dispatch that our forces had taken the upper fort, but not knowing its location we cannot estimate the value of the capture.... We have never feared here but that we would get the fort, unless aid arrives for the rebels from the outside. ... The military operations of the past two weeks have been lively enough, and I anticipate a very stirring activity for some time to come. I do not think the rebels will anywhere be able to repel our advances when at all prudently made. ... One of the most gratifying things is the unexpected development of Union sentiment in all parts of Tennessee. From present indications we shall be almost enabled to hold that State by merely liberating public opinion from the thrall of terrorism in which it has been suppressed. From Tennessee we can easily reach every one of the Cotton States, and they cannot withstand a simultaneous land and sea attack.

On February 17th he wrote cheerfully:

The long suspense about the conflict at Fort Donelson, Tenn., was today relieved by the welcome news that the garrison, (about 16,000 including three generals) surrendered to our forces (General Grant) yesterday, Sunday morning. The President yesterday sent a long telegram to General Halleck suggesting several important points of military strategy not to be lost sight of.

Tonight the Secretary of War brought over the nomination of General Grant to be Major General of Volunteers, which the President signed at once. Talking of the surrender and the gallant behavior of the Illinois troops, the President said, "I cannot speak so specifically about the fighting qualities of the Eastern men, or what are called Yankees— not knowing myself particularly to whom the appellation belongs—but this I do know. If the Southerners think that man for man they are better than our Illinois men, or Western men generally, they will discover themselves in a grievous mistake.

Another note shows that February 25, 1862, was the date on which military censorship went into effect:

An order was issued today by the Secretary of War and telegraphed all over the Union, forbidding the publication of intelligence concerning military operations, whether received by telegraph or otherwise. Papers violating the order to be debarred from use of the telegraph entirely.

During this same month a severe domestic affliction came upon the President. Willie, the older of his two young sons, sickened and died. After describing to Therena Mrs. Lincoln's grand party—the one which was not at all "accidental"—my father had written:

Since then one of the President's little boys has been so sick as to have absorbed pretty much all his attention; and the next, the youngest, is now threatened with a similar sickness.

The President was unremitting in his attentions. He gave them their medicines and spent as much time as possible in the sickroom. On February 18th my father reported, "Willie continues to sink and grow weaker. The President evidently despairs of his recovery." Two days later: "The same routine today. The President very much worn and exhausted."

At about five o'clock this afternoon I was lying half asleep on the sofa in my office when his entrance roused me.

"Well, Nicolay," said he, choking with emotion, "my boy is gone—he is actually gone!" and, bursting into tears, turned and went into his own office.

Browning came in soon after, bringing some enrolled bills from the Senate, to whom I told the news of Willie's death. He went and saw Mrs Lincoln and promised at once to bring Mrs Browning. Later I went to see the President, who had lain down to quiet Tad, and asked him if I should charge Browning with the direction of the funeral.

"Consult with Browning," said he.

On the 21st my father wrote Therena:

The Executive Mansion is in mourning in consequence of the death of the President's second son, Willie, a bright little boy of about twelve years, which happened yesterday at noon. He had been very low for a number of days, so that his death was not altogether unexpected. He is to be buried on Monday next.

On that day all the departments of Government were closed. Tad recovered, and after Willie's death the President was even more tender and indulgent toward him than before, if such a thing were possible. During his convalescence Mr. Lincoln took his writing into the sick room to sit beside him, placing his table where the boy could watch every pen stroke.

The lad seemed never to want his father out of his sight. The bond that had always been uncommonly close between them grew stronger after the older boy's death. Mr. Lincoln once told a friend that he wanted to give the boy "everything he could no longer give Willie." Tad had been born with a speech defect, and not everybody could understand his torrent of rapid, imperfect words. He was always sure his father would know what he was saying, and knew also that he would take his part and protect him from domestic discipline, no matter how outrageous his conduct might have been. Sometimes the boy would take refuge in his father's office and remain there until he fell asleep, when Mr. Lincoln would pick him up and carry him off to bed.

John Hay once wrote in his diary, "Tad laughs uproariously whenever he sees his father's eyes twinkle."

My father, who then had a bachelor's opinion of obstreperous children, ignored Tad and his escapades as much as possible, and never ceased to marvel at the President's patience with this youngest son of his. Even when Tad, beating his drum and demanding attention, broke vociferously into the room where his father was holding an important conference, Mr. Lincoln did not seem to mind. He would only ask, "My son, can't you manage to make a little less noise?" and go on with the matter in hand. Others perforce kept silence, reflecting meanwhile upon what they would do to that boy, if they had half a chance.

It was on March 6, 1862, that the President sent to Congress his message urging gradual compensated emancipation, recommending that the Border States be encouraged to free their slaves and be paid "for the inconveniences, public and private, produced by such a change of system." Three days later my father made this note:

I went this morning to read the President the additional articles in the *Tribune* and *Herald* concerning his emancipation message, both papers continuing to warmly endorse and advocate it. Before this he had brought me a letter to copy which he wrote and sent to Hon. H. J. Raymond, concerning the *Times's* opinion of the impracticability of his scheme on the score of expense. After thanking him for the favorable notice of it he asked if he had studied the fact that one half-day's expense of this war would buy all the slaves

GRAND RECEPTIO

From *Harper's*

Foreground figures, left to right: Hay, Nicolay, General McDowell, General Peck, General Franklin, General Heintzelman, General McCall.

THE WHITE HOUSE

anuary 25, 1862.

amon, President Lincoln, Mrs. Lincoln, Secretary Chase and daughter, Mercier,

in Delaware at $400 per head—and that eighty-seven days'
expense of the war would buy all in Del., Md., D. C., Mo.,
and Ky., at the same price. And whether it would not shorten
the war more than 87 days, and thus be an actual saving
of expense. "Think of this," said he, "and let there be another
article in the *Times*."

While I was still reading to him Mr Blair came in. "I
sent for you, Mr Blair," said he, "about this: Since I sent
in my message, about the usual amount of calling by Border
State Congressmen has taken place. Although they have all
of them been very friendly, not one of them has as yet said a
word to me about it. Garrett Davis has been here three times
since, but although he has been very cordial, he has not yet
opened his mouth on the subject. Now I should like very
much, sometime soon, to get them all together here, and
have a frank and direct talk with them about it. I desire to
ask you whether you are aware of any reason why I should
not do so?"

Mr. Blair suggested that it might be well to wait until
the Army did something further.

"That is just the reason why I do not wish to wait,"
said the President. "If we should have successes, they might
feel and say the rebellion is crushed, and it matters not
whether we do anything about this matter. I want them to
consider and interest themselves in it as an auxiliary means of
putting down the rebels. I want to tell them that if they will
take hold and do this, the war will cease—there will be no
further need of keeping standing armies among them, and
that they will get rid of all the troubles incident thereto.
If they do not, the armies must stay in their midst. It is impossible to prevent negroes from coming into our lines.
When they do, they press me on the one hand to have them
returned, while another class of our friends will on the other
hand press me not to do so," &c, &c.

Mr Blair said he would try and see the Border State con-

gressmen during the day and have them all come and see
the President at nine o'clock tomorrow.

This meeting was held, and later both houses of Con- '
gress passed resolutions endorsing the President's policy,
but the Border States refused to accept the offer of compensated emancipation.

Sunday, March 9th was one of the days on which news
came in abundance. My father's notes tell us,

Today has been eventful. Hardly had Mr Blair gone when
Mr Watson, Asst. Sec. War, brought in a dispatch from Gen.
Wool, saying the *Merrimac* was out—had sunk the *Cum-
berland*, compelled the *Congress* to surrender, and that the
Minnesota was aground and about to be attacked by the
Merrimac, *Yorktown* and *Jamestown*. Two other dispatches
soon came along. One, from the captain of a vessel arrived
at Balto., which had left Ft. Monroe at 8 P.M. yesterday,
and another from the *New York Tribune*, giving more details.
The Sec. War came in very much excited, and walked up
and down the room like a caged lion. The Sec. Navy, Sec.
State, Gen. McClellan, Watson, Meigs, Totten, Comm. Smith,
and one or two more were sent for. The President's carriage
being just ready, he drove to the Navy Yard and brought
up Capt. Dahlgren. For a little while there was great flutter
and excitement, the Pres. being the coolest man of the party.
There were all sorts of expressions of fear. One thought
the *Merrimac* would go to New York and levy tribute—
Another, to Phila.—A third to Balto., or Annapolis, where
a large flotilla of transports has been gathered—Another
that she would come up and burn Washington. Several concluded it was part of a plan and the beginning toward moving
down the army to invest and take Ft. Monroe. After much
rambling discussion it was determined and ordered that the
restrictions upon the telegraph be suspended, and that all
news concerning the affair be permitted to go. Messages
were sent to Balto., Phila., N. Y., and all the seaboard cities,

apprizing them of the facts, and saying what preparations could hurriedly be made. Messages were sent to the governors of N. Y., Mass., and Maine, that naval men here thought timber rafts the best temporary defense and obstruction. Gen. McClellan went to his headquarters to give orders to have the transport flotillas at Annapolis moved as far as possible out of danger up into shoal water; also to prepare a number of vessels to be sent down to the "Kettel Bottoms" to be sunk as obstructions in the channel in case of necessity.

Great anxiety was felt to hear further news, when, at about 4 P.M. it was announced that a cable had been laid across the Bay, giving us telegraphic communication with Ft. Monroe. Soon news came that the *Merrimac* did not get out to sea. Then a dispatch was received from Capt. Fox who went to Old Point yesterday, informing us that the *Monitor*, our new ironclad gunboat, had arrived at the Fort at about 10 o'clock last night—had gone up immediately to where the *Minnesota* was still aground, to defend her—that at 7 A.M. today the *Merrimac* and two other steamers and several tugs had come out to attack the *Minnesota*. That the *Monitor* met and engaged them—the wooden boats withdrew at once. The *Merrimac* fought from 8 A.M. until 12 M. when the *Merrimac* withdrew, it was thought, disabled.

Much other important news has come in today. From General Hooker we learn that the Potomac batteries are reported about to be abandoned. Later dispatches from him confirm this. They have spiked their guns, burned their camps and tents, blown up their magazines, and burned the little steamer *Page* which has been blockading Aquia Creek all the fall and winter. Reports also came in, brought by contrabands, that the rebels are retreating from Manassas. Gen. McClellan went over the river this afternoon to satisfy himself as to their truth.

Tonight he telegraphs that we have Fairfax Court House and Sangster's Station. That he has ordered movements to cut off as far as possible the retreat of the rebels.... We have dispatches that the flotilla has actually raised our flag over Cockpit Point, and McClellan's dispatches to-night report that Manassas is being abandoned.

Of all this momentous news the most dramatic was that of the fight between the *Merrimac* and the *Monitor*, that "cheesebox on a raft" as her critics contemptuously called her.

Two weeks later my father mentioned the movement of Union troops down the Potomac to Fortress Monroe, and wrote that the *Merrimac* had not ventured from Norfolk since her encounter with the *Monitor*. Early in May he reported that the President had left the city for the first time since his inauguration, going with the Secretaries of War and of the Treasury "and some others" to Fortress Monroe. Reports had it that he had gone to Newport News to look at the *Merrimac*, "which lies in sight. I suppose he will be home in a day or two—if the rebels don't catch him." Two days later a triumphant letter was dispatched to Therena Bates:

Before you receive this you will have rejoiced over the glorious news which reaches us this morning from Fort Monroe. General Wool yesterday crossed over and landed sufficient troops and advanced upon and occupied Norfolk, Portsmouth and the Navy Yard; and this morning, seeing themselves hemmed in on all sides, the rebels set fire to, burned and blew up the famous *Merrimac*, thus forever laying this terrible ghost which has haunted us so long.

The *Monitor's* career was likewise short. Less than a year after her famous exploit she foundered in a gale off Cape Hatteras, taking two officers and twenty-eight men down with her. My father wrote that losing her was like losing a friend. But even beneath the waves she was victorious. Shortly after she foundered he wrote Therena:

We had an amusing letter from Commodore Porter, describing how he one night built an imitation *Monitor*, which so frightened the rebels that they sent down a hurried order and blew up the *Indianola* lately captured from us. Chinese warfare seems to pay best, and I am getting decidedly of the opinion that we should give the Celestial tactics a fair trial. At any rate, we are even with the rebels on "Quaker guns."

12

"McCLELLAN'S BODY-GUARD"

IN THE EAST GENERAL McCLELLAN'S BRIL-
liant promise withered, just as Frémont's had done in
the West, but from entirely opposite causes. Frémont's
failure had been due to recklessness; McClellan developed
overcaution. Called from the West after Bull Run to
command the troops in and around Washington, he
quickly cleared the city of stragglers, and did wonders in
organizing the Army of the Potomac out of the new three-
year volunteers who came pouring into Washington. In
three months he made of them a fine fighting machine of
150,000 men. Unfortunately, his egotism grew in proportion to his success, and he developed two hallucinations—
first, that there was a conspiracy to thwart him; and second, that the enemy in front of him always had from
twice to four times as many soldiers as he had himself.

At first McClellan had been astonished at the warm
reception accorded him. He wrote his wife that everybody
deferred to him and that the President and General Scott
gave him "full swing in everything." "Who would have
thought when we were married that I should so soon be
called upon to save my country!"

Soon he entered into differences with General Scott that

caused the old general to ask to be retired. After General Scott's retirement, McClellan succeeded him as head of the Army. This, he said, was an "immense relief," since it placed him in direct contact with the President and Secretary of War "without intervention."

In 1861 the Administration hopefully looked forward to his leading a movement against the enemy during the fine autumn weather—the very best season of the year for campaigning. But he was never quite ready. He always made excuses, and the date was constantly put forward. Then he fell ill. Winter set in. The soldiers in various camps put up huts to shield them from snow and storms, and soon the Army of the Potomac was practically, if not by order, in winter quarters. The monotonous phrase, "All quiet on the Potomac," repeated day by day in newspapers throughout the North, ceased to be an expression of disappointment and became one of sardonic criticism. Yet the General continued to have many admirers, especially among the soldiers.

Mr. Lincoln's secretaries would have found it easier to think charitably of McClellan if he had showed more courtesy toward their chief. Mr. Lincoln had been especially friendly, going freely to the General's house night or day for consultation. McClellan, however, seemed to regard this as a sign of incompetence rather than of neighborliness. Contemptuous mention of the President in private letters passed into acts of open disrespect, which culminated one night when the President went to the General's house in company with Mr. Seward and John Hay. Learning that he was not at home, but was expected to return soon, the President waited for an hour. The General came in, but, paying little heed to the servant who told him he had visitors, passed the door of the room in which they sat, and went directly upstairs. After waiting another half hour the President sent word that he was still there. The answer returned was that the General had gone to bed.

Nothing was said as they walked away, but after Mr. Seward had been left at his own door, John Hay's wrath blazed forth. Mr. Lincoln only answered that "in times like these" it was best "not to be making points of etiquette and personal dignity." But his secretaries noted with satisfaction that Mr. Lincoln ceased going to the General's house. Instead, he summoned him to the Executive Mansion when he wished to consult him.

My father's own feelings toward McClellan are mirrored in the private notes and confidential letters he wrote during 1862. A note dated February 27th reads:

It is understood that McClellan has been gone a day or two to superintend a movement from Banks's division on Winchester . . . for the purpose of permanently opening the Baltimore and Ohio Railroad. This evening, 7 P.M., the Sec. War came in, and after locking the door, read the President two dispatches from the General. [The first one reported that a pontoon bridge had been successfully thrown across the Potomac at Harper's Ferry; that a portion of the troops had crossed, in excellent spirits though it was raining; and that they seemed ready to fight anything. This was in preparation for an attack on Winchester.]

"The next is not so good," remarked the Sec. War. It ran to the effect that the "lift lock" had turned out to be too narrow to admit the passage of the canal-boats through the river (as one of the facilities and precautions, arrangements had been made to build a permanent bridge of canal-boats across the Potomac, and a large number of canal-boats had been gathered for that purpose.) That in consequence of this, he had changed the plan and had determined merely to protect the building of the bridge and the opening of the road—leaving the obvious inference that he proposed to abandon the movement on Winchester. In fact he so stated [because] the impossibility of building the permanent bridge as he had expected would delay him so that Winchester would be reinforced from Manassas.

"What does this mean?" asked the President.

"It means," said the Sec. War, "that it is a d——d fizzle. It means that he doesn't intend to do anything."

The President was much cast down and dejected at the news of the failure of the enterprise. "Why could he not have known whether his arrangements were practicable?" &c. &c.

The Sec. State came in and the three had a long conference.

Afterward General Marcy [McClellan's father-in-law] for whom the President had sent earlier in the evening, came in and the President had a long and sharp talk with him.

"Why in the Nation, General Marcy," said he excitedly, "couldn't the General have known whether a boat would go through that lock before spending a million dollars getting them there? I am no engineer, but it seems to me that if I wished to know whether a boat would go through a hole or a lock, common sense would teach me to go and measure it. I am almost despairing at these results. Everything seems to fail. The general impression is daily gaining ground that the General does not intend to do anything. By a failure like this we lose all the prestige we gained by the capture of Fort Donelson. I am grievously disappointed—almost in despair."

This is almost the only time in all my father's notes that he mentioned seeing the President shaken out of his usual calm.

General Marcy endeavored to palliate the failure—said no doubt the General would be able to explain the cause— that other operations would go on, etc., and that he was satisfied—plenty of activity in movements, &c.

"I will not detain you any further now, General," said the President; and though Gen. Marcy showed a disposition to talk on, the Pres. repeated the dismissal and the Gen. took his hat and went away.

When he chose to do so, this backwoodsman could act in a very kingly manner!

On May 21st my father wrote:

Expectation is all on tiptoe again at hearing that McClellan's army moved forward to the Chickahominy yesterday, and that a battle is imminent—perhaps already in progress. . . . My own apprehension is that the rebels will fall back, and cause another and tedious delay. I am beginning very much to fear that we shall have to have a new general before we can get any decisive results from the Army of the Potomac.

On June 2nd:

Our usual budget of Sunday news came along yesterday— *viz* That a very considerable battle was progressing before Richmond. . . . We got no more information until near noon yesterday, when we heard that after a seven hour conflict during the forenoon we had finally repulsed the enemy at all points. . . . It seems that they attacked us at about one o'clock on Saturday and whipped us pretty badly until night, but that we recovered our losses during the next morning. We have as yet no particulars of the affair, though one or two dispatches received this morning indicate that it is more of a success for us than we at first supposed.

June 5th—I still adhere to my old opinion that if we can somehow scatter or destroy the present armies of the rebels, they will never be able to raise new ones. In the West we seem to be in a fair way to accomplish this result. I confess I am not so sanguine as to our eastern operations. McClellan's extreme caution, or tardiness, or something, is utterly exhaustive of all hope and patience, and leaves one in that feverish apprehension that as something *may* go wrong, something most likely *will* go wrong. Risks of battle are proverbially uncertain, but I am beginning to feel that the apprehension of defeat is worse than defeat itself. . . . I am getting very nervous at the long delay before Richmond. The battle fought there the other day seems to me hardly decisive enough to pay for the very large loss it involves.

June 12—We have little news that is pleasant.

June 23—This morning we get a report by way of the Richmond papers that a battle was fought a week ago today near Charleston, S. C. . . . Matters seem to be drawing to a crisis before Richmond. I think there must be a battle or an evacuation before long.

June 27th—So far the week has been pretty quiet, excepting of course the President's sudden visit to West Point, which set a thousand rumors to buzzing as if a beehive had been overturned.—The Cabinet was to break up and be re-formed. The generals were to be removed and new war movements were to be organized. You have no idea how rapidly rumors are originated and spread here . . . notwithstanding the fact that they are daily served with the most extraordinary Munchausens. My own impression is that the President merely desired and went to hold a conference with General Scott about military matters, and that no immediate avalanches or earthquakes are to be produced thereby. That eventually results will follow I have no doubt.

On the next day he made and placed in his private file a hurried memorandum. Joy in the President's firm stand was to be read in every pencil stroke:

There is a letter on file in the State Department addressed by Mr Lincoln to Mr Seward, under date of June 28, 1862, in which the President, after detailing the military situation—*viz*—our western movements arrested, and McClellan unable to attack at Richmond, &c, &c, says we must have 100,000 more troops, and continues:

"I expect to maintain this contest until successful, or till

I die, or am conquered, or my term expires, or Congress or the country forsake me."

He then goes on to say that he would make public appeal to the nation, but for the fact that it might create a panic, and bring about the very end it was designed to avert.

For this reason the letter was a private one to be used by Mr Seward among friends at the North to facilitate the raising of troops.

It has just been sent by Mr Seward to Mr Fish, and placed on file in the State Department.

On June 29th he wrote Therena:

There has been fighting before Richmond for three or four days and very important strategic movements have been made by the whole army. What it will result in we cannot even guess. . . . I suppose that nearly all, if not the whole army has been engaged in the battles (for there have been several) and that the fate of the whole army, and perhaps the whole country, is to be decided by the result.

We have so far only enough news to lead us to believe that up to the last advices, we were even in the game. I am however beginning to look upon great pitched battles as the worst and most barbarous species of gaming, so that to me it is neither a cause of much hope nor great fright.

Our army had pressed forward upon Richmond until it became evident to the rebels that they must either attack and beat us back, or slowly but surely give up the city. It seems that they decided to do the former, and accordingly began on Thursday last. Since then the success appears to have alternated, sometimes for, sometimes against us. . . . The final result we have not yet heard.

The city here is almost wild with rumors and suspense. The news has been so completely kept from the public that up to this morning no one had a serious suspicion of what was going on. This morning however several persons reached the city who left Fortress Monroe yesterday, and of course brought with them all the rumors prevailing there. These have been caught up here with great avidity and repeated with their usual additions and embellishments. Some enterprising news-gatherer has collated these, sifted an intelligent report out of them as nearly as he could, and posted it up on the bulletin of the hotel. [Willard's.] I think it makes the story better for us than it really is. The bulletin board is surrounded by a crowd about ten deep, all making frantic efforts to read the news. As reliable reports from the War Department have been heretofore posted up at the same place, many will go off much deceived as to the value of their intelligence. Of course the suspense is terrible.

When finally confirmed, the bad news was accepted with almost stolid resignation. Perhaps after such intense apprehension this result was inevitable. On the national holiday my father wrote Therena:

I think that for fourteen years I have never had so dull a Fourth as today. The day is literally like any other. There has been nothing whatever going on in the city. The little boys have even shot away the bunch of firecrackers they bought this morning, and on account of the hard times and prospective taxation can't afford to buy a second bunch, so that there is not even the usual noise in the street. I have been at work at my desk most of the day.... The news from Richmond comes in slowly: the following is about the substance of it. There were battles on last Thursday, Friday, Monday and Tuesday, in all of which the victory was substantially with us, the enemy's loss exceeding ours. But as it was a sort of running fight, during the movement of the army by which Gen. McClellan changed his position so as to open a communication by the way of the James River and abandon that by way of the York and Pamunkey, we have been consistently getting farther and farther from Richmond and have therefore *appeared* to retreat. Our loss is perhaps 15,000 killed and wounded. We have however established our communications with the James River, and secured a new and good base of operations. Of course everybody here has been terribly blue about it for several days. I do not however see anything very discouraging in this affair taken by itself, although it is to be deplored that we lose the prospect of the early capture of Richmond.

July 6, 1862. . . . Our last advices from the Peninsula state that the Army of the Potomac is for the present where it can according to every appearance maintain itself, and is therefore reasonably safe. . . . In the city there is no excitement of any kind except the arrival of the wounded . . . who are filling up the hospitals pretty rapidly. When they shall all be full there will be a very large number of patients here, nearly all the churches in the city having been fitted up to receive them. . . .

July 13, 1862. . . . The President made a flying visit to McClellan's army on the Peninsula this week. . . . I have not yet had much opportunity to talk with him about the result of his observations, but my impression is that he came home in better spirits . . . having found the army in better condition and more of it than he expected.

That month my father went to Minnesota on a presidential mission. Before he left Washington, McClellan's efforts to capture Richmond had signally failed, and the General had sent his insubordinate letter of June 27th to Secretary Stanton, throwing blame for the failure entirely on the administration: "If I save this army now, I tell you plainly that I owe no thanks to you or any other persons in Washington. You have done your best to sacrifice this army," he wrote.

Even this did not move Mr. Lincoln to dismiss him, though it is easy to imagine what would have happened in similar circumstances under almost any other government or ruler. "Save your army at all events," the President answered. "If you have had a drawn battle or a repulse, it is the price we pay for the enemy not being in Washington"; and being utterly without personal resentment, he went on doing his patient best to persuade the dilatory general to more energy. To those who were harsh in their criticism of General McClellan he answered that though he might not fight well, he excelled in making others ready to fight, and reminded them that it was necessary "to use the tools we have." When Senator Wade, who was not the most patient of men, urged him to supplant General McClellan he answered:

"Well, put yourself in my place for a moment. If I relieve McClellan, whom shall I put in command?"

"Why, anybody!" said Wade.

"Wade," replied Mr. Lincoln with weary resignation, "*anybody* will do for you, but not for me. I must have *somebody*." So he continued to "use the tool he had," seeing none better. When my father returned from Minnesota, McClellan was still in command of the Army of the Potomac; though when he took the field at the beginning of his disastrous Virginia campaign, Halleck had been assigned to replace him as General in Chief.

By October it was evident that McClellan's failure to advance was becoming chronic. My father wrote to John Hay who was away in his turn: "The treadmill goes on. The President keeps poking sharp sticks under Little Mac's ribs, and he has screwed up his courage to the point of crossing the river today." And in a later letter: "I have but little hope until we can somehow get McClellan out of the way. He won't fight offensively." General Buell also seemed inclined to procrastinate. My father's impatience boiled over in elaborate sarcasm. "It is rather a good thing to be a major general—one can take things so leisurely " was his comment.

That autumn, after the rebel cavalry repeated its insult

of the early summer by again riding entirely around the Army of the Potomac he wrote Therena:

It is a little thing, accomplishing not much actual harm, yet vexatious and mischievous. The President has well-nigh lost his temper over it. I wish he would sometime get angry enough to dismiss about half the officers of the army. I think the remaining half would do more work and do it better by the example.

Returning to McClellan's unfortunate army in Virginia, he continued:

I discovered no signs of life in the Army of the Potomac. The President is anxious that it should move and fight, and I still have hope that even if McClellan refuses or neglects to take the responsibility, the President himself will give the order "forward march."

What the President really thought about McClellan was summed up in a single stinging phrase, spoken one night as he and his friend O. M. Hatch stood together looking down on the tents of the sleeping Army of the Potomac. He sighed, and called it "Only McClellan's body-guard."

13

A BATTLE WITH THE SENATE

OCCASIONALLY, MR. LINCOLN FOUND IT convenient to have an unprejudiced observer at some distant point. In July, quite unexpectedly, the President asked my father to go west to report on the Indian situation. The Sioux were already on the warpath and the Cheyennes were restless and threatening. My father had just time to write hurriedly to Therena that he was leaving "day after tomorrow" for a trip to Minnesota where he was to meet the Commissioner of Indian Affairs William P. Dole, and go with him to conclude a treaty with the Chippewa chief Hole-in-the-Day. He would probably be gone about five weeks.

A party of Pittsfield friends suggested joining him at St. Louis for the trip up the Mississippi. The reason they did not do so is evident in the first message he sent back from St. Paul.

It is perhaps as well we did not all come together up the Mississippi River. At Duluth I learned that the Missouri guerillas have occasionally been firing into a boat, and that they have to barricade the Secesh side with hay-bales for security.

St. Paul seemed to him "primitive," and the International Hotel smelled strongly of pine and kerosene, but the week he spent there was so filled with pleasant excursions that he pronounced the region ideal for summer residence "provided of course one has wealth and leisure."

He joined Commissioner Dole at St. Cloud, about eighty miles from St. Paul, and, with a venturesome United States Senator, the local Indian Superintendent, and "several experienced frontiersmen," they started for wilder country. A week later they were all back in St. Paul, the trouble with the Sioux having developed into one of the bloodiest Indian massacres ever to occur in the northwest. The Chippewas, like the Cheyennes, were restless, though hostilities had not yet broken out. One cause of their discontent was the erratic behavior of an Indian agent named Walker, whom the Commissioner had already seen. Later he had fled from his agency, had become completely deranged, and had committed suicide. My father wrote John Hay:

Since Walker left Hole-in-the-Day has sent word down here to Commr. Dole that he wished him to come up there to see him, and Dole has concluded to go. So our party starts again today to Fort Ripley—at a rough guess 150 miles from here. A company of Volunteers has already gone to the Fort, and we take two additional companies with us, so that we will have about 300 fighting men at the Fort. As it has turned out that Walker was crazy, I suppose the Commr. will be able to settle the difficulty with Hole-in-the-Day without war—at least he is going to try.

Fort Ripley was an unfinished fort, garrisoned until very recently by only about thirty soldiers. Eighty women and children had fled to it for protection, and the soldiers worked feverishly to complete the stockade.

The muss with Hole-in-the-Day is a complicated affair, involving official frauds on the one hand and Indian depredations on the other. The Indians are in bad temper and the young braves want to fight; but they are poorly armed and have little ammunition, and therefore hesitate. Hole-in-the-Day is a shrewd and intelligent and able diplomatist, and has the counsel and assistance of interested whites.

Up to this time it is very uncertain what he will do— whether he will meet the Commissioner in council, or whether the tribe will get ready and attack the whites. Robberies they have already committed, but so far they have killed no one. If the Indians should agree to meet the Commr. in council, still the result is uncertain, because they allege a long string of real or fancied grievances, difficult of investigation. If the Indians come to council I shall yet be here several days. If they refuse I shall before long return to St Paul and Illinois. I shall know more about it tomorrow.... P.S. In the paper we get here tonight (only one comes to the Fort) I see that the rebels are almost in Washington. How does your head feel? It looks very much as if it were about as safe as my scalp here.

An unsuccessful attempt to capture Hole-in-the-Day had already been made, during which the whites had gained possession of his most cherished belonging, a fine Colt revolver, given him years before in Washington by President Pierce. In his skillful hands it was a weapon of uncanny accuracy: even in the hands of his enemies he could still use it to advantage.

"Where is my gun?" he asked. "When my gun is returned to me, I will tell the Commissioner when and where I will see him."

After eight days of what he called "shilly-shallying," my father wrote John Hay they had "utterly failed to get indemnity for the past or security for the future." Still, the Commissioner would remain at Fort Ripley a couple of days longer before returning to St. Paul. "What the morrow will bring forth we cannot tell. If they should come down into this neighborhood within two days we are cooped up here for the Lord knows how long, with no impossible chance of having our scalps hooped."

However, according to latest news from the East his chances seemed as good as John's.

Our last advices from Washington show the C-sesh between Fairfax and the Capital, and our forces retiring into the impregnable diggins along the Potomac. I still think it is about an even chance whose scalp will be in chancery first, yours or mine. Pray have the rebels removed from their close proximity to *la Maison Blanche* before I get there.

Hole-in-the-Day finally consented to a conference, but it came to nothing. "I left Fort Ripley this morning," my father wrote Hay on September 12th, "and am this far on my way to St. Paul. My scalp is yet safe, but day before yesterday it was not worth as much as it is tonight." He described to Therena the scene at the conference.

At about twelve o'clock the Indians appeared approaching from the ferry. They came on down to the place where the troops and our party and lookers-on were—(I suppose there were perhaps 130 white men altogether, nearly all armed, while there were, as we afterwards counted, 108 of the Indians.) When they had reached the place arranged for the council two or three of them went to the bank of the river, raised their voices and shouted out some sort of signal or order, when, judge our surprise at seeing another party of the red-skins, 82 in number, emerge from the bushes and come down into the road behind us, completely surrounding us! They quietly took possession of the road, and detained as prisoners two white settlers who were coming to look on. They were however on demand of the Commissioner released and permitted to come to us. The Commissioner also asked that the Indians behind us be ordered 'round in front, but Hole-in-the-Day evaded, saying he could not control them, and he feared the attempt to remove them would produce trouble. In this situation we went into council. Hole-in-the-Day was quite bold and impudent. An hour or so was spent in preliminary talk, when the Chief proposed that the council be postponed 'till next morning—a proposition that the Whites were deuced glad to accept.

When the Commissioner and his party went to the meeting place next morning, they took with them sixty soldiers and a howitzer, and posted guards to prevent another such surprise.

The Commissioner sent a message to the Indians. The Indians took possession of the messenger's horse. The Commissioner demanded the restoration of the horse. Ye Gentle Savages refused, and negotiations were broken off.... I shall make but a short stay in Springfield and Pittsfield and then hasten to Washington to relieve you—Stonewall Jackson willing.

My father entertained no sentimental illusions about the North American Indians. He had grown up too near frontier times in Illinois to regard them as other than cruel and savage enemies whose moral code (granted they had one) was different from that of the whites. Yet he recognized in Hole-in-the-Day a man of strong character and marked ability.

A new Congress was to be elected in November 1862, and even before my father went west he had written Therena that practically everybody "except the President and Cabinet" seemed "very blue" over election prospects.

I don't think I have ever heard more croaking since the war began than during the past ten days. I am amazed to find so little real faith and courage under difficulties among public leaders and men of intelligence. The average public mind is becoming alarmingly sensational. A single piece of accidental ill-luck is enough to throw them all into the horrors of despair.

Military news during the summer continued to be alternately good and bad, and not all of the failures could rightfully be attributed to McClellan. The country's diplomatic relations seemed precarious, for both England and France appeared really to desire the success of the South —at least, when vessels, manifestly destined for use by the Confederates, were built in their shipyards, they took little notice of these breaches of neutrality. Unrest increased in Mexico, urged on by France. France made the suggestion that Russia and England act as mediators between our warring sections. When this was refused, she recommended a six-months' truce.

Washington was almost thrown into a panic by rumors of rioting in Baltimore; and the situation grew no better so far as the Army of the Potomac was concerned: "We have no real news" was the burden of almost every letter my father sent to Therena that fall. Shortly before the election he wrote her that the Republicans had "lost almost everything" in Pennsylvania, Ohio, and Indiana, and that Iowa, not yet heard from, seemed likely to follow the general drift.

Five days after the election he wrote her that the war program had "somewhat changed."

The President's patience is at last completely exhausted with McClellan's inaction and never ending excuses, and he has relieved him from command of the Army of the Potomac. The President has been extremely reluctant to do this. In many respects he thinks McClellan a very superior officer. This, with the high personal regard for him, has led him to indulge him in his whims and complaints and shortcomings as a mother would indulge her baby, but all to no purpose. He is constitutionally *too slow*, and has been fitly dubbed the Great American Tortoise. I am sure sensible people everywhere will rejoice that he, and not the Army, goes into winter quarters.

Looking forward to possible political results, since the General was still very popular with the soldiers, he continued:

It is barely possible that the secession element of the Democratic party will endeavor to make him a leader of an opposition movement and party, but I think his popularity is too fictitious for that. He has been made a hero by a most vigorous and persistent puffing in the newspapers. I do not know that he has instigated this; but he could hardly help knowing that his friends and hangers on were doing it, and that too always in connection with an attack on somebody else. He should not have permitted this. During his country's peril every man should avoid even the imputation of selfishness. If any man ever had reason to be not only unselfish but humbly grateful to the Administration and to the country, it was McClellan. They have given him position, power, confidence and opportunity without stint. He has illy repaid the generosity.

A week later he wrote:

We have nothing new here since the removal of General McClellan. So far there has not been the least excitement about it; he has had the prudence and good taste to submit quietly to the President's decision, and to go home without saying anything on the way. Whether he will continue to behave himself properly or not is of course a question, though I think he will. He can't help knowing something of how great a failure he has made, and what glorious opportunities he has wasted.

My father supposed that either General Hooker or General Burnside would succeed to the command of the Army of the Potomac and earnestly hoped for speedy movements. Defeat, he thought, could scarcely be worse than the endless suspense the country had endured under McClellan. His hopes for victory went unfulfilled. "We have no real news" continued to be the burden of his messages until General Burnside, who was appointed in McClellan's place, suffered serious defeat at the battle of Fredericksburg on December 13th. Shortly afterward my father, curious to see the results, rode out to Fredericksburg.

The town has been badly battered by the bombardment, and seemed almost entirely abandoned [he reported]. The soldiery were in the houses in some instances, apparently helping themselves to what they desired. The place was within easy reach of the rebel batteries, and as there was a reasonable expectation that they would begin shelling it at almost every moment, I only stayed long enough to ride through two or three of the principal streets and get off and drink a cup of coffee with some of the officers who were lunching in one of the houses.

The next battle about which he wrote Therena was a contest between the Senate and the Administration, whose final show of strength took place on December 19th in the White House itself. A faction, very unfriendly toward the Secretary of State, had developed in the Senate. The President believed Mr. Chase primarily to blame for it. The faction became so critical that Mr. Seward tendered his resignation. Mr. Lincoln, who did not want to lose his services, brought the troublemakers unexpectedly together at the Executive Mansion, and so managed the encounter that Mr. Chase also felt it necessary to tender his resignation in writing. The President accepted it with an alacrity that must have surprised his Secretary of the Treasury. Then, having what he wanted—offers from both ministers to resign—he persuaded both to remain in the Cabinet. Expressing his satisfaction privately to a friend soon after, he said, "Now I can ride. I have a pumpkin in each end of my bag."

"The trouble is all over for the present," my father assured Therena.

The President was determined that he would retain both Mr Seward and Mr Chase, meddling outsiders to the contrary notwithstanding. I think the Cabinet and the Government is much stronger than it was before the shaking up it received. Mr Seward particularly has achieved a triumph over those who attempted to drive him out, in this renewed assurance of the President's respect and esteem.

Robert Lincoln once gave me the following version of this incident, saying it was as his father had told it to him. Senator Trumbull and two other senators came to the President "and demanded that Seward be kicked out of the Cabinet," charging that he had said something inexpressibly offensive in a Cabinet meeting, the substance of his alleged remarks being that he had classed the secessionists and the extreme anti-slavery men as working together to bring on a servile war.

"Gentlemen, will it be convenient to meet me here at nine o'clock tonight?" the President asked.

When they presented themselves they were thunderstruck to find the entire Cabinet present, seated with much more formality than usual, Lincoln at the head of the table, Seward at his right hand, Chase on his left, and so on. The Cabinet was equally startled by the incursion of these senators into a Cabinet meeting, a thing unheard of in the history of the Government.

The senators were greeted by the President and also given seats at the Cabinet table, after which Mr. Lincoln, turning to Mr. Seward, said:

"Mr. Secretary of State, will you be kind enough to tell us what you recall happened and was said at the meeting of the Cabinet on such a day?" Mr. Seward, manifestly astonished, did as he was asked.

When he finished, Mr. Lincoln turned to Chase. "Now, Mr. Secretary, will you please tell us what you remember about that meeting?" Chase hemmed and hawed—then made a statement practically upholding Seward. Lincoln asked for the recollection of each member of the Cabinet in turn. They were practically unanimous.

The President thanked them, saying, "I am very much obliged to you for this—I am sorry to have been obliged to inconvenience you this evening," and dismissed them.

Trumbull approached the President, his eyes blazing. "Lincoln," he said, "somebody has lied like hell!"

"Not tonight," answered the President, quietly.

While the Cabinet might show a united front in an emergency, its members were not harmonious among themselves. Several of them constantly deplored Mr. Lincoln's lack of ceremony. The Secretary of the Interior wrote that there was scarcely a formal Cabinet meeting during his term of office. Secretary Seward might come in, throw himself down upon the couch, and, lying at full length, give the President a report on some important state paper he was preparing. Secretary Stanton was so outraged by the President's habit of turning suddenly from laughter and jesting to the consideration of some very solemn matter that he could scarcely force himself to stay more than ten or fifteen minutes. The Attorney General agreed that this was annoying and that it indicated levity of character. He also thought the ceremonious state receptions could be better managed. Mr. Lincoln, who had once carried a whole post office in his hat, saw no reason, now that he was in the White House, for gold-laced aides in the East Room, or stiff etiquette at Cabinet meetings. He rarely sat down during Cabinet meetings, preferring to walk about the room as he talked with his advisers. He had not chosen them because they thought as he did, but because they all differed with him, yet each represented a large section of public opinion. Small wonder therefore that they were critical of him and of each other. Stanton and Chase were at loggerheads; Stanton and Welles seldom agreed. Welles and Bates believed that Seward tried to interfere in the affairs of the Navy. Only the President's informal yet masterful way of doing business saved the day.

Officially, he was fully aware of the dignity of his office, and of his importance and power as President. For all his simple manners he gave orders as one born to the purple. "You will hear all they may choose to say, and report it to me. You will not assume to definitely consummate anything," he instructed Secretary Seward when the latter went to meet the Confederate Commissioners at Hampton Roads. And his directions to General Grant, when the war came to its close were quite as regal. "You are not to decide, discuss or confer upon any political question. Such questions the President holds in his own hands, and will submit them to no military conferences or conventions."

But he was never impressed by a sense of his own personal importance and his democratic leanings continued to manifest themselves in unexpected ways and places. One morning an early passer-by saw him at the White House gate, peering down Pennsylvania Avenue.

"Good morning," he said as the gentleman approached. "I am looking for a newsboy. If you see one when you reach the corner, please send him up this way."

14

THE EMANCIPATION
PROCLAMATION

JANUARY 1863 HELD TWO DATES OF ESPE-
cial interest to my father. One, purely personal, was
January 20th, when he was admitted to practice before
the Supreme Court of the United States, his sponsor being Attorney General Bates. This marked a real achievement, since, without the stimulus of law schools, or the
companionship of others engaged in the same pursuit, he
had strength of purpose, amid all his duties and distractions, to carry on systematically the necessary reading.
This proved too great a strain, and brought on the beginning of the serious eye trouble from which he suffered
during the rest of his life. He went to his doctor for advice, and the latter wrote in his casebook, "Asthenopia
from excessive use of organs—Has been studying at night
for some time."

The other date, January 1st, was important to half
the world—on that day, President Lincoln signed his proclamation freeing the slaves. Strangely enough, there is
no mention of this in the notes my father made at the time,
or in his letters to Therena. Thirty-seven years later,
when John Hay was Secretary of State, my father an-

swered, at Mr. Hay's request, an inquiry sent to the State Department by A. W. Bachelder of Gloucester, Massachusetts:

No list of the names of the persons who were present when President Lincoln signed the Emancipation Proclamation of January 1, 1863, has been preserved, and it is no longer possible to reconstruct it. My strong impression is that neither Mrs Lincoln nor any other lady was present. It was not known at what hour the President would sign it, and therefore no concerted or formal meeting took place to witness it.

In *Abraham Lincoln: A History* the authors tell us that "those who were in the house came to the Executive Office merely from the personal impulse of curiosity, joined to momentary convenience." Once my father told an interviewer that it was he who handed Mr. Lincoln the pen.

January 1st was always a busy day at the White House, beginning with one of the most colorful social events of the season, the reception at eleven o'clock in the morning, to which all officialdom came to wish the President and his wife a happy New Year. The diplomats wore their ceremonial garments and all their decorations, the Army and Naval officers their showiest uniforms. After they and the senators and representatives and the judges of various courts had been received, the general public trooped by for two hours. It was on such a day, after at least three hours of continuous handshaking, when his right hand was almost too numb to hold a pen, that Mr. Lincoln went to the Executive Office to sign the momentous document. One who was there recorded that the President laid the pen down and took it up again several times, remarking that if ever his name got into history, it would be because of this act, and that he did not wish his signature to look as though he had hesitated, or as if his hand had trembled. Then he wrote "Abraham Lincoln" firmly and slowly, looked up and smiled, and said to the men who stood near him:

"That will do."

Politics gained in importance with the opening of the New Year. On January 11th my father wrote:

I think we have great dangers to apprehend from the treasonable attitude which the Democratic party of the North is everywhere preparing to assume. Under the subterfuge of opposing the Emancipation Proclamation they are really organizing to oppose the war. It is a very bold issue for them to take, and I do not think they can succeed with it, but they may give us great trouble.

Again there was a long period of military uncertainty, during which almost every letter he wrote to Therena told her, "We are all in a state of feverish excitement," or "No definite news has come as yet." On January 23rd he wrote:

Nothing of interest ... except the trial and dismissal of Major General Fitz-John Porter. From the great ability with which his legal counsel conducted his defense at the trial, public opinion had settled down to the belief that he would certainly be acquitted. It however turns out otherwise, and of course all his friends are howling with indignation. ... Whatever may be the justice of his sentence, I have no doubt the result of the trial will have a salutary influence on the discipline and *morale* of the Army, teaching the officers that the principle of accountability to the Government is not yet obsolete.

And on the following Sunday:

I walked up this morning to the Senate Chamber to hear a sermon by Moncure D. Conway, an Abolitionist, but one of the most eloquent men of the country. I should be willing to go to church every Sunday if I could hear a sermon of equal power.

The Unitarian church of which Mr. Conway was then pastor had been the first to offer the Government the use of its building as a hospital, and in recognition of this the congregation was invited to hold services in the Senate Chamber.

February was ushered in by a heavy snowstorm, and for weeks thereafter the effort of walking three blocks to Willard's in search of food seemed to my father almost more than the meal was worth.

If there were any possible prospect of getting a week or two's sleighing out of it, the discomfort might be borne with fortitude [he grumbled]. When I get rich I am certainly going to spend a winter somewhere in the North where I may once have some of the benefits and pleasures of extremely cold weather.

He must have been quite desperate when he wrote those words, for his considered definition of a sleigh ride was "A thumping and ear-freezing amusement."

The bad weather practically stopped military operations. He wrote: "The Army of the Potomac is for the present stuck in the mud, as it has been during nearly the whole of its existence. We hope however that it may yet do something, by accident at least, if not by design."

Reporting perfunctorily to Therena on society's last full week of gaiety before Lent, he mentioned "a little reception given by Mrs Lincoln to Tom Thumb and his bride." One of the guests present noted the great respect with which the queer little pair in their wedding finery looked up and up into the President's kind sad face and the gentleness with which he took their little hands into his great one, as though they were fragile birds' eggs, and the grave courtesy with which he presented them to his wife. He did not show by the quiver of an eyelash that he was conscious of anything odd or unusual in the meeting— he so tall, they so abnormally short—he the president of a great nation, they, little playfolk being signally honored. Yet later in the evening, when they were unconscious of his scrutiny, this guest saw the President's eyes following them with amused and kindly sympathy. He looked very tall and gaunt. He was all in black, save for the white gloves, which seemed rather ghastly on his huge hands. He presented a great contrast to plump Mrs. Lincoln so dressy in her rose-colored, low-necked frock, with hoops, and wearing pink flowers in her hair. Tad entered into the scene, as he did into so many where small boys were not supposed to penetrate. That evening he was very practical and took it upon himself to see that the guests of honor should be able to eat their supper "comfortably" off something no higher than a chair.

About the middle of March John Hay went to Hilton Head, South Carolina. The newspapers had it that he went to accept a place on General Hunter's staff. This, my father wrote, was "not correct. He does hope to help the General take Charleston, but in an amateur and not a professional capacity." The real reason was that John's brother Charles, serving under General Hunter, had been very ill, and the kindly President sent him down so that he could be with Charles for a time.

"Why in the name of Mars don't you tell me what your title is?" my father demanded impatiently after he thought he had waited a reasonable length of time for a letter from Hilton Head:

How am I to know whether to address you as Brig. Genl. or Acting Rear Admiral? . . . You simply stated you had been announced as a Vol. A.D.C. with too high a rank (the only instance in addition to McDowell's where modest merit has protested against its blushing honors.)

"Our reverses still continue," he wrote Therena, but he assured her he would not lose hope, even if he had to wait a great while longer. He believed a healthy reaction was in progress against the Copperheads—but copperheadism was a subject on which he could not trust himself to talk or to write. "The battle against it should be one of swords, not words." In April he told her that dislike of the draft was causing public unrest.

If I were not of a very hopeful disposition I should feel blue about military affairs. Grant's attempt to take Vicksburg looks to me very much like a total failure, with the possible danger that the whole Yazoo expedition may be cut off and captured. At Port Hudson we are held at bay; at Charleston our chances for success are too small; and the Army of the Potomac, in addition to seeming *fated* never to accomplish anything even under the most favorable contingencies, is still hopelessly weatherbound. Do not understand that I am despairing, I only mean that the present progress looks unsatisfactory to me. But if the present progress fails we will devise and try a new one. We must and *will* succeed.

He wrote Hay that nothing had been accomplished in Washington since he left, "except finally to get Prado and Miss Lisboa married." The President had gone to visit the Army. Next day, Mr. Lincoln had not yet returned. "I guess," he added, "the Tycoon has concluded to follow your example and go on Hooker's staff."

In early May, when the Army of the Potomac was fighting its losing battle at Chancellorsville, he wrote that Washington was wild with rumors. At that very moment, the funeral of General Berry, who had been killed in action, was moving along Pennsylvania Avenue with shrouded banners. A few days later he admitted that after fluctuating between good news and bad, the stern fact was established that Hooker's attempt to beat the rebel army had failed. "In the bitterness of disappointment I can add no comment."

As soon as they learned that Hooker and his army had recrossed the Rappahannock, the President and General Halleck went to satisfy themselves about its true condition. They found it better than they dared hope:

Only three of the seven army corps were much in the fight. ... All indications are that the enemy suffered much more severely than we. ... An intercepted dispatch from Lee to one of his subordinates states that their loss was "fearful."

Exchanged prisoners who were in Richmond at the time state that our cavalry penetrated within sight of the city, and the force (some 400 strong) ... could have easily gone into it and captured it, or at least destroyed all the valuable rebel stores, buildings and machinery, as there were no soldiers left in it ... but of course our troops had no means of knowing this fact. Fortunately Porter and Grant seem to be making some headway on the Mississippi ... and that occupies and diverts public attention somewhat.

May 17th—The President has just been in my room for a little while ... [He] told me that Senators Wade and Chandler, who returned from the army yesterday, report that it is in good spirits and courage, and that they think it would be able to cross and whip the enemy now. The pickets stationed along on each side of the Rappahannock have gone back to their old pastime of bandying wit and repartee across the river:

"I say, Yank," shouted over one of the rebels, "where is fightin' Joe Hooker now?"

"Oh, he's gone to Stonewall Jackson's funeral," shouted Yank in reply.

It is nearly time we were hearing something from Grant.

May 25—The success of Grant's operations around and about Vicksburg is really glorious. ... Our last news is to the effect that Grant, after having fought a successful battle nearly every day for a week, has finally invested Vicksburg. ... The praise of our Western soldiers is on every lip. ...

Three times between May 31st and June 9th he reported on the siege of Vicksburg, a subject of engrossing interest to Therena, because her young brother Dorus, known at home since childhood as "Major," was fighting there under Grant. He lost an arm at Vicksburg and was carried from the battlefield by his colored servant "Rosey" (Rosecrans), who accompanied him to Pittsfield. Here Copperhead sentiment was strong enough to make a Negro's life miserable. But my mother defiantly taught him to read. Later he became enshrined in literature as Banty Tim in John Hay's *Pike County Ballads*.

Learning of Dorus's misfortune, my father wrote Therena a long letter of sympathy, mentioning by name several officers who had achieved brilliant success after sustaining similar injuries, and continued:

Having chosen the profession of arms, and made this much sacrifice for it, Major should rather be encouraged by this event to strive for a higher accomplishment and usefulness as an officer. It is a profession in which the head is of much the most value. It is a field worthy of the highest talent and ambition, and rewarding as surely as any other all the industry and energy and ability expended in it. I trust Major will remember that he is just at the beginning of a useful and honorable career.

Lee led his Confederate army up into Pennsylvania, capturing on the way a wagon train within ten or a dozen miles of Washington. My father confessed to Therena that this "produced quite a little panic among the inhabitants." General Hooker was relieved at his own request, and General George G. Meade, appointed to succeed him, not only won the battle of Gettysburg early in July, but seemed on the point of capturing Lee's whole army. But Lee evaded him, crossed the Potomac, and retreated to familiar camps in central Virginia. An entry in John Hay's diary, under date of July 15th tells us, "Robert Lincoln says the President is grieved silently but deeply about the escape of Lee. He said, 'If I had gone up there I could have whipped them myself.' I knew he had that idea." Meade followed Lee southward and for months thereafter the two commanders played a skillful game of strategy, neither being able to break through the other's guard. The beginning of 1864 found them encamped not far south of positions their respective armies had occupied two years earlier.

15

THE GETTYSBURG ADDRESS

THE WORK THAT MY FATHER DID IN MIN-
nesota in 1862 must have pleased both the President
and Mr. Dole, for late in the summer of 1863 he was again
directed to meet Mr. Dole, this time to act as secretary of
a commission that was to accompany the Governor of
Colorado Territory down to Connejos in the San Juan
Valley and to conclude a treaty with the Utes.

My father looked upon that visit to Colorado as one of
the rare experiences of his life. The Indians, however, who
had furnished most of the interest and all the excitement
the year before, sank to a very minor place in the accounts
he sent back to Therena and John Hay. The incidents of
travel—the hunting, particularly a buffalo hunt on the
plains—the virile young life of mining camps—and the
jewellike beauty of Colorado's wild flowers and sunsets—
interested him on this trip.

He was to join the Governor's party at Denver, and the
council was to take place early in September. But owing
to engagements already made by the Governor the meeting
with the Indians had to be postponed a month, which gave
him a chance to see much more of the fabulous country.

Adventures began almost at the start. The public stage in which he traveled from Atchison, Kansas, came to broken bridges and got stuck in a slough. The seventy-hour journey over the desert from Fort Kearney to Denver had to be made on a seat without a back, shut up in a stage with "six passengers, and a nigger baby," while express packages bounced on the roof above. In Denver a fire routed him from his hotel before he had been there long enough to take a nap.

But it was all high adventure. The buffalo hunt near Fort Kearney was as satisfying as a small boy's dream. "Very exciting sport, and not without danger.... Just the experience I wanted.... To see thirty horsemen charge and scatter a herd of buffaloes over the prairie, grouped around those brought to bay, or pursuing the flying with a continuous popping of revolvers in all directions is a very pretty sight."

A little black notebook that he carried in his pocket fairly explodes with adjectives praising the beauty of the scenery, the fantastic grades at which alleged roads climbed steeplelike peaks, only to drop again into valleys in a way to make a traveler's head swim.

The little town of Central City, where Gregory and his band of roving Georgians had discovered gold only five years before, amazed him. Hundreds of miners had rushed to the spot, only to leave a year later, ruined and sadly disillusioned. A few remained, and when my father saw the place in 1863 an almost impassable trail had been widened to a road. The town consisted of two streets whose houses burrowed into the mountainside at one end while the other extended out over empty air, supported by an occasional trestle. There were stores where anything could be bought from a hoop skirt to a quartz mill. There were banks and a hotel, a post office, a neat Gothic church, and two theaters, where he saw *Money* and *Rob Roy* performed "in very passable style." What astonished him most of all was that there seemed to be no municipal government, and gambling places were wide open, yet he neither heard nor saw, during his four days' stay, the least sign of disorder.

From Central City my father went on for a season of hunting in Middle and North Parks, then joined Mr. Dole and the Governor for their meeting with the Indians. It proved a distinct anti-climax. Only eighteen hundred Indians presented themselves: fifteen thousand had been expected. They were of a stolid inert type that he found most objectionable. They seemed far more interested in consuming their government rations of beef than in treaty making.

Much as he enjoyed the outing, consciousness of the struggle in the eastern half of the United States rarely left him, and he was glad to get back.

He returned to Washington in time to accompany Mr. Lincoln to Gettysburg for the dedication of the National Cemetery. The President had received a formal invitation to take part two weeks before the date set, but press of work in Washington was so great that it was settled only on November 17th—forty-eight hours before the dedication—that he could be present. Secretary Stanton prepared a schedule by which the party would leave Washington at eight o'clock on the morning of the 19th and return that same night. This, Mr. Lincoln vetoed in a characteristic note:

I do not like this arrangement. I do not wish to so go that by the slightest accident we fail entirely; and at best the whole [will] be a mere breathless running of the gauntlet— But any way—"

He left Washington at a few minutes past noon on the 18th, accompanied by Mr. Seward, Mr. Usher, and Mr. Blair of his Cabinet, my father and John Hay, the Minister from France, M. Mercier, the Minister from Italy, M. Martinelli, Mr. McDonald who represented Canada, with diplomatic secretaries and attachés from their respective countries, Mrs. Wise, the daughter of Edward Everett who was to give the principal address and her husband Captain H. A. Wise, and the guard of honor from Company A, First Invalid Regiment, which was to take part in the parade. Other military officers joined the train at various stations between Washington and Gettysburg.

Mr. Lincoln, Mr. Everett, and the Governor of Pennsylvania were guests of Mr. David Wills who had first suggested the creation of the National Cemetery. Mr. Seward was given a room in the house next door, and other members of the President's party were taken care of in the homes of hospitable citizens. Never had Gettysburg been so crowded. Hotels overflowed with guests and every place of public entertainment was filled to capacity. After the supper hour the streets swarmed with people. A serenading party went from house to house calling upon prominent visitors for speeches. Calls for a speech were loud in front of Mr. Wills's house, but the President showed himself only long enough to make the few commonplace excuses demanded by politeness.

Much controversy has arisen as to how, when, and where the Gettysburg Address was composed—whether Mr. Lincoln wrote it in Washington or on the train, or scribbled it hurriedly after reaching Gettysburg. My father's recollection was published in *The Century Magazine* for February 1884. He tells us that Mr. Lincoln received his formal invitation on November 2nd, and that this was accompanied by a private note from Mr. Wills, asking him to be his guest. He was very busy at the time with complicated military affairs, and besides was considering his annual message to Congress, which was to meet the following month. The *Century* article says:

There is no decisive record of when Mr Lincoln wrote the first sentences of his proposed Address. He probably followed his usual habit in such matters, using great deliberation in arranging his thoughts and molding his phrases mentally, waiting to reduce them to writing until they had taken satisfactory form.

The President's old friend, James Speed, says that Mr. Lincoln told him "on the day he left Washington" that he had found time to write "only about half his speech." My father assures us that "there is neither record, evidence, nor well-founded tradition that Mr. Lincoln did any writing, or made any notes on the journey between Washington and Gettysburg." In fact, writing would have been practically impossible amid the confusion of the journey and the greetings in which he had to take part as group after group joined the train. When he left Washington, he carried in his pocket the autograph manuscript of as much of the address as he had already prepared. It was written in ink and filled one page of the letter paper used at that time at the White House.

After breakfast on the 19th my father went to the upper room in Mr. Wills's house where the President had spent the night and remained with Mr. Lincoln until he was called downstairs to take his place in the procession that was about to start for the cemetery. It was during this short time that Mr. Lincoln finished writing his address, in pencil, on a sheet of bluish gray foolscap of large size such as he habitually used for long or formal documents.

The Grand Marshal for the day had planned an imposing procession, which was to leave Mr. Wills's house for the cemetery at precisely ten o'clock. Mr. Lincoln, dressed in his customary black, and wearing white gauntlets, mounted his horse but was no sooner in the saddle than the throng pressed forward so persistently to shake his hand that the marshals had difficulty in persuading them to let him sit quietly on his horse. The usual delays occurred, and curiosity to see the battlefield had already drawn away so many who were supposed to take part in the procession that it did not make the imposing display expected. Mr. Lincoln reached the cemetery at about eleven o'clock, half an hour before Mr. Everett.

It was fully noon before Mr. Everett began his two-hour address. Then, after a musical interlude, the President rose to speak. "It was entirely natural," wrote my father, "for everyone to expect only a few perfunctory words, the mere formality of official dedication." Probably the assemblage looked upon Mr. Everett as the true spokesman for the occasion and took it for granted that Mr. Lincoln was there merely in his presidential capacity—the final official decoration of an elaborate pageant. Totally unprepared, therefore, for what they heard, they did not immediately realize that his words, not Mr. Everett's, were to carry down to posterity the concentrated emotion of the occasion.

Newspapers stated that Mr. Lincoln read from a manuscript in his hand. My father sat only a few feet away, and his distinct recollection was that the President held the manuscript but did not read from it, his delivery being far more than a mechanical reading of written words. My father's recollection is borne out by the fact that the speech as taken down in shorthand by the Associated Press and printed next morning in the newspapers does not follow exactly the written words. My father thought it most likely that, during the ride to the grounds and the delivery of Mr. Everett's oration, Mr. Lincoln fashioned the phrases anew in his silent thought and had them ready when he rose to speak.

Contrary to the often made statement that Mr. Lincoln's address was little appreciated by those who heard it, the Associated Press report shows that during the short period of its delivery he was interrupted six times by applause.

That evening the presidential party left Gettysburg on its special train, reaching Washington about midnight. The next day Mr. Everett sent the President a note of thanks "for your great thoughtfulness for my daughter's accommodation yesterday, and much kindness to me and mine at Gettysburg." He added:

Permit me also to express my great admiration of the thoughts expressed by you with such eloquent simplicity and appropriateness at the consecration of the cemetery. I should be glad if I could flatter myself that I came as near the central idea of the occasion in two hours as you did in ten minutes.

Mr. Lincoln replied:

In our respective parts yesterday you could not have been excused to make a short address, nor I a long one. I am pleased to know that in your judgment the little I did say was not a failure. Of course I knew that Mr Everett could not fail.

Confusion about the exact text of his address is natural —for the odd reason that we have too much evidence.

There are three distinct and apparently correct authentic versions: (1) Mr. Lincoln's original draft; (2) his spoken words as reported by the Associated Press; (3) still another version made by Mr. Lincoln himself at the request of Mr. Wills, who asked for a copy of the historic document. This request was later repeated by several individuals who wished autograph copies for exhibition and sale at Sanitary Fairs. In all, half a dozen or more such copies were painstakingly made by the President, to correspond word for word with his final revision.

16

MANEUVERS, SOCIAL
AND POLITICAL

BY THE END OF 1863 THE COMING PRESI-
dential election, although nearly a year away,
already loomed large. Military success and political
strategy inevitably reacted on each other, and the end of
the war still seemed far distant. Notable military gains
had indeed been made. The Mississippi River was open,
Grant had captured Vicksburg, and Meade's victory at
Gettysburg had been further dramatized and made memorable by the words spoken by President Lincoln at the
dedication of that battlefield as a national cemetery. But
it had been necessary to resort again to the draft, and ill
luck still followed the Army of the Potomac. In spite of
his defeat, Lee had managed to save his army and lead it
down into Virginia, where, ever since, it had held General
Meade and the Army of the Potomac at bay. Already
President Lincoln was longing to bring General Grant
from the West to infuse the soldiers with his energy. A
note made by my father on December 7, 1863, reads:

The President this evening read me a telegram from Foster
saying that Sherman had reached and joined Burnside at
Knoxville, that Longstreet was in full retreat up the Valley

into Va., that he, Foster, would obey orders and vigorously follow up the pursuit, &c.

"Now," said the President, "if the Army of the Potomac was good for anything—if the officers had anything in them —if the army had any legs, they could move thirty thousand men down to Lynchburg and catch Longstreet. Can anybody doubt, if Grant were here in command, that he would catch him? There is not a man in the whole Union who would for a moment doubt it. But I do not think it would do to bring Grant away from the West. I talked with Gen. Halleck this morning about the matter, and his opinion was the same. 'But you know, Mr President,' said the General, 'how hard we have tried to get this army to move toward the enemy, and we cannot succeed.' "

"This," said the Pres., referring to Sherman's junction with Burnside, and Longstreet's retreat, "is one of the most important gains of the war. The difference between Burnside saved and Burnside lost is one of the greatest advantages of the war—it secures East Tennessee."

Political malcontents were making the most of every opportunity. One center of dissatisfaction was in Missouri. Missouri, being a slave state that had remained in the Union, was exempt from the provisions of the Emancipation Proclamation, yet critics of the President as diverse in opinion as those who thought he should not have issued it at all, and those who blamed him for not making it more drastic, united in expressing dissatisfaction. A deputation was sent to Washington to protest against many things, but chiefly to urge the removal of General Schofield from local military command. Mr. Lincoln answered these gentlemen in a long and careful letter addressed to them by name, in which he pointed out that some of their objections were irrelevant, and told them why he did not think it necessary to remove General Schofield. It was this deputation of Missourians to which Mr. Lincoln referred in a conversation recorded by my father on December 8th, when he wrote:

Today while comparing the engrossed and printed copies of his message to Congress, the President, by way of comment on some part he was reading, said:

"When the Missouri delegation was appointed and it was known that they were coming to see me, Seward asked that until I should hear and decide their case in my own mind, I should not say a word to him on the subject, or in any way ask his opinion concerning the controversy, so that hereafter we might both say that he had taken no part whatever in the matter, to which I agreed. Yet Wendell Phillips said in a later speech that Seward had written the whole of that letter."

Several notes made by my father during the first half of December 1863 had to do with the activities of the Peace Party in the North. This party, active since the beginning of the war, contended that the only thing to do was to enter at once into negotiations with the rebels. It had fared badly in the congressional elections of 1862, but was by no means ready to give up its opposition to Mr. Lincoln. The Clerk of the House of Representatives, Emerson Ethridge of Tennessee, whose duty it was to pass upon certificates of membership presented by members of the new Congress, had formerly been a staunch Republican, but he had become estranged from his old associates and was now an ardent member of the Peace Party. He thought he saw a chance to give control of the new House of Representatives to the Peace Party by leaving off the roll of membership all those whose certificates did not follow the exact wording of a law hastily passed in the closing days of the last session. My father wrote on December 6th:

Saw Colfax this morning and learned from him the particulars of Ethridge's plan to revolutionize the House. He insists that members' certificates which do not specify that they were elected "according to the laws of the State or the United States" (quoting the language of the law) are invalid. He therefore proposes to leave off the roll as not having proper certificates, the members from Vermont, Maryland, Missouri, Minnesota, California, Kansas, Oregon, Virginia and West Virginia.

When I reached home the President sent for Colfax. He showed him a blank certificate which he had two months ago sent to the Senators of the States, calling their attention to this law, to the probability that a contest would be made over the members' certificates, and suggesting that they have them made in several different forms, so as to cover all the points which might probably be raised. In some of the States it seems that this precaution had been neglected notwithstanding his warning.

"The main thing, Colfax," said the President, "is to be sure to have all our men here. Then if Mr Ethridge undertakes revolutionary proceedings, let him be carried out on a chip, and let our men organize the House. If the worst comes to the worst a file of 'Invalids' may be held convenient to take care of him."

Our active center of the Peace Party was in New York. My father's notes of December 14th indicate that Fernando Wood, recently elected a member of Congress from New York, came to the White House oftener than Mr. Lincoln liked as an advocate of this faction.

This morning early Edward came into the President's office and announced that Mr Wood was here to see him. "I am sorry he is here," said the President. "I would rather he should not come about here so much. Tell Mr Wood that I have nothing as yet to tell him on the subject we conversed about when he was here last." Edward went out to deliver the message.

"I can tell you what Wood wants," said the President to me. "He came here one day last week to urge me to publish some sort of amnesty for the northern sympathizers and abettors of the rebellion, which would include Vallandigham, and permit him to return; and promised that if I would do so, they would have two Democratic candidates in the field at the next Presidential election."

Mr. Vallandigham was a congressman from Ohio, whose violently incendiary speeches against the draft resulted in his arrest and trial before a military tribunal which sentenced him to imprisonment for the duration of the war. Mr. Lincoln regretted the arrest, but felt he could not annul the action of the military tribunal. He modified the sentence, however, and sent Vallandigham beyond the military lines instead of to prison. Vallandigham went to Richmond, from there to Bermuda, and finally to Canada, where he issued a political address. The Democrats of Ohio, taking up his cause with great enthusiasm, unanimously nominated him for governor, while sympathizers in New York and in Ohio sent imposing committees to Washington to tell Mr. Lincoln what they thought of him. He answered both these committees forcibly in writing. But one sympathetic question in his letter to the New Yorkers proved even more convincing to many who had joined the movement. "Must I shoot a simple-minded soldier who deserts," the President asked, "while I must not touch a hair of the wily agitator who induces him to desert?" Vallandigham was defeated for governor by more than 100,000 votes; and the operations of the draft were not delayed a single day.

But as always in our country when people are dissatisfied, much criticism rolled in on the President—a large part of it irrelevant. In the early days of the war a letter had come to the White House, asking earnestly if it could be true, as stated, that Mr. and Mrs. Lincoln had driven out "on a Sunday" to review the Army, "when the

ink was scarcely dry on a proclamation for a fast day."
Now objection was made that the President's answer to
the Albany Committee had first appeared in a Copperhead
journal. My father, through whose office the letter was
given to the press, felt called upon to explain that this
had not happened by design, and that "there is no disposition on my part to furnish disloyal sheets with special
privileges."

The *Chicago Tribune*, acknowledging receipt of its
copy of the President's letter, pronounced it "a crusher"
which the Copperheads would find hard to answer, then
turned to a grievance of its own. Historically, the incident
is of little value, but as evidence of my father's devotion
to the President, his answer deserves reading:

Private   Executive Mansion, Washington, D.C.
                              June 19, 1863

Gentlemen: I have received your note of the 16th inst. in
which among other things you say: "By the way, we are told
the President said to Senator Sumner recently, that he had
not seen a copy of the *Chicago Tribune* for four months.
Now, as it is mailed regularly we wish to know whether it is
received at the White House. If it miscarries we will have that
corrected. If he does not want it—declines to read it—we will
discontinue sending it. Please answer. Yours respectfully,
                              Tribune Company."

To this let me answer:

The *Chicago Tribune* is received very regularly, opened
and kept with other papers on the newspaper table in my
office; it is very regularly examined by myself, and especially
sought after by the western men who happen here.

That so far from desiring to place the *Tribune* under ban
in the Executive Mansion the President requests me to say
that he will be very glad to receive it here as long as in your
kindness you may please to send it;

And to this much from him, let me add a word on my own

responsibility. Excepting the Washington City dailies, in which he carefully reads the telegraphic dispatches, the President rarely ever looks at any papers, simply for want of leisure to do so. In this the *Tribune* fares as well as and no worse than all others. Still I think that during the two years of his stay here he would have been attracted to your journal more frequently, as to an old and familiar friend, if it had not in that time contained so much which he had a right to expect it would *at least have left unsaid.*

I can assure you of what you ought to be able to guess, that the President's task here is no child's play. If you imagine that *any man* could attempt its performance, and escape adverse criticism, you have read history in vain, and studied human nature without profit. But was it not to be expected that those of the President's friends, who have known him long and intimately—who understood his integrity and his devotion to the country and the cause entrusted to his charge—would at least abstain from judging him in the blindness of haste, and condemning him in the bitterness of ill-temper? It does seem to me that this much was due to generosity and charity for the fiery trial which he is called upon to pass through here, if not to political or personal friendship.

Let me repeat that these are exclusively my own thoughts and not the President's, and even I would not have written them if I could without misconstruction have otherwise answered the implication in your note to which you specifically requested a reply.

Let me add that I desire to continue reading the *Tribune,* reserving only the privilege of finding as much fault with it as it finds with the Administration which I know is unselfishly endeavoring to do its whole duty in the crisis.

Your obt. servant
Jno G. Nicolay

In spite of criticism it was evident that the majority of Republican voters desired the renomination of Mr.

Lincoln. Residents of the District of Columbia have no vote, but they do hold political opinions. In a letter written to John Hay in December 1863 my father mentioned a public meeting at which "Miss Dickinson made a telling harangue," complimenting the President, and when she alluded to his second term "the house came down with continued and repeated rounds of applause." He thought this "a gratifying evidence of the strength of the tide here."

There was opposition, however, even in the Cabinet. Well-informed circles knew that Secretary Chase coveted the presidential nomination in 1864, and had not frowned upon efforts to influence public opinion in his behalf. When, one night, John Hay heard Mr. Chase say rather grandiloquently

It is singularly instructive to meet so often, as we do in life and in history, instances of vaulting ambition, meanness, and treachery, failing after enormous exertions; and integrity and honesty march straight in triumph to its purpose,

this young hot partisan of the President was moved to copy the speech, word for word in his diary, and to add, ironically, "A noble sentiment, Mr. Secretary!"

Mr. Lincoln knew of this desire of Mr. Chase's, but ignored it, and continued to appoint his partisans to office. Young Hay even ventured to remonstrate with his chief, but confided to his diary afterwards that "He seemed much amused at Chase's mad hunt after the presidency."

The efforts in Mr. Chase's behalf culminated in February 1864 in a secret letter or circular signed by Senator Pomeroy of Kansas, which more than hinted that Secretary Chase was the man to correct all President Lincoln's mistakes and lead the party triumphantly forward. Alluding to this, my father wrote to John Hay on February 17th:

The Treasury rats are busy night and day and becoming more and more unscrupulous and malicious. They are circulating a scurrilous anonymous pamphlet to injure the President, and today I was shown a circular signed by Pomeroy as "Chairman of the National Executive Committee," proposing a Chase organization throughout the country. The adherents of this faction in the House and Senate are malicious and bitter, but dare not openly attack the Tycoon. Winter Davis showed his teeth in the House yesterday, but got no backing except from two or three Members. Things have been drifting along chaotically for two or three weeks, but active work must begin soon. Dufrees has gone to Indiana to look after matters there, and we shall probably have a good endorsement there.

Corruption and malice are doing their worst, but I do not think it is in the cards to beat the Tycoon.

Mr. Lincoln refused to look at the Pomeroy circular. Soon after it got into print. Secretary Chase wrote to him offering to resign, but assuring the President that he had known nothing about it until he saw it in the newspapers. Mr. Lincoln kept the Secretary's letter a week before replying. Robert Lincoln, who was home at the time, remembered that his father strolled into his room after dinner one evening, showed him Mr. Chase's letter, asked for writing materials, and sitting down wrote his answer, to the effect that he had not read Mr. Pomeroy's letter and did not think he would; that he knew just as little about such things as his friends allowed him to know; that neither of them could be held responsible for acts committed without their knowledge or approval, and ended:

Whether you shall remain at the head of the Treasury Department is a question which I will not allow myself to consider from any standpoint other than my judgement of the public service, and in that view I do not perceive occasion for a change.

He showed this answer to his son, who asked in surprise if he had not seen the circular. Mr. Lincoln stopped him almost sternly, saying that a good many people had tried to tell him something he did not wish to hear, and that his answer to the Secretary of the Treasury was literally true. "Thereupon," Robert Lincoln added, "I called a messenger, and the note was sent."

To one of his secretaries Mr. Lincoln had said, months before, that Mr. Chase made a wonderful Secretary of the Treasury, and that he preferred to know nothing about his outside political activities. "If he becomes President: all right. I hope we may never have a worse one." He was scrupulously careful not to allow personal considerations to influence his official acts. About an entirely different matter he had said, "I shall do nothing in malice. The issues I deal with are too vast for malicious dealing."

But he had his opinion of the good taste displayed by his would-be successor. In June 1864, a difference of opinion with the President regarding certain appointments led the Secretary of the Treasury to offer his resignation twice in rapid succession. The second time Mr. Lincoln accepted it—possibly to Mr. Chase's surprise. He went home to Ohio. In early December Mr. Lincoln made him Chief Justice of the United States Supreme Court. At some time during the interval his secretary had brought Mr. Lincoln a note from the former Secretary of the Treasury.

"What is it about?" the President asked.

"Merely a kind and friendly letter."

"File it with his other recommendations!" Mr. Lincoln said quickly. Chief Justice Taney had died meanwhile, and the President knew Mr. Chase coveted the office.

Probably no other man than Lincoln would have had, in this age of the world, the degree of magnanimity to thus forgive and exalt a rival who had so deeply and unjustifiably intrigued against him [my father wrote Therena]. It is however only another and marked illustration of the greatness of the President in this age of little men.

In spite of Mr. Lincoln's fine attitude, Mr. Chase's aspirations had repercussions in the White House. Washington was full of cliques and jealousies. Since the capital was on the border line between North and South, sad family divisions had occurred between the intensely loyal and those whose sympathies drew them toward the Confederacy. There was a sharp cleavage, too, between the social leaders of Buchanan's day and those of the Lincoln administration. Then there were the natural dislikes that develop between individuals. As wife of the President, Mrs. Lincoln held a position of leadership that she prized highly. She could be very gracious when she saw fit, but was too impulsive to hold an even course through troubled waters, or to restrain her temper when annoyed. Kate Chase, daughter of the Secretary of the Treasury, was as ambitious as Mrs. Lincoln, and possessed the immense advantages of youth and quite unusual beauty. In addition, she was enjoying the glamour that surrounds a bride, having made what was looked upon as a brilliant marriage with the governor of Rhode Island. We have no means of knowing how much the political aspirations of Mr. Chase had to do with the friction that developed between the two ladies, but it is hard to imagine either of them taking such a matter lightly.

Even in his letters to Therena my father rarely mentioned domestic affairs at the White House, feeling that both discretion and good taste enjoined silence; but two very private "off the record" letters written to John Hay while the latter was at Hilton Head, tell this story. One of his duties was to see that invitations to state dinners and other official functions were issued correctly and that the entertainments themselves were conducted with dignity. When it came time to address invitations for a Cabinet dinner in January 1864, he found that the names of Secretary Chase and his son-in-law and daughter, Mr. and Mrs. William Sprague, had been stricken from the list. Foreseeing all sorts of complications, he took the matter to the President:

I referred the "snub" to the Tycoon, who, after a short conference with the powers at the other end of the hall, came back and ordered Rhode Island and Ohio to be included in the list. Whereat there soon arose such a rampage as the House hasn't seen for a year, and I am again taboo. How the thing is to end is yet as dark a problem as the Schleswig-Holstein difficulty. Stod. fairly cowered at the volume of the storm, and I think for the first time begins to appreciate the awful sublimities of Nature. Things have subsided somewhat, but a day or two must of course bring them to a head.

Later he reported:

I came out of what Uncle Jem called the *imbroligo* of the cabinet dinner with flying colors. As I wrote before, after having compelled Her S. Majesty to invite the Spragues I was taboo, and she made up her mind resolutely not to have me at the dinner. She fished around with Stod. to try to get posted about managing the affair, but I instructed Stod. to tell her, 1st, that there was no way of his obtaining the requisite information, and 2dly, that if there were, yet as it was exclusively my business he *could* and *would* not do anything in the premises. Stod., I think, carried out my instructions faithfully. She expressed her great regret, but still announced her determination to run the machine without my help. Things ran on till the afternoon of the dinner, when Edward came up to tell me that she had backed down, requested my presence and assistance—apologizing and explaining that the affair had worried her so she hadn't slept

for a night or two. I think she has felt happier since she cast
out that devil of stubbornness. The dinner was got through
creditably. On Wednesday last she sent out cards for the
diplomatic dinner. While she has not in all matters done so,
she has in the main adopted my advice and direction in this.

Society flourishes. I couldn't begin to count the parties
on all my fingers. They are beginning to double up. Phren-
andowood had a grand blow-out last night to which he didn't
invite me. Bob has been home about a week, and Neil Den-
nison is with him.

The Tycoon is taking the Arkansas matter in hand as you
will see by the papers. I have not yet had time to get you
Grant's address, but will do so.

Therena Bates had relatives in Washington. She visited
them to get a glimpse of life at the capital, which, that
year, was very gay. She used her dark eyes to advantage in
the White House, as is plain from questions she asked
about the furniture—details that my father had never
even noticed. Doubtless she knew or divined the relations
existing between the President's wife and his private secretary, which were polite and correct, but never cordial.
The only possible allusion to the "imbroligo" in my
father's letters to her is one telling her he had suffered
considerably from the blues since she left, and that "it
seems as if circumstances surrounding my position are
getting worse every day. I am beginning seriously to
doubt my ability to endure it a great while longer."

Because of Mrs. Lincoln's southern family connections
she was the victim of much cruel and unjust criticism—
some of which actually accused her of disloyalty to the
United States. She received so many abusive letters that
she finally told "Stod" to open and read them all before
bringing any to her—excepting only those from her
sisters.

Two letters written by my father in later years in answer to questions about Mrs. Lincoln have been preserved. In one of them we read:

"The statement that Mrs Lincoln gave a confidential map to anybody anywhere, or at any time is, in my opinion, pure invention with no word of truth."

The other, written in 1887, is a better summary of the subject than I have seen elsewhere:

These accounts are very much overdrawn. I was in the official family of Mr Lincoln during his entire term, and never saw anything to justify such statements as have been made about Mrs Lincoln at that time. That she was very eccentric there is no doubt, but that she went to the extremes reported I do not believe. . . . She had her likes and dislikes. For instance, she never liked Secretary Seward. . . . I don't think she liked me, but I never knew her to so far forget herself as to make a fuss about it. At the Executive Mansion she would receive of evenings fifteen and twenty ladies and gentlemen without any exhibitions of undue nervousness or excitement. She was a woman of great frankness and would speak her mind out.

Referring to a revival of these stories, he continued:

It is noticeable that ———— is in the habit of saying things about people who are dead and therefore unable to defend themselves against any statements that might be made. I think this one about Mrs Lincoln at the time referred to can be accepted *cum grano salis*. . . . The shock of the assassination did ultimately disturb Mrs Lincoln's sanity, so that her son was obliged to ask an order of the Court restraining her of her liberty. Such imaginative coloring of peculiarities or mannerisms of people who have passed away are an act of injustice to the memory of the dead, and sooner or later must react upon their inventors.

17

GRANT, LIEUTENANT-
GENERAL

THE NOTES THAT MY FATHER MADE
when Grant was called to Washington to receive his
commission as Lieutenant-General are quite full.

Executive Mansion, March 8, 1864—In obedience to an invitation from the Sec. of War Gen. Grant reached the city about 5 P.M. By some sort of negligence there was no one at the depot to receive him, but he found his way to Willard's with the two members of his staff who accompanied him.

Reception tonight. The weather was bad; but the *Republican* having announced that Grant would attend the reception, it brought out a considerable crowd. At about 9½ P.M. the General came in—alone again excepting his staff—and he and the President met for the first time. The President, expecting him, knew from the buzz and movement in the crowd that it must be the General; and when a man of modest mien and unimposing exterior presented himself, the President said:

"This is General Grant, is it not?"

The General replied, "Yes."

and the two greeted each other more cordially, but still with that modest deference, felt rather than expressed in word or action, so appropriate to both—the one the honored ruler, the other the honored victor of the nation and the time.

The crowd too partook of the feeling of the occasion. There was no rude jostling, or pushing, or pulling, but unrestrained the circle kept its respectful distance, until after a brief conversation the President gave the General in charge of Seward to present to Mrs Lincoln, at the same time instructing me to send for the Secretary of War. After paying his respects to Mrs Lincoln the General was taken by Seward to the East Room, where he was greeted with cheer after cheer by the assembled crowd, and where he was forced to mount a sofa from whence he could shake hands with those who pressed from all sides to see him. It was at least an hour before he returned, flushed, heated and perspiring with the unwonted exertion.

The *New York Tribune's* account of the reception added the interesting detail that the General was "literally lifted up," and that Secretary Seward preceded him to his eminence on the sofa. After this there was a promenade of the receiving party through the East Room, the President walking with Mr. Seward, and Mrs. Lincoln with the guest of honor. Then they returned to the Blue Room and sat down.

The President went upstairs, and returning in a little while, sat down near where the General, the Secretary of War and I were sitting.

"Tomorrow," said the President to the General, "at such time as you may arrange with the Sec. War, I desire to make to you a formal presentation of your commission as Lieut. Genl. I shall then make a very short speech to you, to which I desire you to reply for an object; and that you may be properly prepared to do so I have written what I shall say —only four sentences in all—which I will read from my MS. as an example which you may follow and also read your reply, as you are perhaps not as much accustomed to speaking as I, myself—and I therefore give you what I shall say that you may consider it and form your reply. There are two points that I would like to have you make in your answer, 1st, to say something which shall prevent or obviate any jealousy of you from any of the other generals in the service, and 2d, something which shall put you on as good terms as possible with this Army of the Potomac. Now, consider whether this may not be said to make it of some advantage; and if you see any objection whatever to doing it, be under no restraint whatever in expressing that objection to the Secretary of War who will talk further with you about it."

The General asked at what time this presentation would take place.

"The Secretary of War and yourself may arrange the time to suit your convenience. I will be ready, whenever you shall have prepared your reply."

"I can be ready in thirty minutes," said the General.

One o'clock tomorrow was finally fixed as the hour, after which the General took his leave, accompanied by the Sec. of War.

The President, as I learned in reply to a question to him, is contemplating bringing the General East to see whether he can not do something with the unfortunate Army of the Potomac.

During the reception a dispatch was brought to me announcing that the Union ticket had been today carried in N.H. by 3000.

March 9, 1864—The presentation ceremony of General Grant's commission as Lieut.-General took place today at 1 P.M. in the Cabinet Chamber. The newspapers give the proceedings and addresses in full. Both the President and the General read their remarks from MSS. The General had hurriedly and almost illegibly written his speech on the half of a sheet of note paper, in lead pencil, and being quite embarrassed by the occasion, and finding his own writing so very difficult to read, made rather sorry and disjointed work of enunciating his reply. I noticed too that in what he said, while it was brief and to the point, he had either forgotten or disregarded entirely the President's hints to him of the night previous.

During this afternoon Gov. Chase sent the President a copy of his letter to Judge Hall of Ohio withdrawing his name from the presidential canvass.

Toward the end of March my father wrote Therena:

The armies are of course standing still until Grant shall get his new harness well on. He is expected here tonight. After receiving his commission, and visiting the Army of the Potomac, the General had returned to the West to wind up his affairs there. He had gone to Washington fully determined to accept no appointment which required him to leave the western field of operations, but after seeing the Army of the Potomac had made up his mind that he must be in Virginia.

At the moment the main interest was in politics. My father wrote:

Congress is driveling its time away; luckily not doing much harm, if it is doing no good. Chase having retired from the presidential contest, the tide continues to set as strongly as ever to Lincoln, and politicians therefore have but little to intrigue about. A few malcontents in the Republican party are stewing around trying to make Butler, Frémont, or anybody they can get, the nucleus of a little faction in opposition to Lincoln, but there is not the remotest prospect that their eggs will hatch. It is a time of general calm—most likely a calm before a storm—for we shall undoubtedly have events and excitements enough during the year.

He told Therena that Hay, who had been in Florida, was probably on his way home, doubtless "a good deal annoyed at the way his name has been bandied about in the newspapers when there was not the shadow of foundation for it." The cause of this visit was that, some time before, Mr. Lincoln had offered full amnesty to men connected with the rebellion provided they took an oath to support the Constitution of the United States and legislation freeing the slaves. Only those who had resigned office under the United States government or who had maltreated colored soldiers were excluded from this amnesty. The President had further made it known that when one-tenth of the voters in any of the seceded states took this oath and established a government, it would be protected by the Federal authorities.

Union men in Florida had thereupon asked young Hay to come down there and seek election as their representative in Congress. When he told the President of this invitation, Mr. Lincoln looked upon it as an opportunity to test his scheme and sent the young man to Florida, saying,

"Great good luck and God's blessing go with you, John."

But the effort was premature. The necessary 10 per cent of voters could not be secured, and Hay was coming back to his old position.

Soon after his return my father went to New York on a delicate and troublesome errand that had to do with a change of appointees in the Custom House. While there he talked with many politicians about Mr. Lincoln's renomination, "about which," he reported, "there seems to be more diversity of views and interests than anywhere else in the country," though the general opinion, even among those who opposed him, was that the President's renomination and re-election were practically certain.

Whatever diplomacy the President's secretary possessed must have been called actively into play in the matter of the Custom House. Personal feelings were deeply involved, and there were charges that men in a certain bureau were actively aiding the rebellion. My father sent the President a private report of his interview with Thurlow Weed, who had impatiently awaited his arrival at the Astor House. Mr. Weed's criticism of Mr. Lincoln was that he "did too much for those who sought to drive him out of the field." His personal grievance was that the President exercised his own judgment instead of always taking Mr. Weed's advice. My father wrote:

Private. Mr President: Mr Weed was here at the Astor House on my arrival last Saturday morning, and I gave him the note you sent him.

He read it over carefully once or twice and then said he did not quite understand it. He had written a letter to Judge Davis which the Judge had probably shown you, but in that he had said nothing about Custom House matters.

He said that all the solicitude he had was in your behalf. You had told him in January last that you thought you would make a change in the Collectorship here, but that thus far it had not been made. He had told you he himself had no personal preference as to the particular man who is to be his [the present Collector's] successor. He did not think Mr. Barney a bad man, but thought him a weak one. His four deputies are constantly intriguing against you. Andrews is doing the same. Changes are constantly being made among the subordinates in the Custom House, and men turned out for no other reason than that they take active part in primary meetings &c. in behalf of your renomination.

His only solicitude he said was for yourself. He thought that if you were not strong enough to hold the Union men together through the next presidential election, when it must necessarily undergo a great strain, the country was in the utmost danger of going to ruin.

His desire was to strengthen you as much as possible, and that you should strengthen yourself. You were being weakened by the impression in the popular mind that you hold with much tenacity to men once in office although they prove themselves unworthy. This feeling among your friends also raises the question as to whether, if re-elected, you would change your Cabinet. The present Cabinet is notoriously weak and inharmonious—no Cabinet at all—gives the President no support. Welles is a cipher, Bates a fogy, and Blair at best a dangerous friend.

Something was needed to reassure the public mind and to strengthen yourself. Chase and Frémont, while they might not succeed in making themselves successful rivals, might yet form and lead dangerous factions. Chase was not formidable as a candidate in the field, but by the shrewd dodge of withdrawal is likely to turn up again with more strength than ever.

He had received a letter from Judge Davis, in which the Judge wrote him that he had read his (Weed's) letter to you, but that you did not seem ready to act in the appointment of a new Collector, and that he (the Judge) thought it was because of your apprehension that you would be merely getting out of one muss into another. A change in the Custom House was imperatively needed. . . .

The ambition of his life had been, not to get office for himself, but to assist in putting good men in the right places. If he was good for anything, it was as an outsider to give valuable suggestions to an administration that would give him its confidence. He feared he did not have your entire confidence—that you only regarded him with a certain degree of leniency . . . as being not quite so great a rascal as his enemies charged him with being.

The above are substantially the points of quite a long conversation. This morning I had another interview with Mr Weed. He had just received Governor Morgan's letter informing him of the nomination of Hoogboom to fill McElrath's place and seemed quite disheartened and disappointed.

How deeply hurt this well-meaning gentleman was, and how his self-esteem had been wounded, is shown in a letter he addressed to the President, which closed with these words:

But I have a letter from Governor Morgan informing me that John P. Hoogboom has been appointed General Appraiser. This appointment, after what I told you of the character and condition of the Appraisers and their Department shows how egregiously I have mistaken my position. But I am instructed now, and will not hereafter trespass upon your time nor subject myself to future mortification.

Pray do me the justice to remember that I have never consumed your time or asked your attention but upon subjects which concerned the general welfare, so that while a useless, I have not been an expensive, friend.

In spite of Mr. Weed and several other worries, my father got some pleasure out of his visit to New York, notably, several nights at the opera. He saw the opening of the great Sanitary Fair, but it hardly came up to his idea of what such a fair in New York should be. The part he enjoyed most was the exhibition of paintings held in the private gallery of William H. Aspinwall on 10th Street, which brought together probably the largest collection of good works of art seen up to that time in the United States. "It alone well repaid me for having stayed to see the opening of the fair," he wrote.

He had several matters to attend to in connection with the fair. Flowers from the White House had been promised for the opening night. As transit between Washington and New York consumed long hours in 1864, there were instructions to be sent back relative to getting the flowers there in good condition and on time. A greater worry had to do with a promised manuscript written by the President.

My father found that the one chosen and sent by the State Department was a Thanksgiving Proclamation, composed by Mr. Seward and in his handwriting. To advertise it as a Lincoln autograph would be untrue. Yet to attribute it to Mr. Seward would seem to confirm a statement widely circulated by the President's detractors that "all the President's important papers are written by Mr Seward." He instructed Hay to find out whether the sending of this document was the result of a trick or a mistake. "It is of no serious consequence in any event," he wrote, "yet it will be a pestiferous annoyance to have the newspapers gossip and wrangle about it." If it was a trick "then we had better have it announced that the document is Seward's composition, and so end all controversy at once." If a mistake, another manuscript should be substituted.

But the matter that delayed his return still further was considerably more "pestiferous."

I had determined to start home tonight [he wrote], but seeing the villainous unfair and untrue editorial in the *Tribune* of this morning, I have determined to stay till I can have another talk with Greeley and Gay and tell them a fact or two, so that if they print misrepresentations in the future they shall do so knowingly. As Mr Greeley only comes to his office very late in the evening I do not know how soon I may be able to get off.

The "villainous unfair and untrue" story, which had been circulated manifestly for its political effect, was a sample of the persecution to which the President and his family were subjected, on account of Mrs. Lincoln's southern origin. The President had lately given a pass to Mrs. Lincoln's sister, Mrs. J. Todd White, permitting her to visit Richmond. The story, originally sent from Washington on March 28th by a correspondent of the *New York Tribune*, was to the effect that Mrs. White had not only objected to having her luggage searched, but had defied the officers to touch it, boasting that her trunks were filled with contraband, and had flourished the President's autograph pass "under their noses," saying in substance, "Here is the positive order of your master!" At first the story had been pronounced by the *New York World* "a *Tribune* romance" but later the *World* retracted this, saying the tale, after investigation, proved to be "even more damning" than as at first related.

In spite of my father's effort to see Mr. Greeley and "tell him a fact or two" the story circulated so persistently that on April 12th, he wrote to General Butler, in whose military district the incident was said to have occurred, enclosing a copy of the current version, and saying:

Now the President is not conscious of having given this lady a pass which permitted her to take anything more than the ordinary luggage allowed, nor which exempted her from the existing rules of inspection. He certainly gave her no such extraordinary privileges as are above described and implied. Will you please inform me whether Mrs White presented to you what purported to be more than the usual pass on which persons have been sent through our lines, or which purported to entitle her to carry more than ordinary baggage?

(1.) Did she take with her more than customary baggage?

(2.) Was, or was not, her baggage inspected?

(3.) Did she use the language alleged in the above statement?

Your obedient servant

Jno. G. Nicolay

P.S. Are such passes usually taken up by our officers? If so, please send me this pass, or a copy of it.

General Butler answered speedily and satisfactorily. He denied all the damaging statements and added a paragraph that indicated that the "contraband" Mrs. White was alleged to be carrying consisted merely of some wedding presents she was bringing to a relative in Richmond.

In acknowledging his reply, my father enclosed a brief editorial written by himself which appeared in the *Tribune's* editorial columns. "I felt sure the whole *canard* was too silly and trivial to merit an official contradiction," he wrote General Butler, "but thought that a correction in this shape was due and proper, and therefore troubled you with the matter only that I might get the exact facts."

His editorial stated the accusation and the denial, and ended:

As the Copperhead papers throughout the country are quoting the *Tribune* as authority in this matter, we hope they will give this statement a speedy and wide publication.

He sent the editorial to Mr. Greeley, marked "Private," on April 25th, asking him to publish it or its equivalent in his editorial columns, since the original story had been printed in the *Tribune's* Washington correspondence.

Mr. Greeley answered:

I thank you heartily for your note of yesterday. I shall of course publish the enclosure tomorrow.

Please send me anything of public interest you may at any time have to publish. Though I am an earnest one term man, I want to publish all the truth I can get, and as few falsehoods as possible.

But even so, the slanderous tale had been in circulation more than four weeks before the President's secretary was able to stop it.

18

LINCOLN RE-ELECTED

BEFORE RETURNING FROM THE WEST TO establish his headquarters in Virginia, General Grant had conferred with his trusted friend General Sherman and agreed with him upon the very simple military plan to be followed during 1864. There were to be two leading campaigns. Sherman was to start from Chattanooga with his combined forces against the Confederate army under Bragg, while Grant in the East would conduct operations against Richmond and Lee's army, retaining General Meade as commander of the Army of the Potomac, to carry out his daily orders. The two Confederate armies were eight hundred miles apart. If either gave way it was to be followed relentlessly to battle or surrender. They must not be allowed to join.

At first all went well. Grant crossed the Rapidan. General Butler took up a position where he might either menace Petersburg or advance upon Richmond. General Sherman started on his famous march toward the sea. For a few days the end of the war seemed very close. My father confessed that he had not felt so nervous and anxious for a year. "Our spring campaigns have so generally been failures that people are beginning to feel superstitious about them." He regarded the people who for one reason or another wished to substitute some other candidate for Mr. Lincoln as being consciously or unconsciously in league with the enemy. "There is not a rebel on either side of the Potomac who does not feel that the presidential canvass is full of promise for their cause," he wrote disgustedly.

The President is cheerful and hopeful—not unduly, but seeming confident; and now as ever watching every report and indication with quiet unwavering interest. If my anxiety is so great, what must be his solicitude, after waiting through three long weary years of doubt and disaster for such a consummation, to see the signs of final and complete victory every day growing so bright and auspicious.

But then the weather changed, and with it the fortunes of war. Grant encountered obstacles that gave literal meaning to his obstinate assertion that he meant to fight it out on that line if it took all summer. The Peace Party clamored louder than ever. "Still," my father wrote, "there seems to be constant activity. Grant's wounded are being taken care of, and his reenforcements are arriving, which will about replenish his losses in the late battles."

Perhaps it was at this time that he wrote an undated memorandum to remind himself that public opinion could still be relied on.

When the *Herald* endorses Sumner's plan for amending the Constitution of the United States to abolish slavery—

When Brooks makes a speech in the House declaring it dead—

When Bryant in the N.Y. legislature offers a series of resolutions declaring it should be extinguished—

When the Democratic paper at Cincinnati hoists the name of Frémont for President—

The people may well take courage that the country is progressing.

The Republican National Convention met in Baltimore early in June. The *New York Tribune* advocated postponing it until midsummer or later, but it was the Democratic Convention that was postponed, finally nominating General George B. McClellan as its candidate on the last day of August.

My father attended the meetings of the Republican convention, as a spectator, just as he had done four years before. The renomination of Lincoln was a foregone conclusion since the large delegations from New York, Pennsylvania and Illinois had been instructed to cast their votes for him. "I suppose a similar unanimity has not occurred during the whole history of the country" he wrote. But there was great uncertainly about the vice-presidency. Before going to Baltimore, my father had asked Mr. Lincoln about his preferences, and Mr. Lincoln had replied, as he had to others, that since all the aspirants were good men and good friends of his he did not wish to influence the Convention in any way. At the same time he made it clear to my father that so far as his personal feelings were concerned, he would be glad to see the old ticket of Lincoln and Hamlin renominated.

Before the Convention was organized my father wrote John Hay:

Hamlin will in all probability be nominated V.P. New York does not want the nominee—hence neither Dix nor Dickinson have any backers. Andy Johnson seems to have no strength whatever; even Dr Breckinridge and the Kentuckians oppose him. Cameron received no encouragment outside of Pennsylvania, and he is evidently too shrewd to beat an empty bush. The disposition of all the delegates was to take any war Democrat, *provided he would add strength to the ticket.* None of the names suggested seemed to meet this requirement, and the feeling therefore is to *avoid any weakness.* It strikes everybody that Hamlin fills this bill, and Pennsylvania has this afternoon broken ground on the subject by resolving on Cameron's own motion, to cast her vote for him. New York will probably follow suit tonight, which will virtually decide the contest.

The delegations being so unanimous for Lincoln are in a great measure indifferent about the other matters. All day everybody has been asking advice, nobody making suggestions. The Convention is almost too passive to be interesting—certainly it is not at all exciting, as it was at Chicago.

Next day he wrote to Hay:

The Vice Presidency goes begging. Yesterday as I wrote you the current set toward Hamlin. But New England does not support Hamlin, or at least Massachusetts does not, because, it is shrewdly suspected, she hopes something may turn up in a new deal which would enable her to push Andrews. New York leaned decidedly to Hamlin yesterday evening; but the main thing New York wants is *not* to have the V.P. because that would obstruct Seward's future. So, this morning, New York, fearing that through Hamlin's failure Dickinson might succeed, determined to go for Johnson. So the matter drifts. . . .

First of all, an attempt was made to nominate the old ticket of Lincoln and Hamlin by acclamation. That failed, and finally the choice for Vice-President fell on Andrew Johnson, who, when the Convention opened, seemed to have "no strength whatever."

Gradually during the summer the political barometer fell. There were no outstanding military victories, and factions within the Republican party grew vociferous, declaring that although he had been nominated, Mr. Lincoln could not possibly be elected. As early as June a small group, meeting in Cincinnati, denounced the President's policies as "imbecile and vacillating" and nominated John C. Frémont as their candidate. He accepted the nomination, but withdrew before the campaign was over. Mr. Chase had already withdrawn. Another faction favored General Benjamin F. Butler; still another General Grant, but he was too busy at his task of winning the war to pay much attention. The Democratic Convention, meeting in Chicago, had nominated McClellan. Many of its members agreed with the Peace Party that negotiations should be opened at once with the rebels. But there were also many sturdy War Democrats who believed with the President that such a course would be worse than a military defeat. The way was therefore left open for General McClellan to indicate in his letter of acceptance which course he favored—but he chose to evade the issue.

Early in the summer Therena had hoped my father might make her a short visit, but Copperhead sentiment flared so hotly in Pittsfield, near the border line, that she began to wonder if it would be safe for him to come. He wrote that he might not be able to leave Washington, but added:

I think you over-estimate the possible danger. . . . While of course the Copperheads in Pike County dislike me more because of my close personal relations to the President, I have no idea their animosity would be so intense as to move them to seek my personal injury. . . . At all events when I get ready to come out to see you, I shall not delay or defer my visit on that account.

He made his visit and went on to the Rocky Mountains in search of sorely needed strength. At St. Joseph, Missouri, he met two friends who were to accompany him. But from the outset this trip, as a vacation, was unsuccessful. He and his friends made an inventory of their belongings and found that they had everything heart could desire for the trip, except an ambulance in which to cross the plains. They had ordered one, but it was nowhere to be found. Lively telegraphing, in which the commander of the post took a prominent part, finally located it at Quincy, Illinois, neatly stored away with freight "deferred for next year." Disentangled at last, it reached St. Joseph, and my father, who had made one trip across the desert in a public coach, feasted his eyes on its perfection. "We have a magnificent outfit," he wrote Therena.... "I doubt whether any team and party so well provided has started from here this spring." But to Hay he wrote:

How we shall get along after we are started is not so certain. The Plains are full of emigrants, and the Platte has been on a "high," and whether we shall find anything for ourselves and our mules to eat is not yet certain. Add to this that the Arapahoes are on the rampage, and you get a lively idea of the situation.

Later advices assured them that the Indian rumors were more of a scare than a menace, but already they were beginning to wonder whether the ill-fated trip was worth continuing. "If you hear of my having a sudden call to return, don't get alarmed," my father wrote.

He went on as far as Fort Kearney. But the swarms of mosquitoes buzzing around them every night added the final touch of annoyance.

There is no protecting against them [he wrote]. They bite through my buckskin gloves without wincing, and I think that nothing short of iron-clad armor would even bend their bills. I am beginning to believe the legend of the man under the iron kettle.

"I have taken the back track," he wrote Hay, "I will be in Washington—as soon as I get there.... Fight the good fight till I come and reinforce you with pluck at least, for strength I have gained none. I think I am thinner than when I started. . . . This expedition has so far proved a lamentable failure." At heart he was glad to get back near the center of the political campaign. When Therena sent him clippings from certain Illinois newspapers, he answered:

Do the Democratic papers accuse me of cowardice because I did not run into the jaws of the Indian devils? I had not yet seen it. Well, it won't worry me much, so long as I am not craven enough to join them in asking that the victorious flag of the Union shall be disgraced by lowering it to traitors in arms as they are doing every day.

During the next few weeks his letters reflected the growing anxiety among Mr. Lincoln's friends. To General C. B. Fisk, who had not only helped get his ambulance out of cold storage, but was advising and helping him to buy a farm in Kansas, my father wrote:

You gather the situation about as well from the newspapers as I could give it to you in a dozen pages. Although the country generally is in a feverish and unsatisfied condition at our failure to obtain great military successes ... the President is, as ever, patient, plucky and confident.

After a fortnight in Washington he wrote Therena that there was rather a bad state of feeling among weak-kneed members of the party, due to the lack of decided military success, and to impatience over the necessity for a new draft. Croakers were talking about the impossibility of re-electing Mr. Lincoln "unless something were done"— though nobody seemed able to define exactly what that something should be. He believed this was mainly due to anxiety and would pass after the Democrats nominated their candidate and an active campaign got under way. On August 25th he wrote to Hay:

Dear Major: Hell is to pay. The N.Y. politicians have got a stampede on that is about to swamp everything. Raymond [Henry G. Raymond, editor of the *New York Times*] and the National Committee are here today. R. thinks a commission to Richmond is about the only salt to save us, while the Tycoon sees and says it would be utter ruination. The matter is now undergoing consultation. Weak-kneed d——d fools like Chas. Sumner are in the movement for a new candidate to supplant the Tycoon. Everything is darkness and doubt and discouragement. Our men see giants in the airy and unsubstantial shadows of the opposition and are about to surrender without a fight.

I think that today and here is the turning-point in our crisis. If the President can infect R. and his Committee with some of his own patience and pluck, we are saved. If our friends will only rub their eyes and shake themselves and become convinced that they themselves are not dead, we shall win the fight overwhelmingly.

Three days later he reported to Therena:

I wrote you that the Republican party was laboring under a severe fit of despondency and discouragement. During the past week it reached almost the condition of a disastrous panic—a sort of political Bull Run—but I think it has reached its culmination, and will speedily have a healthy and vigorous reaction. It even went so far that Raymond, the Chairman of the National Executive Committee, wrote a most doleful letter here to the President, summing up the various discouraging signs he saw in the country, and giving it as his opinion that unless *something* was done (and he thought that "something" should be sending commissioners to Richmond to propose terms of peace to the rebels on the basis of their returning to the Union) we might as well quit and give up the contest. In this mood he came here to Washington three

or four days ago to attend a meeting of the Executive Committee of the National Committee.

The President and the strongest half of the Cabinet—
Seward, Stanton and Fessenden—held a consultation with
him, and showed him that they had already thoroughly considered and discussed his proposition; and upon showing
him their reasons, he very readily concurred with them in the
opinion that to follow his plan of sending commissioners to
Richmond would be worse than losing the presidential contest
—it would be ignominiously surrendering it in advance.

My father was in New York (again on that troublesome
Custom House business) when this visit of Mr. Raymond
and his Committee occurred. On his arrival in New York
he had found much discouragement among Mr. Lincoln's
partisans, but during his stay several happenings gave
them renewed hope. One was Admiral Farragut's success
at Mobile Bay. Another was the Chicago Democratic nomination and platform. He believed that chances for Republican success had very much improved during his stay. In
particular the surrender platform adopted by the Democratic party had filled many War Democrats with indignation.

"If things continue as favorable as they seem today, we
shall beat Little Mac very handsomely," he wrote Therena
after his return.

Unless the Republicans are recreant to every sentiment
of duty and honor we shall send this Chicago program to a
speedy oblivion. The Lord preserve this country from the
kind of peace they would give us! It will be a dark day for
the Nation if they should elect the Chicago ticket and purchase *peace* at the cost of Disunion, Secession, Bankruptcy
and National Dishonor and an "intimate" Slave Empire. I
cannot think that Providence has this humiliation or disgrace and disaster in store for us.

While the President was far from admitting, during this period of discouragement, as rumor insisted he did, that he was "a beaten man," he was too astute a politician not to know that the campaign had gone badly, and too great a statesman not to see what must happen if the Republicans lost the election. On August 23rd, two days before the visit of Mr. Raymond and his despondent Committee, pondering the situation, he had done a very characteristic thing. Drawing a sheet of paper toward him he had written:

This morning, as for some days past, it seems exceedingly probable that this administration will not be reelected. Then it will be my duty to so coöperate with the President-Elect as to save the Union between the election and the inauguration, as he will have secured his election on such grounds that he cannot possibly save it afterward.

He folded and pasted the paper in such a way that the writing could not be seen, and at the next meeting of his Cabinet asked each member as he came in to write his name on it without examining its contents. That done, he put it away to await the result of the election, gathering strength from this strange act in some mysterious fashion, to meet the decision of the country's voters, whatever it might be. If it should be their will that he go down to defeat, he would go down "like the Cumberland, with colors flying."

My father was in Springfield on election day, for, shortly before, Mr. Lincoln had "quite unexpectedly" asked him to attend to a matter of business in St. Louis. It is more than possible that the kindly President, who took a fatherly interest in his secretary, and of course knew of his long-standing engagement with the dark-eyed Pittsfield girl, thought this trip "back home" would be the best possible medicine for him since his effort to reach the

Rocky Mountains had failed. If so, he was right. The traveler wrote John Hay that he was "picking up" although he did not yet weigh two hundred pounds, and he reported enthusiastically on the golden beauty of the Illinois October woods.

But being in Springfield made him feel like an octogenarian. He wrote John that all their companions were gone and the boys who replaced them seemed so young! However, as Springfield was his voting residence, he took good care to be there on November 8th.

Water and ducks being scarce in Pike...I packed my traps and...came to this city in time to exercise my right royal prerogative of shying my mythical oyster-shell at the shins of the Small Unready on Tuesday last. Of course the Argus-eyed Democracy challenged my vote, and caused me to swear, and likewise caused me to cause two other sovereigns to swear for me. My oyster-shell triumphed over all obstacles, and went in. The election went off very quietly— the Copperheads evinced not the least anxiety for the "free fight" they have so long clamored for. Indeed, the only coat-tails that were swung 'round defiantly were those that hung from the jackets of the Lincolnites. Early in the morning, indeed, there was a prospect of a small shindy. Virgil the classic had had a row of tall boards put up before each of the polls, leaving only a very small peep-hole through which outsiders could see what might be going on behind them. Geo. Webber, having his ancient democratic prejudices aroused by this exclusiveness, procured a hand-saw and went vigorously to carpentering a large hole. Whereat Virgil grew wroth, and ordered the Sheriff to remove Webber, but Webber's friends said he'd better not, and he didn't, and Webber sawed boards to his heart's content.

After that the voting proceeded quietly enough, individuals standing in line for hours without grumbling till their turn came; an exercise of patience that required some nerve during the heavy showers of the afternoon, when the line stretched from the Courthouse door out on and along the sidewalk past the banks. Fastidious men groaned in spirit when they saw the ordeal to which they were obliged to submit, but the rain and the crowd were inexorable. The Emperor came along in the afternoon and gazed long and wistfully at the line, hoping it might open somewhere near the polls and let him in without the necessity of sandwiching himself for two hours and a half between two fragrant hod-carriers. I hope his tender sensibilities may have been spared the shock.

There was no enthusiasm on election day, but very deep earnestness. There was scarcely any of the usual electioneering about the polls. Voters came with their minds made up. Even ticket-peddlers on both sides were rather scarce.

Thank God, night brought the right results for the nation, and as it now appears to us for this State. The waiting at the telegraph office for the tardy news—the lunch at midnight over Watson's, furnished by the ladies—the jubilee at the Representatives' Hall, reminded me very much of four years ago, even if they were but faint imitations of the glory of those departed days.

John Hay wrote that in Washington on election day the White House was still and deserted.

Everybody ... not at home voting seems ashamed of it and stays away from the President. I was talking with him today. He said, "It is a little singular, that I, who am not a vindictive man, should have always been before the people for election in canvasses marked for their bitterness. Always but once. When I came to Congress it was a quiet time. But always besides that, the contests in which I have been prominent have been marked with great rancor." ...

At seven o'clock we started over to the War Department to spend the evening .... The night was rainy, steamy and dark. We splashed through the grounds to the side door where a soaked and smoking sentinel was standing in his own vapor with his huddled-up frame covered with a rubber coat. Inside, a half-dozen idle orderlies; up-stairs the clerks of the telegraph.

The clerks handed the President telegrams. He was astonished at the size of the majorities reported in some instances, and asked if the figures might not have been wrongly given.—For instance, should not the telegram from a precinct in Boston, which claimed a majority of 4000 have read 400? He sent the interesting telegrams over to his wife, saying, "She is more anxious than I am." Toward midnight, when supper arrived from some unexplained but highly appreciated source, "the President went awkwardly but hospitably to work shoveling out the fried oysters. He was most agreeable and genial all the evening." He told stories, and was gay and happy, but there was no lack of solemnity and of deep feeling in the little speech he made to the serenaders he found waiting for him in the early morning hours when he left the War Department to return to the White House.

I am thankful to God for this approval of the people; but while deeply grateful for this mark of their confidence in me, if I know my heart, my gratitude is free from any taint of personal triumph.... It is no pleasure to me to triumph over any one; but I give thanks to the Almighty for this evidence of the people's resolution to stand by free government and the rights of humanity.

He spent the following morning at one of his endless tasks—reviewing the court-martial cases that came to him by hundreds. As always, he caught at any fact that would justify him in saving the life of a condemned soldier. "There are already too many weeping widows in the United States," he said. "For God's sake do not ask me to add to the number!"

At the next Cabinet meeting he took a paper from his desk. It was the one on which he had asked the Cabinet members to write their names without examining its contents. He asked John Hay to open it without tearing it, read it aloud, and turned to the men around him.

Gentlemen [he said], you will remember that this was written at a time six days before the Chicago nominating Convention, when as yet we had no adversary, and seemed to have no friends. I then solemnly resolved on the course of action indicated above. I resolved in case of the election of General McClellan, being certain that he would be the candidate, that I would see him and talk matters over with him. I would say, "General, the election has demonstrated that you are stronger, and have more influence with the American people than I. Now let us together, you with your influence, and I with all the executive power of the Government, try to save the country. You raise as many troops as you possibly can for this final trial, and I will devote all my energies to assisting and finishing the war."

One of his hearers said, "and he would have answered, 'Yes, yes,' and on another day, 'Yes, Yes'—and have done nothing at all."

"At least," sighed the President, "I should have done my duty, and have stood clear before my own conscience."

19

THE SECOND INAUGURATION

M Y FATHER WROTE THERENA THAT SEV-
eral unpleasant things had happened to him during
the last few weeks. While in New York before the election

I was drafted, and although I was in the first place erron-
iously enrolled, and in the second, if I had offered myself
would have been rejected by the examining surgeon, I yet
nevertheless thought it best to forestall any evil or ill-natured
criticism by Democratic demagogues against a "shirking
Lincoln official" (as they would have called me) by furnishing
a substitute, which I did yesterday. He ... was accepted and
mustered in, and I doubt not will do my fighting to the best of
his ability.*

Another unpleasantness was the theft of an old watch
he valued for sentimental reasons. "What troubled me
most is that the watchguard you gave me was attached to
it." The third happening was the wreck of the night train
on which he was returning from New York. While nobody
was killed, several people had been seriously hurt. Five
cars were derailed, including the one in which he was

* He was a colored man from North Carolina, named Hiram Child,
who died in battle.

219

traveling. He had been awakened to find it standing at an angle of about forty-five degrees.

He reported that a strange apathy seemed to settle over Washington after the election. There might not even be a quorum of members present for the opening of Congress. "Events that are really important do not seem to make much impression on the public mind.... Sherman's advent in Savannah, Butler's failure at Wilmington, the debate in Congress on the Constitutional Amendment all excite but a momentary ripple of attention." Society was equally sluggish. Receptions at the homes of Mrs. Sprague and Mrs. Seward had both been complete failures.

I do not know to what to ascribe this state of things unless it be to the reaction which follows the intense popular interest in the last presidential election. Public feeling, though silent, was highly wrought up about that.

The pending constitutional amendment was of tremendous importance to him. The last note he was destined to make in the White House with a biography of Mr. Lincoln in mind had this as its subject.

Executive Mansion, Jan'y 18, 1865—I went to the President this afternoon at the request of Mr Ashley, on a matter connecting itself with the pending Amendment to the Constitution. The Camden & Amboy interest promised Mr Ashley that if he would help postpone the Raritan Railroad bill over this session, they would in return make the N. J. Democrats help about the Amendment, either by their votes or absence. Sumner being the Senate champion of the Raritan bill, Ashley went to him to ask him to drop it for this session. Sumner however showed reluctance to adopt Mr Ashley's suggestion, saying that he hoped the Amendment would pass anyhow, &c. Ashley thought he discovered in Summer's manner two reasons—1st, that if the present Senate resolution were not adopted by the House, the Senate would send them another in which they would most likely adopt Sumner's own phraseology, thereby gratifying his vanity and ambition; and 2nd, that Sumner thinks the defeat of the Camden & Amboy monopoly would establish a principle by legislative enactment which would effectually crush out the last lingering relics of the States Rights dogma. Ashley therefore desired the President to send for Sumner, and urge him to be practical and secure the passage of the Amendment in the manner suggested by Mr A.

I stated these points to the President, who replied at once:

"I can do nothing with Mr Sumner in these matters. While Mr Sumner is very cordial with me, he is making his history in an issue with me on this very point. He hopes to succeed in beating the President so as to change this government from its original form, and make it a strong centralized power."

Then calling Mr Ashley into the room, the President said to him, "I think I understand Mr Sumner, and I think he would be all the more resolute in his persistence on the points Mr Nicolay has mentioned to me if he supposed I were at all watching his course in this matter."

Late in January a letter to Therena told her:

Our armies are everywhere active, and military operations will be pushed ahead as fast as the winter weather will possibly permit. The whole military situation has been so much simplified and contracted by Sherman's successful march to Savannah that we all look forward to an early overthrow of the rebel armies with most sanguine hopes.

On February 4th he wrote:

We have been in such a continual whirl of work and excitement here for a week past that the letter which ought to have been mailed to you last Sunday is yet unwritten.... The excitement of the week has been the peace rumors and proceedings growing out of Blair's two trips to Richmond, which I mentioned in a former letter. The substance of what he accomplished was to get from Jeff Davis on the one hand, and the President on the other, an expression of willingness to send or receive commissioners or persons who should be permitted to hold an informal conference about matters with a view to reaching a peace.

In pursuance of this willingness so expressed, Jeff Davis some days since sent Stephens, Hunter and Campbell to our lines to hold such a conference. They were permitted to come to Fortress Monroe, where Seward went to meet them on Wednesday, and the President also went down on Thursday. They had on yesterday a four hours' interview with them. It was a long and rambling talk, entirely friendly and courteous, and also entirely informal. Nothing was written.

Of course it would be impossible to give an outline of a four hours' conversation; but substantially the talk amounted to this: The President told them that he could not entertain any proposition or conversation which did not concede and embody the restoration of the national authority over the States now in revolt. . . . that he could not recede in the least from what he had publicly said about slavery; and that he could not concede or agree to any cessation of hostilities which was not an actual end of the war and a disbandment of the rebel armies.

It was clear that the end of the war was at hand. "There remains only the army of Lee to be caught and overcome," my father wrote Therena. He thought the war would certainly be over within a year—he hoped the end might come before the next Fourth of July.

During the stress and uncertainties of conflict he had never seriously thought of resigning, even when the pinpricks of daily annoyance were most trying. But with victory approaching it was natural he should think of his own future. Loyalty to his chief and to the Union no longer made it imperative for him to remain and to perform duties that were daily becoming more irksome. He would, of course, stay long enough after Mr. Lincoln's second inauguration to get his successor well acquainted with his duties—after that he would be free.

He wrote Therena:

Do not think that because I have written nothing about it I have not been engaged in considering the question as to where I shall stay and what I shall do after next fourth of March. I have thought about the matter almost constantly ever since we talked it over in Delphina's parlor last fall; but I have not as yet reached any definite conclusion.

As the matter now stands I am pretty well resolved not to remain here in my present relation after that time, and I think the chances are also against my remaining in Washington. This feeling does not result from any talk with the President about the matter, although I have once or twice alluded to the subject in our conversations, but from other causes and considerations. I think he does not now wish to be troubled with the question in any way, and therefore I do not repeat it to him. After his inauguration however other changes will necessarily take place, after which I will probably be able to determine my own course. So I remain as patient as I can, three or four weeks longer.

Considering himself a newspaper man, his thoughts turned, naturally enough, in that direction. He had saved a little money. If he could join others in buying a well-established journal, that might be the solution. James C. Kennedy of the Census Bureau had already written him enthusiastically about editing the old *National Intelligencer*, the newspaper that had printed a flattering notice of Nicolay's Improved Rotary Press, years before. It was the one Washington newspaper that had weathered the changes of many succeeding administrations. Mr. Kennedy foresaw a great future for it and believed it could be made "a most productive property" under my father's management. If he were not so worn out with hard work, he would join in the enterprise himself.

"I feel that it could be made of more importance to this government than the donation of $100,000,000 to the Treasury," he wrote. If conducted moderately, in support of the administration, after the return of peace, its circulation throughout the South could be immense.

But the attractive prospect came to nothing. It was also suggested that my father join others in buying and publishing the *Baltimore Sun*. Then suddenly his problem was settled for him. Mr. Seward notified the President that the consulate in Paris had become vacant; that the position ought to be filled before the adjournment of Congress, and that he had sent up the nomination of Mr. Nicolay. The Senate confirmed the nomination without a dissenting voice on the day it was received. "So important an appointment has rarely been conferred on one so young," was the comment of the *National Republican*.

On March 5th my father wrote to Therena:

Inauguration week is happily over and with it most of the hard work of the winter. Lent has substantially stopped the gaieties; the House of Representatives adjourned, and only the Senate remains in special session. The office-seekers will swarm upon us like Egyptian locusts for two or three weeks; but I do not think the President intends to give them much encouragement, and without that the extravagant hotel bills here will exhaust their pockets in a very short time....

The ceremonies passed off yesterday in as pleasant a manner as was possible. The morning was dark and rainy, and the streets were very muddy; nevertheless large crowds were out in the procession and at the Capital. I think there were at least twice as many at the Capital as four years ago. Just at the time when the President appeared on the East Portico to be sworn in, the clouds disappeared and the sun shone out beautifully all the rest of the day. We had a reception here at night, which was without exaggeration the largest crowd that has been here yet. The doors were closed at eleven o'clock, and great numbers went away who had been unable to get in.

The next letter, dated March 12th, brought Therena the news for which they had both been waiting.

You have probably already seen from the dispatches that I was yesterday appointed and confirmed as Consul to Paris. The salary is $5000 per annum.

I have not yet fully matured my future movements. The probability is however that I will not start for two or three months yet, and that meanwhile I shall see you and ask you to go with me. . . . It will be as well for you to be quietly getting your wardrobe ready for the trip.

I think of starting day after tomorrow on a short trip to Charleston, and after my return, may possibly make a trip to Kansas before I see you; but as I wrote above, my plans are not entirely matured. . . .

His contemplated trip to Kansas had to do with buying some of the Indian land lately opened to settlement, in which he had become interested on his last visit West. Since he was going to Paris, buying an interest in a newspaper was out of the question; nor had it seemed quite prudent to accept a proposal that he become vice-president of a company organized to supply Denver with illuminating gas. Not trusting entirely to his own judgment, he asked the advice of "Emperor Nicholas" in Springfield, who answered decisively that Denver was "too new" for such improvements.

He finally bought a section and a half of Indian land, officially described as "the half of Section 1 and all of

Section 2 Township 16 south, range 15 east of the 6th Principal Meridian," but locally known as lying on Dragoon Creek, not far from the town of Lyndon. The care with which he made the selection and his reasons for a personal visit are set forth in a letter he wrote to the agent who was conducting the sale. He explained that if the purchase were only for an investment such care might not be necessary, but that he wanted it for occupancy by a brother who desired to farm it at once. The brother was Jacob, who moved from Macoupin County, Illinois, to the Kansas farm and remained there until his death, the land sustaining him and a large family through years of drouth and wind and grasshoppers. Finally it passed entirely into possession of that branch of the family. I am convinced that during the years the deeds remained in my father's name, its ownership gave him a comfortable assurance that if all other plans went awry, he could settle down on Dragoon Creek and live in comfort, if not in luxury.

For John Hay a certain vineyard near Warsaw, Indiana, served the same purpose of tethering him to the warm Midwestern earth. When officeholding abroad seemed to both of them a precarious occupation at best, they remembered with satisfaction these American acres, and jested about the day when John Hay would return from the courts of Europe to publish the *Warsaw Sentinel*, while my father made history as editor of the *Dragoon Creek Mud Cat*.

He did not go to Charleston at the time originally planned, which was fortunate, since the friends who did go were caught in a severe gale off Hatteras. The letter telling Therena about this storm also told about the visit to Washington of two Pittsfield acquaintances, a married pair on their way to New York.

As the President, Mrs Lincoln and Tad are all away on an excursion to the Army of the Potomac, I was enabled to show them through the rooms in the house, and also to take them into the greenhouse. The expressions of enthusiastic wonder and delight to which Mrs C. gave vent at the sight of what she evidently considered so much stately magnificence, were truly fresh and interesting, and almost enough to make me forget for the moment what an ill-kept and dirty rickety concern it really is, from top to bottom. I wonder how much longer a great nation, as ours is, will compel its ruler to live in such a small and dilapidated old shanty, and in such a shabby-genteel style.

The letter ended:

John Hay (beg his pardon, I should have written Major), has been appointed Secretary of Legation to Paris, and will go out about the same time I do. While he will be in no way connected with my office there, it will be exceedingly pleasant, for both of us, to be there at the same time.

20

TRAGEDY

O N THE 28TH OF MARCH 1865, MY FATHER
wrote:

I start this morning for a short cruise along our southern
coast. The party is made up of Capt. Fox the Assistant
Secretary of the Navy and ten or twelve friends of his,
ladies and gentlemen. We go to Baltimore by rail, and there
embark on the gunboat *Santiago de Cuba*, in which some
temporary staterooms have been put up for the accommodation of the party. We will in all probability sail directly for
Havana, Cuba, and returning from there stop at Savannah,
Charleston, and Hilton Head. I understand that Secretary
Stanton has projected quite an excursion to go to Charleston on the 13th of April, to raise the flag over Fort Sumter.
We will most likely arrange our return with a view of being
there at that time.

We hope to get back here about the 19th of April. As
Captain Fox is taking his family along, you can rest assured
that all possible precautions in regard to safety have been
looked to.

Thus it happened that my father was not in Washington at the time of the President's assassination. On April
1st he wrote to my mother from the *Santiago de Cuba*
lying in Charleston Harbor:

We embarked on this ship on last Tuesday at Baltimore and had very still weather as far as Cape Hatteras, after which the wind freshened up and gave the vessel motion enough to make us all reasonably seasick.... When we arrived off this place, as the weather still promised to be windy, we concluded to run in here for a day or two. We anchored here in the harbor at about noon yesterday, since which time we have been looking at Sumter, Moultrie and the city, finishing up at Calhoun's grave this afternoon. The city looks desolate enough—much battered up by the bombardment, and looking generally very seedy and dilapidated by its four years of wear-and-tear without repairs. A large part of it was destroyed by fire and what is not in ruins is deserted, so that altogether it has a most God-forsaken look. It is to be hoped that its people are satisfied with the "rights" they have obtained by seceding.

Venerable carriages drawn by sorry-looking horses had been assembled to take the visitors sightseeing. "I did not have a chance at looking at things in detail," he wrote Therena, "but judging from the streets it seems to have been a rather pretty place in its palmy days, a great deal of attention having evidently been paid to the embellishment of yards and gardens with shrubs and flowers." Historic Christ Church was occupied by a single soldier "sitting in the pulpit reading a prayer-book and smoking a pipe." The ruins of Fort Sumter were in possession of about a dozen Union soldiers and some carpenters who were putting up a new flagpole in preparation for April 14th, when Major Anderson was to raise the flag he had been forced to lower in 1861.

My father delighted in the warm sunshine of Cuba, and thoroughly enjoyed exploring the picturesque Spanish-tinged island. Fortunately, he did not have to avail himself of all the distractions Havana hospitably offered its visitors. The program for Sunday read:

6 A.M.—Prisoner to be garroted.
10 " " —Palm Sunday services in the Cathedral.
2 P.M.—Cock Fight.
5 " " —Bull Fight.
7 " " —Grand Opera
11 " " —Grand Ball.

On April 8th they visited Matanzas, which he thought a finer city than Havana, though smaller. Here they attended Holy Week services at the Cathedral, where blacks and whites knelt devoutly together. He found it hard to reconcile this spiritual equality with the shocking condition of the slaves on the prosperous sugar plantations, where overseers carried heavy whips under their arms, and the life expectation of a slave was only seven years, because of the hard work.

A picturesque procession of gentlemen on horseback escorted seven *volantes* bearing the guests up a palm-shaded driveway to the dwelling house on a large coffee plantation. The crop had been harvested, but a few red berries remained. About thirty Negroes, with knives in their hands, ran after the procession. When it stopped they vigorously shook the orange trees among which the coffee bushes were planted, stripped the fallen oranges of their skins, and offered the peeled fruit to the guests on the points of their knives; at the same time they suggestively held out their hands and begged, "Me money. Buy backy." The houses of these people were about ten feet square, were windowless, and were supposed to hold five human beings each. They were built around a hollow square, in the center of which stood the cookhouse. Nearby stood a cagelike structure in which were half a hundred little Negro children, stark naked, all chattering and holding out their hands, in imitation of their elders.

On their return, the party on the *Santiago de Cuba*

reached Port Royal in time to learn of the capture of Petersburg and to devour old newspapers with their accounts of seven days' victorious fighting. Next they touched at Hilton Head and went out to the colored settlement on Hilton Head Island to attend a monster abolition meeting. The audience numbered perhaps a thousand, only twenty or thirty of whom were white. William Lloyd Garrison gave the address, and they listened to an eloquent prayer by an old Negro preacher named Donogan, a life-long slave, whose language and clear enunciation would have done credit to a man of much whiter skin.

When they reached Charleston the news of Lee's surrender had just been received by steamer from New York, there being no telegraphic communication between Richmond and Charleston. Gaily decked steamships carried several hundred notables out to Fort Sumter, where the ceremonies were heavily charged with emotion. When Henry Ward Beecher arrived, the audience rose in recognition. As Major Anderson raised the flower-wreathed flag he was visibly overcome. The day closed with a brilliant naval illumination and a grand ball.

No news of the tragedy at Ford's Theatre had reached Charleston when the *Santiago de Cuba* made her way out of the harbor early next morning. It seemed a time for unlimited thankfulness and rejoicing. So when those aboard the ship received the news, the shock was all the greater. My father wrote to Therena from Chesapeake Bay on April 17:

Last night as we passed Cape Henry and took a pilot on board to enter Hampton Roads we had from him the first news of the terrible loss the country has suffered in the assassination of the President. It was so unexpected, so sudden and so horrible even to think of, much less to realize that we *couldn't* believe it, and therefore remained in hope that it would prove one of the thousand groundless exaggerations which the war has brought forth during the past four years. Alas, when we reached Point Lookout at daylight this morning, the mournful reports of the minute guns that were being fired, and the flags at half-mast left us no ground for further hope. I went on shore with the boat to forward our telegrams, and there found a Washington paper of Saturday, giving us all the painful details.

I am so much overwhelmed by this catastrophe that I scarcely know what to think or write. Just as the valor of the Union arms had won decisive victory over the rebellion. the wise and steady guidance that has carried the nation through the storms of the past four years is taken away, and its destiny is again shrouded in doubt and uncertainty. My own faith in the future is not shaken, even by this sad event; but will the whole country remain as patient and as trusting as when it felt its interests safe in the hands of Lincoln?

It would seem that Providence had exacted from him the last and only additional service and sacrifice he could give his country—that of dying for her sake. Those of us who knew him will certainly interpret his death as a sign that Heaven deemed him worthy of martyrdom.

You will readily infer that my own personal plans may be entirely changed by this unlooked-for event. We hope to reach Washington by 4 P.M. today. I will write again as soon as I can, but may not learn anything definite for some days.

Next day a letter in a black-bordered envelope went to her from the Executive Mansion.

Our ship arrived safely at the Navy Yard at about 2½ P.M. yesterday. I cannot describe to you the air of gloom which seems to hang over the city. As I drove up here from the Navy Yard almost every house was draped and closed, and men stood idle and listless in groups on the street corners. The Executive Mansion was dark and still as almost the grave itself. The silence and gloom and sorrow depicted on every face are as heavy and ominous of terror as if some greater calamity still hung in the air, and was about to crush and overwhelm everyone.

This morning the house is deeply draped in mourning, and the corpse is laid in state in the East Room, where great crowds are taking their last look at the President's kind face, mild and benignant as becomes the father of a mourning nation, even in death. The funeral will take place tomorrow.

On April 20th he addressed a formal note of resignation to the new President; and four days later wrote Therena:

After the funeral of the President on Wednesday last I felt entirely too depressed in spirits to write you a letter. Words seemed so inadequate to describe my own personal sorrow at the loss of such a friend as the President has been to me, and my deep apprehension of the new troubles and difficulties in which it would involve the country, that I could not bring myself up to the task of attempting to portray them in language.

I think that I do not yet, and probably shall not for a long while realize what a change his death has wrought in my own personal relations, and the personal relations of almost everyone connected with the government in this city, who stood near to him. And this state of feeling is very much enhanced by the unsettled condition of the country. So far the new President has very favorably disappointed the expectations of almost everyone. He has been quiet, steady and content to let the government run along under the healthy and strong impetus it had at Mr Lincoln's death—the very wisest policy he could have pursued under the circumstances. I have seen and talked with him twice, and all the indications of his personal appearance are very good, except that I think he will not have very great physical endurance, and is in some danger of wearing himself out.

He has not yet come into the Executive Mansion, but has

his business office in the Treasury Department, and does not intend coming here till after Mrs Lincoln goes out, which will not be for two or three weeks yet.

Major Hay and I are still here arranging the papers of the office, which has kept us very busy.

On May 5th he wrote from Springfield:

I left Washington last Sunday evening to come out here to attend the President's funeral . . . but was detained on the way, so that I did not arrive until one o'clock Wednesday night. . . . Today I am attending to some business matters here. Tomorrow morning I think I will go down to brother Jacob's, and from there on to St Louis tomorrow night, and on Monday start from there for Kansas. . . . I go there now because Judge Delaney of Kansas is here and will go with me, and give me the benefit of his acquaintance with the route, and also his knowledge of Kansas in assisting me to look up the land I am going to see, and will thus save me both time and trouble. I do not yet know how much time I may need in Kansas; I suppose not more than a week at farthest. After that I shall return and come to Pittsfield to stay a few days—I cannot tell precisely how long.

The whole pattern of his life seemed disrupted. All was uncertainty. He and Therena might have to postpone their marriage. He wrote her: "I am sorry to say that I think I shall not be able to take you to Paris with me this time— but this I will talk over fully with you while at Pittsfield. I am still trying to get ready to sail about the first of June."

In such a situation the only rational thing to do was to perform each day's obvious duty as it came, and trust that in time the reeling world would steady itself enough for him to see his path clearly again. So after the trip to Illinois and Kansas he returned to Washington to meet

John Hay and finish packing the Lincoln papers, and get their offices ready for occupancy by their successors.

Writing to Therena, he told her he had witnessed part of the Grand Review:

The Review was nearly over for yesterday when I got out, but today I have seen the whole of Sherman's army—really a magnificent sight, as you may well suppose. They passed along Pennsylvania Avenue, going west, and large stands were erected on both sides of the street in front of the Executive Mansion, so that a great many people got a really good view of the procession.

Hay started West today. Just as I was leaving Pittsfield I received his letter saying he had finally concluded to go to Paris.

INTERIM

21

A HOME IN PARIS

GRADUALLY THE BROKEN PIECES OF MY father's life fell into place again. He found he could take Therena to Paris with him. He even knew the name of the ship on which they were to sail, and the date— the *City of London*, leaving New York on June 24th. A telegram from one of the officers of the steamship company had been received offering him and John Hay passage, and adding, "If Mr Nicolay has increased his family by taking a wife, let us know."

The engagement had been of such long standing that their intimates had teasingly wondered whether a wedding would ever take place. Now that it was about to happen, the two resolved to keep it a secret until the very last moment and let it burst as a surprise on the town where both had so many friends. By May 30th plans were complete in his own mind, and he submitted them for Therena's approval.

We will have the ceremony performed either at your house in the presence of a few friends, or at the Congregational Church by Mr Carter, at six or seven o'clock in the evening, and then go out to Mrs Garbutt's and have a party or reception from eight to ten or eleven o'clock as you may decide.

Major Hay will be groomsman, and you must select a bridesmaid for him. If you think Dr and Mrs Hodgen desire to stand up with us, we will also ask them to do so.

I will meet you at St Louis sometime between the 10th and 13th of June. From there, taking Dr and Delphina with us, we will go up to Pittsfield so as to get there on the 14th or 15th. Major Hay will also meet us in St Louis and either go up with us, or go by Springfield to invite and bring with him a few friends from there. ... By this plan no one but your bridesmaid and Mrs Garbutt would need to know anything about the affair until the 14th or 15th. I think Mrs Garbutt would keep the secret. Don't you think it possible to find a bridesmaid who would also do so? I should very much like to surprise the people and gossips of Pittsfield. ... Tell Mrs Garbutt not to worry herself about any elaborate preparations, and we will save her what trouble and expense we can by bringing cakes, confections and berries from St Louis with us in such quantities as you may suggest.

Make a list of Pittsfield people to be invited—only let it be large enough. Let the house be filled to overflowing—a perfect jam—and everybody will be entertained and delighted. We will send out the invitations on the 14th or 15th in something like the enclosed form—but have no regular wedding cards, my range of acquaintances outside of Pittsfield being too large to make it convenient to send to all. After the wedding we will stay at Mrs Garbutt's until we leave Pittsfield, which will be next day by way of St Louis, or on Sunday evening by way of Naples.

I have thought the matter all over, and can devise no better plan than this. I am decidedly in favor of having a large party, and Mrs Garbutt's house is decidedly the best place to have it in. I will be interested to see how sucessfully you will be able to execute the program.

The form of invitation read:

> Mrs P. B. Garbutt will be pleased to see you
> on Thursday evening, June 15th, from 8 until
> 11 o'clock, to meet Mr and Mrs Nicolay.

They succeeded so well in keeping their secret that the wedding was delayed—not, as sometimes happens, by the tardiness of the bride—but because of the non-arrival of the minister. "Brother Carter" was out of town. Another minister was ill, and when at last the Rev. Mr. Burnham had been located and arrangements made to have him perform the ceremony at the bride's home, a sharp thunderstorm, such as Illinois can manufacture very suddenly on a June evening, kept the small company waiting for half an hour. The storm passed; the minister at last arrived. The reception at Mrs. Garbutt's was as much of a "jam" as the bridegroom desired and proved a great success. It went down in local history as the first time ice cream was served in Pittsfield to a large evening party.

Next morning my father sought out the old printing office and set a stickful of type—just to show he had not forgotten how. Then he and Therena set forth on their wedding journey.

One of the letters of introduction they carried with them to Paris was from Horace Greeley to Mrs. Esther C. Cleveland:

> My Sister:—I wish you to know and to advise my friend Mrs J. G. Nicolay, who will make her first experiments in housekeeping in your city, and who will greatly profit by your experience and thrift. I wish you were Mrs Grouch for her sake, but since you are not, I pray you to be as wise and good to her as you possibly can.
>
> Yours,
>
> Horace Greeley.

My mother, being shy, and moreover independent, the letter was never delivered. Another letter they did not carry with them, but which very possibly traveled by the same ship, was from Thurlow Weed to John Bigelow, the former consul, who had been advanced to the post of United States Minister to France. Commenting on the new appointee, Mr. Weed wrote: "Mr Nicolay is an intelligent honorable man. I think you will like him." This speaks well for my father's handling of that touchy gentleman in New York, over the Custom House matter.

I believe my parents thoroughly enjoyed their four years abroad, though my father reviled the climate of Paris, and their first impressions of the Hotel Chateaubriand were not all rose-colored.

"Do you remember how the back room downstairs looked when we went into it on our first arrival here?" my father wrote a year later. Cholera had invaded Paris, and he had taken his wife and baby to Switzerland, then returned to pursue his duties. "Our room looks and feels just as that did then. I feel every evening on going home and going upstairs as if I had just seen a waxed floor for the first time." In America, during the sixties, people in "comfortable" circumstances stretched Brussels carpet over their floors clear to the baseboards, and tacked it down firmly.

To the couple who had grown up in the simplicity, yet comparative lavishness of the Middle West, there was much to criticize and not a little to learn from the careful economy practiced at the Hotel Chateaubriand. They admired some aspects of it and made private fun of the rest. Years later my father could tell a graphically humorous story about the daily table d'hôte, over which M. d'Asterac presided in person, serving his guests if the main course happened to be chicken, from a platter that contained, carefully counted, one piece for each person present, and one skinny portion of neck or back to be left over for manners. This, M. d'Asterac offered hospitably to each person in turn, well knowing that nobody would have the temerity to accept it, and offering it as strictly according to rules of rank and station as could have been followed in seating a diplomatic dinner party.

Although Monsieur and Madame were not in the *pension* business "for their health," they were kindly folk, and when my father's digestion got so badly out of order that Madame began to fear he would starve himself to death, she put all the resources of her kitchen at his disposal and recommended a variety of French remedies which prudence forced him to decline. "The event has had one result," he wrote his wife, "namely, that if we stay in Paris, we shall in all probability keep house in one form or other. My stomach, having patiently endured boarding-house abominations for ten years, is becoming rebellious."

He did a little apartment hunting before Therena's return, but prudently made no decision. In answer to her demand for his daily routine he wrote:

I get up in the morning at eight, take my coffee and *croissant*, seize my umbrella, put on my hat, rush over to the omnibus station, and come down town. I reach the office generally about ten, where I stay until one, when I go to Byron's Tavern, make my breakfast on cold roast beef, bread, butter and water, spiced only with an occasional small radish and a glance at the *London Times*, which the *garçon* brings me regularly in consideration of his daily *pourboire* of four sous. From breakfast I go back to the office, where I generally stay till half past four, which gives me time to walk leisurely to the Madeleine to meet the *voiture*. The *voiture*, by the way, is still the same grand object of interest on the Champs Elysées, all the parties of English sight-seers twisting their necks off to get a good look at it.

He had seen Hay a few times and made perhaps half a dozen calls, but most of his evenings were spent, either in the far-from-gay parlor, or in his own room, tramping back and forth before the empty hearth, like the bear in a cage they had seen at the Jardin des Plantes. He had read only one book clear through since his return—a small book on Egyptian travel—but he considered that an achievement. "People come and go occasionally," he wrote, "but no one turns up in whom I get the least interested."

To a friend in Washington he wrote:

I have a great deal to do, or rather I should say a great deal to look after. The work of the office has doubled since my advent, and while most of it is in reality done by my clerks, yet the supervision costs me a great deal of time, as your position will enable you to appreciate.

Then I live (or rather board, which you know is not living) a long way out of town. I suppose it is two and a half or three miles from my Consulate to where the household gods sit enthroned. It is a twenty minutes' ride or an hour's walk—you may readily imagine however that I indulge in the latter only as a luxury. ... During winter weather in Paris the day is a myth. I am not exaggerating when I say that the sun sets every morning at seven o'clock, and that the rest of the twenty-four hours is a night of clouds and fog. The spring, I am told, will be bright and lovely, and I am awaiting it with all the ardor of a devotee who hopes through faith alone. I am confident in the belief that the religion of Sun-worship originated in this latitude.

As to Paris, what shall I say, and how could I say it in the compass of a single letter? It is a great city, having much to admire and more to condemn; a sort of delta in the great stream of human life; rather an aggregation of *débris* than a fresh healthy organic structure of vital and intelligent forces. As a study, social, political and historical, it is infinitely curious and interesting. As a station of travel it is

central and amusing. But as a place to live in, or to die in—
well, it may do for Frenchmen. . . .

So far, as I have already told you, I have been devoting
myself to business, and have not as yet had much Parisian
experience. Even of the theatres I have as yet seen but little.
Their strong point is scenery. . . . As for music, I can't as
yet say much. I have on several occasions remembered
Grover's dumb fiddles and the clear ringing soprano of
Frederica with regret.

The Paris he was observing was the Paris of the Second
Empire—gorgeous, perhaps a little tawdry, and seething
with political undercurrents, for Napoleon III was already beginning to find himself embarrassed by the forces
that later brought about his downfall.

Baron Haussmann was busy modernizing the city—
ruthlessly cutting streets through warrens of centuries-
old buildings, to transform crooked lanes into wide
handsome boulevards—unroofing, demolishing, letting the
light of day into interiors that had not felt the sun's
rays since they were built. My father was reminded of an
old fable that told how Satan suddenly unroofed a city,
laying bare its secrets and all its sins.

Through the consulate's door, at 79 rue de Richelieu,
a steady stream of visitors passed, and my father found
that a consul's duties were even more varied than those of
a private secretary to the President. Practically every
traveler from the United States called, and usually asked
"a small favor" before he went away. My father became
an expert on sight-seeing tours, leisurely or rapid, to suit
demands, and once boasted that he had shown Paris
"thoroughly" to an American in four hours. Once, when
a plain white card was brought him, bearing the name
"Mr. Fillmore," he realized, with something of a start,
that his visitor could be none other than the former Presi-

dent of the United States, upon whom he had called with some awkwardness and much keen interest during his first visit to Washington in 1852.

He learned that a consul is expected to be especially attentive to expatriates who have been living long in Paris —especially when they grow old and begin to fear for their latter end. He would be called upon to explain to them how a foreigner could die comfortably and legally in France—a complicated process under French law. John Bigelow, his predecessor in the consulate, had been adept at such things, and, when he resigned as Minister in 1868 and went home, he left behind him this kindly letter:

I would advise you to call with your wife on Mrs S. and talk with her about her affairs. Never dispute with her, and take your compensation in the reflection that you are helping to replace one of her old friends to whose residence in Paris she attached an undue value. She is old, infirm, and not blessed with exalted visions of a future life. You can't do a greater charity, you and Mrs N., than to be kind to her.... She does not like to pay in money, though she will not die in debt to you.

The duty that irked my father most, however, had to do with weddings, not funerals. French law required that there be a civil ceremony, which, in the case of Americans, usually took place at the consulate. Years later he explained his dislike of these weddings, saying, "the responsibility was so great!"

Another unpleasant duty was to take action when Americans went crazy in Paris. A note in his private files, hastily scribbled in pencil, and undated save for "9 o'clock A.M. Monday morning," reads: "The wisest plan would be, my dear sir, to have Mr P. carried to the Maison de Santé, Faubourg St Denis, *at once*." Another, more pathetic, is a long letter addressed to the consul from the Cabinet de Maire, asking what is to be done in the case of a young man, left at the Maison de Santé three years before, and apparently forgotten by his family.

By contrast, many other letters were merely amusing. Chief Justice Chase wished confidential information about a young man who was courting a lady of his acquaintance. George Bancroft, Jr., asked for titles of law books to be ordered from America, Paris booksellers being "in perfect ignorance" on the subject. Albert Bierstadt, the artist, demanded that his picture, in the Exhibition, be placed on the line and in a better light because the Czar of Russia wanted to look at it. A French author, about to publish "an extensive and substantial notice of your so lamented grand citizen Abraham Lincoln," solicited an interview. A theatrical manager, wishing to take his troupe across the Atlantic, sought to gain favor by addressing the consul as "Sir John Nicolay." And of course there was a stream of letters asking for help of all kinds—not only for money, but for aid in finding a pair of spectacles, or even a missing husband!

Socially, the position of consul offered many interesting opportunities, although of strictly French social life the Nicolays saw little. Parisian society was jealously exclusive, and they made no effort to penetrate its reserves. But an invitation "to spend an evening at the Tuileries," delivered *"par ordre de l'Empereur,"* represented an official obligation. It was the prelude to an occasion of great elegance and extreme fatigue. Violet-clad chamberlains herded the guests slowly through salon after salon toward the throne room. There was color everywhere, used as only the French dare use it. Walls and furniture glowed with color. *Cent Gardes* stood about in faultless uniforms of blue and gold. Diplomats glittering with orders were accompanied by pale elegant ladies clad in the height of fashion. Occasional flashes of scarlet showed the presence of cardinals who were already a thorn in the flesh to Napoleon III, though adored by his devout Empress.

When at last the throne room was reached, it was disconcerting to find that the brilliant pageant centered on a small man of about sixty, whose legs were too short for his body, whose movements "suggested those of a gouty crab," and whose smile seemed to have fallen down into one corner of his mouth and to be badly out of repair. Even the sight of the Spanish-born Eugenie beside him, beautiful still at forty, was not enough to reconcile the unflattering reality with preconceived notions of imperial splendor.

22

FAREWELL TO EUROPE

M Y FATHER RECEIVED BAD NEWS FROM
America. His only sister died. From Washington
came accounts of political quarrels, not only between
Democrats and Republicans, but between factions of the
party in power. The good impression made by Mr. Johnson on assuming office gave way to increasing criticism,
which culminated in impeachment proceedings. In such
circumstances the Administration found it a great temptation to curry favor by lavish distribution of offices. Inevitably, covetous glances were cast at the Paris Consulate.
How long my mother remained in ignorance of efforts to
supersede her husband, I do not know; but on October 30,
1866, before she had returned from Switzerland, my
father wrote her:

The reports that come from home from time to time that
I am to be superseded evidently have some sort of foundation. I received on yesterday morning a dispatch from the
State Department informing me that representations had
been made there charging me with *negligence, inefficiency,
ignorance* of the business and receipts of the Consulate, and
habitual disrespect toward the President. Isn't that sublimely
impudent?

The truth probably is that the Gibbs* coalition have determined to have me out and some tool of theirs in. Were it in ordinary times I should say they would be powerless to do me injury. But now in a time of such general political *bouleversement* in the United States there is no foreseeing the result. If either the President or Mr Seward have made up their minds that they need this place to stop some one's hunger, why an excuse will be found for removing me, or in case there is none handy, I will be removed without excuse. The triviality and absurdity of the charges they have made only show the desperation of the case. I think there are ten chances to one against my being left here. So if you have any thinking or planning to do for such a contingency, I advise you to employ your leisure moments at it, so that we may be ready to migrate at short notice.

He wrote a private letter to Frederick Seward, Assistant Secretary of State, who, with his father, had been retained by President Johnson in the offices they held under Lincoln.

I confess I felt a passing chagrin that such accusations should appear on the public records; but a moment's reflection reminded me that I could not have a greater compliment to my official character than that the malice of the accuser has been unable to trump up anything else than allegations so trivially absurd, so utterly untrue and so easily disproven. The only embarrassment in the whole matter is that it places me in the awkward situation of being interrogated as to my own "efficiency." One might as well ask a woman if she is beautiful, a scholar if he is profound, or a judge if he is just....

I can only disprove the solidity of a shadow by being

* Mr. Gibbs, appointed some years earlier Special Agent of the Treasury to investigate prices at which merchandise was sent from Europe to the United States, was criticised for the way in which he performed his duties, but had senatorial friends who were influential with both presidents Johnson and Grant.

brought within touching distance of it; therefore I hope you will immediately give me the name of my defamer. . . .

I beg to renew the assurance of my obligations both to your father and to yourself for your many personal and official kindnesses, and to express the hope that your friendship for me may not be shaken by the slanders of persons who have no sincere regard either for yourself, the service, the Administration or the Government.

The answer to this was a formal official letter from Frederick Seward, saying, "Yours, No. 32, seems to fully and clearly refute the charges made against you, and is accepted by the Department as satisfactory." In addition, the Clerk of the Consular Division wrote a letter on plain unmarked notepaper telling him that though it was not the custom of the Department of State to disclose the names of persons making such charges, he wished to say "in order that you may not wrongfully suspect innocent persons," that the charges came from a person unknown to the Department, and probably also to my father, and were undoubtedly prompted by interested motives. He assured him that "this note is written with the knowledge and approval of the Assistant Secretary of State."

John Hay, who was in Washington, wrote him:

You are all right everywhere. That push against you came from cops who want your place. Seward wrote you that letter simply to give you an opportunity to say the charges were lies. He was rather amused at the completeness of your defense—"ten times over justified," he said. Letters like that were written to nearly everyone in the service. . . .

Clippings from Illinois journals were sent to him saying that President Johnson "decidedly refused" to remove Mr. Nicolay or Mr. Hay, though strongly urged to do so. The matter was thus, temporarily, at an end. But knowing the pressure was likely to continue, my father was glad he had bought the Kansas land.

My father remained consul in Paris until 1869 when Grant became President. The charges were renewed from time to time, growing more fantastic at each repetition, until this most abstemious of men was alleged to be an habitual drunkard, and a victim of syphilis. So far as he was able to discover there was "nothing personal" in all this—it was merely a result of political intrigue. Meanwhile, he did his work conscientiously, and when vacation times came, tried to see as much of Europe as possible.

He and Therena had already made a short trip up the Rhine in the autumn of 1865. In the fall of 1867 my father visited John Hay in Vienna where he was American Chargé d'Affaires. After this visit, in his letter of thanks from Paris, he made the following comment on European politics:

Victor Emmanuel dwindles to the effete shadow that he is, and Garibaldi is the only real presence on the Peninsula. But of course France can't afford to let him "loose in the deestrict" and so the Pope's straw-pile will probably be set up again. And so the heap will smoulder for perhaps a quarter of a century longer, and allied King-craft and Priest-craft is still the "worm that dieth not."

Every month that my father and John Hay spent in Europe increased their belief that, whatever its faults, the American system of government was the best yet devised. Hay wrote: "If ever in my green and salad days, I doubted, I am safe now. I am a Republican till I die. When we get to Heaven we may try a monarchy—perhaps." One of the first things my father did, after returning to the United States, was to secure proof of citizenship from the proper court in Illinois. Since he had come to this country when such a small child, probably it had never occurred to him that his citizenship could be questioned. But after four years in Paris he had reached the conclusion that American citizenship was something very precious, to be surrounded by every possible safeguard.

Writing to Hay to return a letter that Hay had received from Robert Lincoln, he said:

I send back Bob's letter, which is certainly characteristic and shows that latent power of observation and comparison which is evidently in the blood. He still looks at politics through a reflecting medium—perhaps I should say an opaque one,—either making him incapable of arriving at a true estimate. Politics is a thing à laisser ou à prendre, but by no means to be despised, either in its nobler or baser relations to the times we live in. Nobody had a clearer perception of that point than his father. A little more age and experience will probably enable Bob to see it as well.

That spring his own political future had seemed more than usually uncertain. Haussmann was intent on sweeping away the old consulate, in order to make way for the rue Réaumur. This made it necessary to find a new location, and to apply to the French authorities for appraisal and indemnity for damages. The small damages awarded became the occasion of controversy, the question being whether the sum rightfully belonged to Mr. Bigelow, who made the original lease, to my father, as the consul then in office, or, on general principles, to the United States Government. Several vigorous but polite letters on the subject passed between my father and Mr. Bigelow, without in the least disturbing their friendly personal relations; but the incident was used as one more bit of ammunition by those working for a change of consuls.

My father wrote John Hay that he had been asked in a roundabout way, by a man who coveted the Paris Consulate, whether he would be willing to exchange it for the position of Minister Resident to Portugal, the man who longed to live in Paris believing he could arrange the transfer. After deliberation, my father had sent word to "go ahead." Any one of three things might happen in consequence. (1) Nothing might come of it, and things would remain just as they had been. (2) It might be that Mr. Seward would find the change a help in straightening out some other appointment tangle. (3) The nominations being made, the Senate might fail to confirm him and he would find himself out of office, having fallen between two stools.

Should the worse come to the worst, and my *caput officium* (Is that good Latin?) roll in the dust, I would retire with dignity to Dragoon Creek, and inscribe myself for the horticultural prize at the State Fair. One of these days I shall have money enough to buy me a Shakespeare, a Goethe, a Cervantes and a Balzac, and then I shall be about ready to leave this country where there isn't sunlight enough to keep Diogenes alive.

Hay's official future was also very insecure. President Johnson nominated a new Minister to Austria, but Congress adjourned without confirming the nomination. "The stars in their courses are betting on you" was my father's congratulatory comment. Then when the Senate in special session confirmed a different man, he wrote:

Enfin, vous voilà prêt à commencer votre rôle du Decapité Parlante. Here you are at a turn in your lane. I have been hoping all along that the *status quo* would be maintained a while longer, so that we might take the boat-ride up the Nile next winter. That, I suppose now we shall have to rub off the slate. What is your program?

Of course you will stay in Vienna until Watts comes. He may be a leisurely man and spend a month or two in getting ready and awaiting his instructions. Stay quietly at your post until he presents his writ of ejectment in person. Take all the chances of sun-stroke and cholera and ice-bergs. Get a friend to quietly suggest to him a season of preliminary German practise at Wiesbaden, or persuade him that his best route to Vienna is *via* Constantinople. He can get himself puffed by his newspapers at home all the same for the directness of his transit. Bancroft might give him a valuable hint or two on that score. At all events take time. That old saw about the forelock is all well enough, but sometimes a good grip on the hind lock is not to be despised.

My father's wife and baby were established for the summer at Houlgate, which he described as "a little bathing-town built to order." Its half hundred cottages were as fresh in color and capricious in design as if newly bought in a Swiss toyshop. The hotel had a deal of plaster ornament and a gorgeous maitre d'hotel in uniform, who lorded it over a retinue of *two* servants, but as it was half-empty, they could do very much as they pleased. "This *laisser aller* style of living is a delicious foretaste of my retirement on Dragoon Creek," he wrote.

If nothing breaks we will remain here a week yet. After that we go back to Paris, and I shall begin getting ready to make way for the rue Réaumur. Upon my experiences of the next six weeks my own movements will largely depend. The condition of my health, the price of rent, &c, will greatly vary my plans and projects. It is not impossible that my own trunks may be packed for Dragoon Creek yet this fall.

But this was not to be until the following spring. He had cabled his good friend Senator Harlan that he did not at all mind resigning, but did object to being removed on false charges. The Senator replied that General Grant assured him he had no intention of making a change, but that there was a "wonderful scramble for office." Another

good friend, U. H. Painter, one of the prominent news-
papermen of Washington, cabled him that some of the
senators were very bitter against him, "having been put
up to it by Gibbs." The President suggested hopefully
that he might appoint Gibbs and not remove Nicolay, but
was told this would be impossible, since there was only one
American Consul in Paris.

The man finally selected was J. Meredith Reid, Jr. A
few months after he supplanted my father he sent him a
friendly letter, saying the business of the consulate was
"now in good running order," and that he liked it although
it was "not a sinecure." Being human, my father probably
liked better the letter he received from David Fuller, the
consulate's efficient colored messenger, who had been asked
to mail him a Paris newspaper now and then. David replied
that he would be glad to serve him in any way, and ventured to add: "Permit me to say that we miss you very
much, and I for my part wish you were still Consul at
Paris." He then courteously expressed sorrow "that your
sight is not entirely restored" and asked to be allowed "to
present my respects to Madame and Miss Helen."

The baby had been named Helen, because, her parents
laughingly explained, they obviously could not call her
Paris—but there was a family reason as well. My father's
mother had been christened Helena.

Before the political echoes of the change in consuls died
away, the matter developed into an official investigation.
The Treasury Department sent General Fred A. Starring
to make a comprehensive inspection of our European con-
sulates and to suggest improvements. General Starring's
report implied that both Mr. Bigelow and Mr. Nicolay
might have managed the office better, but that under Mr.
Reid the investigator could find nothing to criticize. Mr.
Bigelow wrote a long letter of protest to the Secretary of

the Treasury, and the Secretary, transmitting Mr. Bigelow's letter to Senator Sumner, expressed his opinion that "General Starring's report is a censure upon the course pursued by Mr Bigelow and Mr Nicolay which does not appear to be warranted by the facts set forth in Mr Bigelow's letter. Of these I presume General Starring was ignorant."

FULFILMENT

23

GETTING SERIOUSLY
TO WORK

AFTER HIS RETURN MY FATHER VISITED
his brother on the Kansas farm but never took up his
residence there. He was so much out of health that his main
efforts, during the next three years, had to be directed
toward regaining his strength. Winters were spent in
Florida, summers in a northern climate. Florida was still
suffering severely from the aftereffects of the Civil War.
Such hotels as were open did not come up to northern
standards of comfort, but he was most fortunate in finding
entrance into an ideal southern home which was being re-
deemed from wreckage by a wise and sympathetic new
owner. Surrounded by orange trees and stately live oaks,
on land jutting out into the St. John's river, it was well
named Sunny Point, and became a haven of refuge for him
and his family for years.

Early in July 1870 a group of Illinois friends determined to revive the *Chicago Republican*, which was in
difficulties. They meant to make it the only first-class
daily paper in that city to uphold squarely the Republican
administration. They asked my father to act as its editor,
manager, and treasurer. Revived by the Florida winter, he

consented, but resigned after three months, reporting that the venture had been steadily losing money, and that he had neither courage nor physical strength to continue.

The anxious months in Chicago had robbed him of all the health he had regained, and the autumn had been saddened by the death of a nephew he had been instrumental in bringing to Washington. This young man was killed by the accidental discharge of his gun while out hunting, and all the sad duties such a death imposes fell upon my father, since the young man's own father and two other members of his family were critically ill at the time.

The ensuing winter was spent in Florida. Growing stronger again, my father wrote two series of articles for the *New York Times*.—One concerned conditions in the South after the war. The other dealt with Paris as he had found it. I think he hoped to secure a permanent editorial position on the *Times*; but the only one available involved night work, which a friend of his on the staff was sure he would not wish to undertake. He was assured, however, that the *Times* would always be glad to print his interesting articles—at the usual space-rate of ten dollars a column. Whatever disappointment he felt could not have been lessened when William D. Howells, who was editing the *Atlantic*, returned a sheaf of poems he had sent on for criticism. Howells refused to criticize them, on the ground that to do so "must entail partial injustice." "If you write a successful poem it will be from yourself and not from anybody's criticism." He ended his letter with the suggestion that a prose article "on some phase of Parisian life or thought" would be acceptable.

It was very discouraging. He could not go on using his French material forever—and the Lincoln material he considered a sacred trust. Anxious as he was to start the Lincoln book, he knew it would be a long task, and before entering upon it he must make sure of being able adequately to support his family. He surely could not earn a living for them by writing for newspapers at ten dollars a column—or at magazine rates, if his prose happened to please the *Atlantic Monthly*. But he was not yet ready to give up and retire to Kansas to edit the *Dragoon Creek Mud Cat*.

He resolved not to make himself or his family unhappy over something they could not help, but would have them live quietly, and enjoy all the small pleasures that came their way, while he continued his pursuit of health and waited for the chance he hoped would soon come. They spent the summer of 1871 on a farm in New Hampshire, presided over by the sister of their Florida hostess, whose gaunt husband seemed to my mother the embodiment of a "regular dew-tell Yankee."

My father sent a few unimportant manuscripts to various periodicals, some of which were accepted, some returned. He wrote another series of articles for the *Times*, taking New England as his theme. There were two horses available on the Davis farm, more reliable for safety than for speed. He and his family, riding through the country, managed to see a good deal of rural New England. They drove down to the shore for an ocean dip on warm days, made an excursion into the White Mountains, and with the coming of autumn, investigated the camp meetings held in the lake region. New England seemed to him on the whole "a good and comfortable land" in spite of its stony fields. Particularly did he rejoice in the absence of poverty such as had haunted him in France. "Imagine a parish priest abroad saying, 'There are practically no poor in my parish!'" he exulted.

More enjoyable even than their excursions were the golden hours spent on the banks of a little stream that flowed across one corner of the farm. Small water lilies floated on its surface. Little pools along its edge reflected the gorgeous red of cardinal flowers, and there were shade trees near by. My fáther enjoyed such small beautiful things more keenly than any other man I have known. Mountains inspired him as they do most people, but he could also get exquisite pleasure out of the pure curves of a flower. As a little emigrant boy he had longed for the forbidden luxury of drawing lessons. In Paris, before his eyes gave out completely, he had worked with an excellent set of French instruction books and had taught himself to draw accurately and well. That summer, when he needed all the courage and patience he could find, he found both, on the banks of that little river.

But much as he liked New England and Florida, it was Springfield, in Illinois—where he had come to know Lincoln and had entered on the great experience of his life— that seemed most like home. In the autumn of 1871 he bought a rather unattractive little farm of forty acres just outside Springfield's city limits. Here, at least, he could be near old friends, live cheaply, and store his Lincoln material until he should be able to use it. He rented the tillable part of his acres to a neighbor, reserving only the house and its immediate surroundings, which he set himself to beautify by the use of good taste and imagination, in place of hard cash. This was no new idea with him. When scarcely more than a boy he had reminded readers of the *Free Press* that "after all, there was very little money in the Garden of Eden."

Old friends, driving out from town wondered what possessed him to buy such a place. Pointing to a huge solitary cottonwood in the nearest cornfield, they remarked, "Of course you will cut that down."

"Why?" he asked. Instead of destroying it, he made it

the focal point of his garden, planting a wide circle of rosebushes around it, and laying out a broad grassy path directly to it between beds in which vegetables and gay annuals grew amicably together.

As he dug in his garden he tried to plan for the future. The times left much to be desired, for throughout the country the exaltation of spirit that had upheld the people through four years of war seemed strangely absent. Months earlier, he had written: "Gigantic combinations of political and commercial frauds confront us on every hand," and again, "the day is nearly past when the liberty and property of the citizen can be safely trusted to men whose daily and nightly aspiration extends no further than to reach the greatest skill in partizan intrigues and caucus manipulations."

He tried to analyze the causes of the trouble and came to the conclusion that, in this case at least, ignorance was quite as responsible as greed—because in any community the number of clever schemers is small compared to the host of well-meaning, ignorant people, who are often poor. He knew that in St. Louis, where the population was approximately 300,000, there was not a single low-priced newspaper for carrying into poor homes what he believed to be proper daily instruction. This line of thinking led him finally to write to a friend who lived there:

I am anxious to come to the city of St. Louis and establish a newspaper of the class called Penny Papers—of which there is not one in your city, and for which your population of over 300,000 souls offers, as I think, a perfectly clear and most promising field.

My plan is to publish an evening paper about half the size of the *Dispatch* or *Journal of Commerce*, making the compilation and condensation of the news of the day its chief feature. The price would be two cents per copy, ten cents per week, five dollars per year. Its claim to public patronage would consist in giving the reader for five dollars what now costs him ten. It would not conflict with the established papers, because it would reach a different class of readers, who cannot afford to buy the high-priced article.

My telegrams I would obtain from the American Press Association, as there is probably no chance to get into the Associated Press. Until the experiment were sufficiently tried, I would not set up a printing establishment, but get the necessary typesetting and press work done by contract with some job office. I estimate that the total cost of such a publication will be $50.00 per day. I think that if such a sheet were carried for a period of say one hundred days, involving during that time an actual expenditure of $5,000, the experiment would have been sufficiently tried to justify either its further continuance or prompt abandonment. This then, is the measure of actual risk. If the trial promised success, then a further capital of say $20,000 would be needed to improve a little, and still cover a prospective deficit for say a period of twelve months, at the end of which time I believe it would be self-sustaining.

I think the mistake usually made by newspapers is their attempt to jump into full-fledged size, influence and prosperity by unnatural and spasmodic efforts which always fail for want of inexhaustible capital; and, whenever a newspaper flags, it is doomed. I would *begin small* and *grow large*. But only with a natural and healthy growth. That is to say, it would always remain a penny paper; but if prosperity came, I would double its contents without increasing its price, and thus increase its circulation, profits and influence.

But the friend to whom he presented the idea showed no inclination to educate the masses.

That winter was spent on the newly acquired farm. There were stretches of white, snow-covered lawn, followed in the early spring by thaws that filled the roads so full of inky mud, that, near though we were to the post office, the only practicable way to be sure of getting mail was to go after it on horseback, since wheels and human feet alike sank too deeply into the mire.

Once, in Paris, when efforts were being made to remove my father from the consulate, he had told an apocryphal yarn about an office seeker who was asked by cable, "Will you accept the office of Minister to Bogota?" and answered instantly, "I accept. Where in hell is Bogota?" Now, doubtless to his own amusement, he found himself applying for that very office. He wrote to Senator Harlan in Washington:

You will remember that about three years ago President Grant promised you he would not remove me from the Paris consulship, and that it was nevertheless done. He has now a good chance to make amends for the oversight which then occurred in the matter. On yesterday, General Hurlbut, our Minister Resident in Bogota, was nominated for Congress to succeed General Farnsworth. This will of course make a vacancy in that mission, and as it will be not only proper but convenient to send another Illinois man in General Hurlbut's place, I desire the President to give me the appointment. In view of the "Liberal" disaffection right here in the center of this State, the President could not make another appointment which would strengthen him so much among Lincoln's friends. ... Should he feel disposed to appoint me, I will bring him all the recommendations he could possibly ask. If, on the contrary, there be no chance, I do not wish to waste the necessary time to do it.

I do not wish in any way to embarrass the President by office-hunting, and you will yourself testify that I have waited patiently until time should present the opportunity to the President to do me justice. As it has now come I make my application to you direct, in the hope to get a decisive answer from him. Surely after all you have done for him he will at least respectfully consider and frankly answer your request in this behalf.

Of my qualifications, after twelve years of official experience, and a thorough knowledge of the French and German languages, I hope he will have no doubt. Neither will he forget, I hope, that my own hands carried to the Senate every military nomination of his from Brigadier to General.

Providentially, he was not sent to Bogota. Six months later the mutations of politics made R. C. Parsons, Marshal of the United States Supreme Court, a successful candidate for Congress, and in December 1872 my father was appointed to succeed him. He explained to a French correspondent that he had the advantage over other applicants of personally knowing six of the nine judges who composed the court, and that it was *une très jolie position*," which carried with it, besides excellent social standing, a pleasant office in the Capitol, a modest salary, "and not too much hard work."

For the task he had at heart the post was ideal. Not the least of its recommendations was the Court's long summer recess during which his duties as marshal would be at a minimum. Then, too, his office under the Capitol's dome was separated by only a few yards of tesselated marble flooring from the great Library of Congress, whose priceless collections he and John Hay would have constant need to consult. The librarian was Ainsworth R. Spofford, their personal friend, an appointee of Lincoln's.

Milton Hay, John's uncle, writing to congratulate the new marshal, said he would not trade that office for one drawing twice the salary. He thought it high time the authors wrote their book. "God-fearing men make up the reading public," he wrote. "They want a model for all the good little boys to follow, and Billy Herndon's model won't do."

Although my father had been away from Washington scarcely more than six years, many of the men prominent in wartime, who were still there, seemed much older. One of the first calls he made was on Chief Justice Chase. After seeing him, he made this note:

Had a kind reception. He is much changed.—Has let a gray beard grow so as to almost cover his face, which makes a perfect disguise for him.

He spoke of Welles's article in the *Galaxy* on the Emancipation Proclamation as a valuable contribution to history. Asked me if I had read Lamon's book, and what I thought of it. I replied that it contained much insidious depreciation of Lincoln. He said it had made an altogether different impression upon himself. He thought that many things in it, such as the courtship affairs and the effort to prove his irreligion, might have been better omitted, but that as someone would almost inevitably have printed them, it was perhaps as well that they should appear now. Beyond these however the book went to show as he thought that "never in the history of the world had a man risen so high from so low a beginning."

The patriotic fervor that marked Washington in wartime had been succeeded by great interest in the vast political and commercial combinations about which my father had pondered while digging in his garden at Springfield. Few military uniforms were to be seen, but military titles were still on every lip. A saying was current that Washington was "full of colonels, and the colonels full of corn." This was at least half true. Until the day of his death my father answered with pained resignation when addressed as "Colonel Nicolay." He did not protest, from sheer weariness over trying to explain that he had no right to the title.

Locally, the District of Columbia was undergoing an

opéra bouffe experiment in a territorial form of government. It even had an irritating counterpart of Baron Haussmann in "Boss Shepard," once an excellent plumber, who had been made governor. He cut and slashed at will in his praiseworthy efforts to give the town a connected water system; but he cared not a whit what questionable methods were used to reward his friends or to make life miserable for his enemies.

Intellectually, Washington's atmosphere was a little bleak. Few people seemed to care to read and discuss books or listen to music, compared with many who showed deep interest in our country's increasing production of steel ingots. A few old friends, deploring this, thought there might be as many as thirty congenial spirits in the city who would enjoy meeting once a fortnight for an evening of intellectual pleasure. They organized the Washington Literary Society on that basis, but soon increased the membership to forty, not from any fancied resemblance to the French Immortals, but because they wanted to be generous and allow ample room for everybody. My father drafted the Constitution, basing it on the principle that the least possible amount of government is the best. In this instance his theory has stood the test of time, for after more than seventy years the Society still flourishes, and its list of members, past and present, contains many names that will live in history.

My father found that getting down to serious work on the Lincoln biography required time. In May 1873, after Court had adjourned for the summer and he was again at Springfield, he wrote to Robert Lincoln to find out whether the President's papers had yet been transferred from Bloomington to Chicago.

And whether you have done anything toward their examination and arrangement, as you told me you thought of doing.... I ask, because in case you have them with you, I will try so to shape my matters as to come to Chicago and look over them with you in the course of a month or six weeks.... The contemptible assertions and insinuations of Charles Francis Adams in his eulogy on Seward, and the late death of the Chief Justice once more demonstrate the necessity of promptly beginning the collection and arrangement of the materials which John and I will need in writing the history we propose. We must of necessity begin with your father's papers.

Eleven months later, despite the best intentions of everybody concerned, little progress had been made. Again he wrote Robert Lincoln:

I learn from Judge Davis since his return here that he had a short interview with you on the subject of examining your father's papers—that you have had the boxes transferred to Chicago, and opened one of them—and that, following his suggestions, you had concluded to suspend their examination until after the adjournment of the Supreme Court. I could in the early spring come out to Chicago and lend you my assistance about the matter.

This arrangement coincides in every way with my own judgment and desires. I am satisfied that the task is in every way a longer and more perplexing one than either of us yet fully appreciates, and that therefore it will need all the time and patience that both of us may have to give it. I think it in every way most desirable, too, that I should be there at the first overhauling of the papers, as there may be many little things of which note should be taken at the moment, whose importance might not be so familiar to yourself, and would be entirely unknown to any clerk to whom you might confide any preliminary examination. I am also specially anxious—and I press this point particularly—that not a scrap of paper of any kind be destroyed. The merest memorandum, mark, signature or figure, may have a future historical value, which we cannot now arbitrarily determine, and the only good rule is to *save everything.*

I am much pleased that we shall be able so soon to get at this work. It is of immense importance that all accessible material shall at the earliest moment be put into a permanent methodical and convenient arrangement for reference and use. Your father's papers must necessarily form the nucleus. Around this, it is my design to group such documentary collections (printed or MS, original or copied as the case may admit) as the most diligent efforts on my part can bring together. To this end I propose to glean the files and records of the various departments of government here. The captured Rebel Archives, and, as far as I can obtain permission, the personal and private papers of the various Cabinet officers, subordinate civil, and leading army and navy officers, whose careers gave them official prominence or personal intimacy in your father's administration.

I do not flatter myself that this is a trifling work. But I know that no one has equal advantages with myself for doing it, and I hope by very quiet but very persistent effort to accomplish much if not the entire completion of my plans. In the very prosecution of this task, and in progress with it, that History we propose will almost write itself.

There are in this city every winter during sessions of Congress, from one to two hundred individuals from whom accessory or relative information on individual points or incidents may be obtained. Many of these are growing old, and in the course of Nature will not reappear here many winters. As examples I mention Cameron, Blair, Sumner, Wade, Wilson and others, the list of whom is too long for this letter. Whenever I can begin the study of special points, I can go to these men for special papers or reminiscences, but it is of not the least earthly use to go to them until I have a definite inquiry to present. To ask them for general information would be simply asking them to write a book.

You remember that when I was in Chicago last summer you showed me a small open box of papers in your garret which

you told me you had already looked through. Why can you
not nail up that box and forward it to me by express, and let
me utilize the intervening two months between this and the
adjournment of our Court in putting them into shape here?
I shall have plenty of time and more ample facilities than I
can have anywhere else; and I have entire and sole control
of a strong and safe room in the basement of the Capitol
which is more secure than any safe in Chicago against fire.

Meanwhile, he was pursuing his secondary task of
grouping around the President's papers such other collections as diligent efforts could bring together. In June
he wrote Therena from St. Louis that he had arrived only
that morning, but had already called upon Richard Bates,
son of Lincoln's Attorney General. Richard and his mother
had consented to his examining the Bates papers, and
work would begin "tomorrow morning."

24

WRITING THE BIOGRAPHY

AFTER THE LINCOLN PAPERS HAD BEEN entrusted to my father's care, the long task of classification and arrangement was begun. John Hay, who had held several diplomatic posts abroad, resigned as Secretary of Legation in 1872 and came home, but for several years he was too occupied in newspaper work, and in publishing *Castilian Days* and *The Pike County Ballads*, to give my father much active help in the necessary preliminary labors. They kept in constant touch, however, and worked in perfect harmony.

My father, John Hay, Robert Lincoln, and Judge David Davis—whose opinion had great weight with the President's son—were of one mind concerning Mr. Lincoln's greatness, but they did not always see eye to eye on the best use to be made of the documents. Even so, there is no evidence to uphold a statement made, from time to time, to the effect that Robert Lincoln carefully and persistently "edited" the Nicolay-Hay biography. The restraining influence appears more than once to have been my father—not in suppressing evidence, but in determining how and when to use it. One instance of my father's discretionary influence arose after Mr. Seward died in

1872. Charles Francis Adams delivered a eulogy that left the impression that Mr. Lincoln had been a mere figurehead and that Mr. Seward was the guiding force of the administration. In my father's custody were two papers that, taken together, absolutely refuted this impression. One was Mr. Seward's remarkable memorandum of April 1, 1861, in which he virtually offered to assume the whole responsibility of running the government. The other was the President's dignified answer: "If this must be done, I must do it." Robert Lincoln knew that these papers were in my father's hands, and he wanted to publish them at once. Judge Davis apparently agreed with him. My father took a different view and made careful notes of the points he wished to emphasize before writing Robert Lincoln a letter of protest. The letter, as finally sent from Bethlehem, New Hampshire, is dated July 17, 1874, and reads in part as follows:

The boxes containing your father's papers are in Washington, still unopened, and iron-bound as we put them up in Chicago. I brought up here with me the Bates papers which I obtained in St Louis, and am busy with the tedious and long task of copying them, so that if a change of circumstances should necessitate the sudden recall of the originals, I will not be deprived of their use and contents.

You see therefore that at present it is practically impossible to send you the document you wish, without my making a special trip to Washington, and I hope you will content yourself with my sending you the Pope's answer of *non possumus*.

Let me say further however that your design to let Mr Welles use the paper in question is the most rash and inconsiderate step two such sensible men as yourself and Judge Davis could possibly devise. There is quite a shower of publications impending in the general subject of which this particular issue is more or less involved. Warden's *Life of*

Chase is just out; Schuyler's *Life of Chase* is soon to appear; Lamon and Black will issue a second volume whenever they can find a publisher; Sumner's biographies are advertised by the dozen; and Thurlow Weed and Fred Seward are actively at work compiling some sort of biography of W.H.S.

I do not think it probable that the latter will undertake to bolster up the absurd assertion of Charles Francis Adams; and yet against that contingency it is absolutely essential that we hold this particular document in readiness and reserve. If on the contrary they should be courteous and fair, C.F.A. would by that fact alone receive a stinging rebuke, and it would be extremely injudicious in us to place ourselves in the attitude of mere partizans and camp-followers in the Welles-Adams controversy, when we already occupy, and by judicious reticence retain, the immensely higher and more authoritative position of historical arbiters, and possessors of the decisive historical record.

And now let me add, in all kindness but in all candor, that I protest against the injustice you would do myself and Col. Hay in the course you propose. I beg of you to no longer think of us as mere boys, but as men who have reached reasonably mature powers, who have learned something in the school of experience at least, and who believe ourselves capable of doing creditable work, when we have, what all other men have needed before us, the proper opportunity. We find such an opportunity in your father's history. He is our ideal hero. We wish to delineate the grandeur of the era in which he lived, the far-reaching significance and influence of the events he led, and to set him in history as the type, the Preserver and Liberator of the People. In support of this view we wish to present a compact, and exhaustive logical and historical *demonstration*.

On the other hand both yourselves and the public naturally expect great things of us, in the particular course matters have taken, and especially *new things*. If we can have the exclusive use of such leading documents as the Seward memorandum and reply, the 21st of May dispatch, the Greeley letter, &c. &c., together with the matters we shall get from other sources, we shall be able to justify this expectation. In addition to your father's papers I have secured the Bates papers, I am promised the Stanton papers, I hope to be allowed to inspect the Sumner papers, and by special favor, the Chase diaries, or at least to obtain extracts as to particular facts. Mr Fish has promised me the coöperation of the State Department. Mr Belknap has accorded me special privileges among the Confederate Archives (this is confidential). Secretary Bristoe will, I am convinced, do the same with another batch of Confederate Archives in the Treasury Department. Besides this, I expect to secure coöperation in material from as many prominent men as I could write names on this page. Every one I have asked has been cordial in his promises of help, and a large proportion will keep their promises.

But novelty and ephemeral interest are not our only aim. We hold that your father was something more than a mere makeweight in the Cabinet against Seward or any particular Secretary. We want to show that he formed a Cabinet of strong men and great men—rarely equalled in any historical era—and that he, the master-spirit, held, guided, controlled, curbed and dismissed not only them but other high officers, civil and military—and at times the people themselves—at will, with perfect knowledge of men, and almost prophetic forecast of events. And this we believe a logical presentation of the proof will demonstrate. Some things will perhaps need to rest on our mere assertion; and our assertion will carry weight just in proportion as it is accompanied by exclusive documents, showing knowledge of matters not in possession of the public.

Now in proposing to give this paper to Mr Welles you propose to take the strong link out of our chain—the keystone out of our arch. I beg of you to reconsider this purpose; and instead of wasting our powder to celebrate Mr

Welles's already complete triumph over Mr Adams, let us rather so manage matters as that Mr Welles himself shall contribute some new ammunition for the *broadside*.

Again in 1878 a somewhat similar request was made by Robert Lincoln. To this my father replied, that, since he was out of town, it was impossible to send him the desired paper.

But even if I were in Washington I would first most earnestly ask you to recall the request. There is to be no end to these newspaper discussions and you cannot possibly answer them all. Where you do, the central document or fact is rudely torn from its necessary connections and misdated and misquoted, and by the third day flippantly condensed into three lines by the "items" man. Since I have been collecting and arranging, I have been amazed to find how these things sink out of sight and become fossilized in the newspapers.

I pray you to be patient and let us present these matters in authentic shape, and then a hundred sharp newspaper pens will always be on the alert to vindicate true history, from the full record. Besides, new things are yet every little while turning up. Only a few days before I came from Washington I was shown a copy (sent by General Hooker himself to the officer in charge of printing the War Department Records) of an important and very characteristic letter from your father to the General shortly after he had placed him in command.* No copy of it was in the War Department, none among your father's papers, and I had no recollection of it. General Hooker thinks it a compliment, and such it may be, but it would be difficult to find a severer piece of friendly criticism. I mention this to show that your father's fame will not suffer from the delay necessary to present his acts and words in the clearest light and amplest breadth.

* This was the President's letter to General Hooker, dated January 26, 1863.

Beginning in the summer of 1874, several letters passed between my father and Mr. I. N. Arnold, member of Congress from Illinois, who informed him that at the time of the Chicago fire he had a volume of President Lincoln's speeches and writings almost ready for the press. This was destroyed, but he had since rewritten it, and now wished to know when the Nicolay-Hay biography would be out, and whether his book was likely to conflict with theirs. My father answered:

Mr Hay and I are engaged on a life and history of Mr Lincoln as you have heard. He, so far as he can find time besides his present newspaper engagements, and I have given the whole summer to it. We have also always intended to collect, arrange and publish Mr Lincoln's writings, speeches, letters, &c. These are so voluminous that they will necessarily make separate volumes from our main history, but to explain and illustrate which the more fully and completely they will be absolutely essential.

We have for this purpose been given exclusive access to all Mr Lincoln's papers, and I have further made arrangements to secure from the papers of many of his prominent contemporaries all the needed material to make such a collection as complete and full as in the nature of things may be possible. Appreciating fully your own historical ability and your sincere devotion to Mr Lincoln's memory, I regret that our plans should thus cross each other; but considering the scope and necessities of the work we have begun, I do not see how we can deviate from our program—more especially as we hold among Mr Lincoln's papers a large number of unpublished MSS.

We have not yet progressed sufficiently to judge when we may be able to publish. If we wait for the completion of the whole work, several years must necessarily elapse; if we should divide it, a preliminary volume might be got ready earlier. The subject is of such interest and the material so abundant that the great question is, *what to leave out.*

Other letters followed, the friendly conclusion being that their respective books must stand or fall on their own merits. Mr. Arnold's was by no means the first inquiry they received. Almost from the moment of Mr. Lincoln's death, queries and suggestions and offers from publishers had come to them with the regularity of a refrain. In each case they answered politely, as they had answered Mr. Arnold, that their work had not progressed far enough to enable them to set a date for publication. A large proportion of these letters ended with a request for a Lincoln autograph. One inquirer, who described himself as "young and active," and willing to give much energy to publishing their book "in very handsome style" was more comprehensive in his demands, and asked for "some pieces of Mr Lincoln's writing." (Incidentally, more than fifty years ago, the Librarian of Congress told my father that Lincoln autographs had become harder to obtain than those of George Washington.)

Of course they were offered alleged manuscripts, and Lincoln signatures for a price. My father warned John Hay against falling in too readily with such suggestions, telling him of an offer he had recently received. Someone wanted to sell him a signature "for the ridiculously high figure of $150 and two round-trip tickets" from Kentucky to Washington to witness the next inauguration. On examination this bit of writing proved to be only a cleverly executed photograph.

Nor did the two authors escape censure for attempting their task. A friend sent Colonel Hay a clipping from a New York newspaper which asserted that in spite of the close relation in which they stood to Mr. Lincoln during the war years, they were not qualified by experience or mental powers for such work. "There has been altogether too much thin material strained out to the public," the journal pontificated:

Whoever attempts to limn for future ages the characteristics of Abraham Lincoln...must perforce possess the ability to survey very much more than comes within scope of ordinary mortal vision.... It will require powerful treatment; indeed, such vigor and masterful touch as a Carlyle might display.... Mr Hay had better stick to his versemaking. Mr Nicolay is a brilliant writer in his way, but his specialty is in airing the light nothings of fashionable society.... Time enough for them to try biography when they are forty.

John Hay scrawled his disgusted comment in blue pencil on the margin of the clipping and sent it to his coauthor: "That scoundrel D---- has persuaded these idiots that you and I are about nineteen years of age, and that you, especially, are the most frivolous of *petits crevé.*" Both were well over forty when their first volume of *Abraham Lincoln: A History* appeared in book form. My father was fifty-eight, and Hay only six years younger.

From the time during the campaign of 1860, when my father made his first notes for the book, to 1890, when their ten volumes had all appeared, with two volumes of Lincoln's letters and speeches still to follow, this labor of love occupied thirty years. No book was ever more carefully written or more conscientiously verified. It was a matter of greatest satisfaction to both authors that not a statement in the entire work had been made from personal bias or without written evidence to sustain it. In the mere matter of hunting down typographical errors, the proof sheets were read nine times in our house—three times in galley, three times in page proof, and three times more after the pages had been finally cast—all this in addition to the reading Colonel Hay gave it, and to the care lavished upon it at the printing office.

During these thirty years the project had never been out of their minds. Much of the time, my father was fighting his battle against ill health. There were periods after the Paris days when his eye trouble made it necessary to remain in a darkened room for days together. He gave up all other forms of reading, rarely went out into society, and conserved every bit of his strength for this work. During these same years, John Hay was an editor in New York, Assistant Secretary of State in Washington and United States Ambassador in London.

John Hay described himself as "obstinately an optimist, but not a fatalist." In the matter of the Lincoln biography, however, he was not so steadily optimistic as my father. Just as devoted and loyal to the President, and as sure that the book must be written, he doubted at times whether the public would care for it after it was done. "It is a better book than the people deserve," he wrote in a fit of pessimism. "If it had been one quarter as costly and one tenth as good, it might have sold as many copies as one of Gunther's or Albert Ross's immortal works."

Capping all other delays in its preparation was the reluctance of certain well-meaning underofficials to allow the authors to inspect government records that it was imperative to see. Long years of interviewing men prominent in wartime, and of listening to "reminiscences" of men not so prominent, who yet claimed to be custodians of Mr. Lincoln's most secret thoughts, had left them with little respect for recollections unaccompanied by written proof.

They especially wished to consult official records of the Union and Confederate armies. Congress had authorized the printing of these, but getting them into type required time. Even after that was accomplished, sticklers for the letter of the law held that they should be kept secret until Congress passed a law opening them to the public. When my father made application to be allowed to consult the records in the War Department, he received in reply a long, embarrassed refusal that is worth quoting as an example of extreme official rectitude.

December 26, 1876. Dear Mr Nicolay: I am very anxious you should not misunderstand my opposition to your application to examine the Records of the Department. Personally, I should be only too glad to assist you in what I regard as a praiseworthy undertaking, and one that can hardly be compensated for by the sale of your work. But officially I am firm in the belief that such portions of the records of the Executive Mansion in your possession as are of a public nature are the property of the Government and should be filed in the Departments of the affairs to which they relate.

I am sufficiently wrapped up in my own literary labors to understand and appreciate your position and how desirable it is, from an individual standpoint, to retain exclusive control of what you have, but that does not alter the position that the records of the Executive Mansion are *public* and not the property, and *cannot* belong to private parties— even to Mr Lincoln's heirs.

I assure you that it is not without embarrassment and pain that I have deemed it my public duty to oppose you on these grounds, and on the additional one that as the Department is publishing its records, they should be kept from the public until Congress orders their distribution. It is only from my great personal regard for you that I am prompted to explain my endeavors to thwart your wishes.

Yours very truly
W. F. Barnard.

It was not until the next year, when the President himself became interested and intervened, that my father was allowed to consult the printed files. Even then permission was granted grudgingly and in an ungracious letter signed by a lesser official who implied that such favoritism was "manifestly unfair" but that the privilege would be granted as an exception in his case, provided the books were speedily returned and that my father did not allow anybody else to use them.

In November 1875 my father was able to send John Hay "a first instalment of material—a lot of manuscript notes of my Springfield interviews, and a small lot of books—Lamon's, Holland's, Arnold's, and Brockett's lives of Lincoln, works of positive value, with a lot of smaller trash good for little except by comparison of bulk, to illustrate the hugeness of the topic." He sent "along with the others N. W. Edwards's memoirs of his father," which he thought might be useful for its pictures of early days in Illinois, and a volume of the National Almanac, which contained "part of the best chronology of the civil war ever compiled."

A few months later my father reported that he was "getting together quite a little lot of books" which might be the foundation of a Lincoln library that he and Hay would find it pleasant to own. "Of course we will never get our money out of it again. If however we have that much to spare after buying our daily bread, it is perhaps as commendable a waste as we can indulge in." He asked Hay's suggestions for a distinctive bookplate, but they never took time to settle that weighty question, and they soon gave up altogether the idea of amassing a Lincoln library, buying thereafter only the items they felt they would need in their work.

When the writing fit was upon him, the younger man was eager to get on with the task.

Can you not send me some other topic for which you have the notes all ready? [he wrote] I am working like ten turks.

... I am more anxious than I can tell you to make progress. I can manage half a dozen chapters before winter, if you can furnish the material. Then, next winter we will make things hum—'f I'm spared.

He sent on a chapter he had just written, asking for criticism. "As a rule I like compliments better than criticism, but this time is the exception."

I choose this because it is the last I have done, and I want you to say with entire frankness whether you think it is up to the mark. Of course I mean *our* mark. I don't compare it with Gibbon or Thucydides. As to style, arrangement, effect am I, in your opinion, holding my own? I confess I cannot tell. I never could, when I get into a streak of working hard, whether it is pretty good or pretty bad. Read it and tell me as soon as you can.

The two would never divulge how the actual writing was divided between them. They seemed to take a mischievous delight in keeping it a secret, saying they were coauthors, and that was all the public need know. Still respecting their wish, it can be said that they had no set schedule. Each wrote the part he felt ready at the moment to handle. They sometimes wrote alternate chapters, and again one of them might write a whole volume. It was literally a composite work. Every chapter was talked over and submitted to the frankest criticism, possible only between friends as thoroughly in accord as these two. John Hay expressed their aim in one of his racy letters. They had, he said, "no desire to write a stump speech in eight volumes, octavo." Again he wrote, "We ought to write the history of those times like two everlasting angels who don't care a twang of their harps about one side or the other."

Both men resided in Washington during the years when they were busiest with the biography. Hay lived in the house that the architect H. H. Richardson designed and built for him across Lafayette Square from the White House. My father's solid home stood near the Capitol. Messages and manuscripts shuttled so continually between the two houses that my mental map of the city is etched deep with the lines of the route they traveled. A chapter would make the trip many times before it was pronounced complete. Messages between the two authors varied from letter length to a laconic "Dear H" or "Dear N, I agree." Sometimes a pungent comment would be scribbled on the margin of a document enclosed for the other to read. It was often easier to write "like everlasting angels" after they had expressed themselves privately with devastating frankness. Expressions like "That idiot So and So" or "Blank is such a frivolous old liar that I don't like to read him" are not absent from these intimate notes.

We kept no carriage. Colonel Hay probably had several, but when he wanted to confer with my father on the book, he was likely to leave them to other members of his family and take one of the horsecars that plodded at intervals along Pennsylvania Avenue from Georgetown to the Navy Yard.

The house my father had bought stood on land now covered by the white marble annex to the Library of Congress. Built when Washington first woke to the consciousness that it was to be a dignified National Capital, it had large, square rooms. My father's study, on the second floor, faced the south; its windows, unimpeded by drapery, let in floods of sunshine. With the single exception of the guest room, whose furnishing was considered strictly a woman's business, there was not a single piece of window drapery in the house. My father believed that windows were made to let in the light, not to be shrouded in dry-goods. Practical "Hartshorn" shades were there in case the sunlight became oppressive, but nothing else. Several pictures hung on the study wall, the most interesting being a large photograph of President Lincoln and his two secretaries, taken in a Washington studio about the time Mr. Lincoln made his Gettysburg Address. My father had had it colored by a skillful miniaturist, who put in, as background, details of the furniture in what was then called the Cabinet Room. This is probably the only authentic record of how the room looked in 1863. Below the pictures were bookcases whose contents overflowed into a small room near by.

The most impressive piece of furniture was the huge desk that my father had used in the White House. He had the good luck to secure it at one of the sales of "decayed furniture"—as they are called—that take place in Washington when some official decides to modernize his office. It is still in my possession. It is about as big as a capacious double bed, without counting four wings that may be extended to make it larger. All told, it offers about thirty-three square feet of flat top, fifteen drawers, and a built-in safe. One of the drawers, uncommonly deep and furnished with a letter-box slit, was used as the mail box in my father's White House office, being emptied and refilled several times each working day.

This desk seemed to bring old days very close to that study on Capitol Hill. My father could almost see Mr. Lincoln's tall figure pause beside it for a moment as he crossed to his private office.

Perhaps John Hay found more of the spirit of the sixties there than in his own more luxurious library. He would come in, greet us brightly, and settle into a chair. If the session promised to be long and serious, he would relieve me of my seat across the desk from my father. Because of the latter's eye trouble, I had early been pressed into service for such assistance as a young and willing, if untrained helper could give.

The whole movement of our household was geared to the writing of the Lincoln book. Because my father could work better in the morning, the breakfast hour was seven-thirty. Thus he was able to accomplish something before duty called him to the Capitol where the Supreme Court convened at noon. After he had headed the dignified procession of judges in their silken robes into the courtroom, he could come home for a midday meal, returning to the Capitol for several hours in the afternoon.

Only once in the long years was the work temporarily halted for another literary task. In 1880, Charles Scribner's Sons asked my father to write the initial volume in their series *Campaigns of the Civil War*. He was glad to do this, not only because he was familiar with the material, but because the little book would serve as a trial balloon to test his style and ability. So for a time we concentrated on events leading up to the battle of Bull Run. All this activity culminated on a frosty October day, when John Hay joined my father in a long horseback ride over the battlefield, from which they returned late, tired and windblown, but happy as two boys, bringing with them treasure-trove of persimmons looted from a tree that overhung the road.

The meticulous care my father gave to this volume, *The Outbreak of Rebellion*, is disclosed in the letter he sent with the manuscript to Mr. E. L. Burlingame of the firm of Charles Scribner's Sons.

The first thing an author thinks of is, of course, the proper appreciation of his work. Of its literary quality you can form your own judgment. Other features however I may without vanity be permitted to speak of. As I say in the preface, I have taken every possible pains to secure historical

accuracy. If errors be found in it, I think they will belong
only to the following classes. (1) Mere accidents or over-
sights regarding unimportant details. (2) Points in controversy where the evidence is meagre or conflicting. (3)
Omissions compelled by the brevity of the narrative, where
some exception of detail could neither be included in the
sentence, statement or summary, nor yet allowed room for
a separate sentence.

Nor have I been content to entirely trust my own judgment. I suppose it rarely happens that a book goes into the
publisher's hands which has had so searching a preliminary
criticism as this, as you will see when I tell you that the
following chapters have been read and substantially approved by the persons named.

Chapters *Secession, Charleston Harbor, Confederate
States' Rebellion* and *Lincoln,* which involve political, constitutional and legal points, by Mr Justice Wm. Strong,
lately retired from the bench of the U.S. Supreme Court.

Chapters *Charleston Harbor* and *Sumter* by Capt. G. V.
Fox, who commanded the Sumter relief expedition.

Chapter *Lincoln* by Mr Robert T. Lincoln son of the
President.

Chapter *Missouri* by Chief Justice Drake of the Court of
Claims, who was a member of the Missouri State Convention.

Chapter *Kentucky* by Mr Justice Harlan of the U.S.
Supreme Court, a resident and active Unionist in Kentucky
in 1861.

Chapter *West Virginia* by Mr Spofford, Librarian of Congress, who was in 1861 a newspaper correspondent at the first
Wheeling Convention.

Chapters *Sumter, Manassas, Bull Run* and *The Retreat* by
Major General Meigs, Q.M. Gen. U. S. Army, who was at
Centerville and near the Stone Bridge on that eventful day of
July 21st, 1861.

Finally, Col. Hay has carefully read the whole work and
given me the benefit of his eminently valuable literary and
historical judgment upon it.

I am not authorized by these persons to publicly say the above, but I mention it privately to you, to show the pains I have taken to avoid mistakes and attain reliable history.

After the book was printed and successfully launched, he wrote the publishers this grateful and spontaneous letter of thanks.

Dear Mr Burlingame: Now that the *Campaigns of the Civil War* are fairly and I hope successfully launched, permit me to express my personal thanks to the publishers for the very handsome print and binding in which the volumes are presented to the public, and especially to yourself for the unflagging and painstaking supervision you have been pleased to give the whole enterprise. More particularly do I wish to acknowledge my appreciation of the friendly interest, I may say enthusiasm, with which you have followed that portion of the general task confided to me, and the very flattering commendation you have so generously bestowed on the volume I have had the honor to write. I deem it a high privilege to have made my literary *debut* in such distinguished company, and under auspices so favorable as to compensate for the many defects which I am fully conscious exist in my own work.

He did another thing that was characteristically gracious. It was the first manuscript I had entirely copied, and he took care to have a copy especially bound for me, adding an autograph inscription that made me very proud.

The Outbreak of Rebellion proved an unqualified success. My father's friend John Bigelow wrote him:

I have never given you credit for such mastery of the narrative style. You have given us the best account of the origin of the Rebellion, and one that is sure of a permanent place in the historical literature of the country. Your friends will now be more impatient than ever for the long-desired biography of the hero of the war to which this book will serve as an introduction.

Robert Hitt assured him that it had "one of the best qualities a book can have—it is interesting." General David Hunter who commanded the main column of Mc-Dowell's army in the disastrous Bull Run campaign, wrote feelingly "I had lost all faith in history till I received your book."

Highly encouraged, he returned to work upon the longer task. This went on through illness and great personal sorrow. In 1877, George Bates Nicolay, the only son born to him, died when only three months old. In November 1885, my mother passed away. The letter my father wrote John Hay at the time of her death, and his answer, show better than volumes of comment what this meant to all of us:

You can best appreciate my loss when I tell you that since the day you assisted at our wedding she has kept my life young and enabled me to smile complacently at my gray hairs. Now I am sundered from the past by a chasm which can never be bridged. . . . But another and immediate loss will be the absence of her cheer and help in our work. For ten years past she has neglected no opportunity to contribute by her mind and hand to its progress. . . . If our volumes ever reach the full dignity of the binder's art, they will be in some degree a monument to her zeal and labor as well as our own.

His friend answered:

She asked so little for herself—she was so full of help and brightness for others. . . . There is no one outside of my own blood whose death can be such a loss as hers. I have not such another friend left in the world to lose.

We carried on as best we could. I sat across the big desk from my father to take dictation in longhand. He composed slowly, planning his sentences with care before committing them to paper. Since I was easily able to keep up with him, he never suggested that I learn stenography. His patience with his amateur secretary was unbounded. He never forgot that the task might seem long and tedious to one comparatively young, and he encouraged me to keep two sheets of paper before me: one for his manuscript, the other on which to set down whatever I chose—a sketch or an attempt at a poem, or whatever literary rainbow I might at the moment be chasing.

When Colonel Hay came to dispossess me of my chair, I would retreat to a corner and listen. Devoted to both of them, and immensely proud of the work they were doing, I was yet too young to realize fully the unusual privilege I enjoyed in listening to their lively talk and pungent comment. Had I been older, I might have kept notes. They both talked well. Occasionally, my father used the picturesque phrases of the frontier. John Hay had an almost uncanny faculty for suggesting much more than he actually said. I would give a great deal for an accurate transcript of those conferences; but all their details have vanished, never to be recaptured.

25

THE BOOK IS PUBLISHED

IT WAS NOT UNTIL 1885 THAT THE IMPOR-
tant question of who was to publish *Abraham Lincoln:
A History* was decided. Through the years offers had come
to the authors from many sources. The choice finally nar-
rowed down to the old, established firm of Harper and
Brothers and the younger eager Century Company, which
had achieved recent brilliant successes. In March 1885,
Roswell Smith, president of the Century Company, wrote
Colonel Hay that the Lincoln biography was "Our kind
of book. The Century wants it. The Century must have
it!" It is doubtful whether at that time the Century Company realized its length, for the first idea was to make it
one of a series, whose units were to be entitled *The Re-
former, The Journalist, The Stateman,* and so on. This
proposal being turned down, the publishers suggested
printing first "the cream" of the work in a series of articles
in their magazine, and afterward issuing the whole of it in
book form. When my father objected to skimming "the
cream" in this way, they proposed to print it all in the
magazine; whereupon John Hay exclaimed, "It would tire
out the continent!" As a matter of fact, about two thirds
of it did appear in the magazine. In June 1885, my father

wrote Mr. Gilder, editor of *The Century Magazine*, that he and Mr. Hay agreed that the Century Company might print their work in the magazine and in book form also, "subject to the following conditions":

1. If upon examination of the MS. The Century Co. is satisfied with the character and quality of the work,

2. If we are satisfied with the price and terms to be offered.

3. If mutual agreement can be reached upon the style and mode of publication—that is, size, typography, arrangement of volumes, and so on.

4. —(and most important) That we shall be held only to reasonable diligence consistent with health in completing the MS. and not be required to finish it on an arbitrary date.

If we keep our health, we think we can have it done at the period proposed, namely, November 1898. Ill health on the other hand, would necessarily delay us beyond that time.

He suggested that Mr. Gilder meet him at Bethlehem, New Hampshire, where he said he would "turn him loose" among their hundred-odd chapters, "You can select your own stopping-place. I shall probably go to one of the smaller cottages, as being easier to get out of with my bundle of papers in case of fire." Years before, when he had been in one of the flimsy White Mountain hotels, a night alarm was sounded, and he retained a vivid memory of the scenes that followed.

John Hay was in a pessimistic mood. "I do not believe Gilder will want the stuff for his magazine," he declared. "There is too much truth in it." But when the meeting took place, my father wrote him: "Gilder plunged into the MS. at the beginning, and has read ever since as busily as a beaver. . . . This (Sunday) morning he is taking a few chapters before going to Church 'just to get the secession taste out of his mouth,' he says." They were then about half through the reading, and Gilder had said several times that he hoped to find a chapter dull enough to skip—but so far he had found only one page he thought might be condensed.

When the contract for publication of *Abraham Lincoln: A History* was signed in November 1885, Mr. Gilder sent my father a little note expressing his pleasure, to which he replied:

I heartily reciprocate your satisfaction—...I have in it the full realization of my hope and expectation ...that the *book* would find a publisher—not the authors. Their sole duty was to *write the book*. That accounts for our having said so little about it. I feel now that it has not only found a publisher, but the right one.

Later he wrote:

It seemed to me that up to the time of entering upon our agreement my duty as one of the authors was to allow our plan and our work to exert upon yourself and your associates merely that attraction which it would naturally have upon every intelligent worker in the field of letters. In other words that you should judge it coldly and prudently upon its probable relation to market values and business interests.... Our work will make a long serial, it is true, but I do not know where, in all the range of modern literature, one could be found appealing more strongly to the attention of the American reader.... A million of American soldiers and their children are to read this story which comes home locally to almost every hearthstone in our land. We have fifty millions of people, forming a reading public. ... The greatest advantage however lies in the average literary ability and judgment of this vast reading public ... to which we may now with confidence appeal.... The bent of the American mind is not flippant, but serious.

When he received the number of the magazine in which the first instalment of the serial was printed, he wrote Mr. Gilder:

It is not without emotion that I have examined these first pages of our work in serial magazine form. Seeing them thus, about to be launched into the great sea of literature, I am not unmindful of the debt of friendship we owe to you and your associates of *The Century* for the thought and care bestowed upon their favorable presentation.

Continuing, he mentioned the "flattering editorial notice" with which their work was introduced, and the technical details that only one like himself, trained in the rigorous school of an old-time printing office, could have discerned. Apparently such praise was as welcome as it was unusual, for in his next letter to Mr. Gilder he wrote:

Your words of commendation are very welcome. Under such warm appreciation something of the long years of waiting and work through which our chapters have grown from purpose to performance is made to disappear.

The friendliest relations continued. Publishers and authors spoke their minds frankly and freely. When differences of opinion developed, they gallantly gave way so far as they could, while still holding to their basic opinions.

My father never lost the red-hot scorn with which, during the war years, he had regarded the instigators and perpetrators of the rebellion. The only criticisms voiced against his *Outbreak of Rebellion* had arisen from its "aggressive Northernism." This had astonished John Hay at the time, because when he read the little book in manuscript it had seemed to him so eminently fair. "But I am of that age and imbued with all its prejudices," he admitted. Yet he was always a little more willing than my father to accept the changes wrought by the lapse of years. Once he wrote him:

The war has gone by. It is twenty years ago. Our book is to be read by people who cannot remember anything about it. We must not show ourselves to the public in the attitude of two old dotards fighting over again the politics of their youth.

My father's attitude, on the other hand, was expressed in a reply he sent Mr. Gilder when the latter asked him to modify some statement in regard to Lee.

I will look up the exact language I used in reference to Lee. I think the phrase to which you called my attention was merely used in conversation, and then only as a hypothesis of military law. I do not mean to say, even in conversation, that as a matter of policy the penalty he rendered himself legally liable to ought to have been inflicted. But I do mean to say that his adherents and admirers ought to be grateful to the people and the government of the United States for the Great Pardon with which they have covered all these offenses against law and humanity.

And again:

As to possible accusations of partizanship, we stand in no awe of them. We deny that it is partizanship to use the multiplication table, revere the Decalogue, or obey the Constitution of the United States. When logic, morals and law all unite to condemn the secession and rebellion of 1861, he will be a rash critic to pronounce censure upon anyone who helped put down that rebellion, or who ventures truthfully to record its incidents.

For anything personally connected with the secession leaders, he felt a physical distaste. When an acquaintance asked him for an unmounted photograph of President Lincoln, offering in exchange a pen once owned by Jefferson Davis, he sent an engraving of Lincoln, having no photograph at hand, but declined the pen on the ground that "I have no admiration for the character of Jefferson Davis as a politician and statesman, and could derive no pleasure from the possession of a memento of him. I beg therefore that you will bestow it upon someone else who will appreciate it more thoroughly." But he did not omit a word of thanks for the friendship that prompted this offer.

Mr. Gilder, as editor of a popular magazine, was even more inclined than John Hay to regard the issues of the Civil War as belonging to past years. While the publication was going on in *The Century* he wrote my father:

We are all in, for better or worse, for life and eternity; and as if between husband and wife, we must be frank and help each other all we can with our bottom thoughts.

The other night St Gaudens, who has been and is a great admirer of the *Life*, and the only reader, you know, outside of here (it will tell favorably upon his statue for all time), turned to me suddenly at the Century Club and said, of the last parts he had read, far on into your chapters, "How damn partizan it's getting!" I asked him to say what he meant, and he said there was so much "pitching in, calling names, etc." This effect upon a most interested and sympathetic reader recalled my own feeling about some of the adjectives and passages we read over in the mountains, and very much of which you struck out.

In writing this way I am under the imputation of taking the attitude of a frightened editor or publisher. But I trust you know me and all of us better than to suspect that! We have here had for a lifetime the constant experience of the responsibility of disseminating some criticisms of human beings. We have always regretted the slightest unfairness or bitterness, or insistence upon a totally un-

friendly opinion. Satan himself has some good points....
The world loves generosity.... Lincoln represents in his
public acts and utterances the very principle of sympathy,
and the public will revolt at a different tendency in his biographers.

Next day, sending on an installment of magazine proof,
he wrote:

How magnificently the old boy comes out in this chapter
on Lincoln and Trumbull.... I find here and there some remains of the only element that can make the *History* anything short of a great success for us all. Your sanction of
right and natural indignation at wrong sometimes injures
the necessary philosophical equipoise.... Yet, just think
of it, here is the longest contemporaneous history of a
contemporary character almost ever written. The actors in
it—or their heirs, widows, friends—are still living, and the
work is laid on nearly a quarter of a million parlor and club
tables, where all the world *must* see it. No other history
ever had such an audience. How tremendously is increased the
danger of giving needless pain by anything short of omni-
scient knowledge and accuracy of judgment!

My father answered:

Herewith I return the proofs. You will see that I not
only agree with you in the principle laid down in your letters,
but that I also follow your practice. I believe I have adopted
all your corrections, and I think the text the better for them.
I will be glad if you will be equally free to mark in future
chapters anything which you think had better not go in,
and I do not apprehend that we shall often disagree.

But he continued to believe in the multiplication table,
the Decalogue, and the Constitution of the United States!

Praise coming from the South occasionally astonished
him. Returning two letters sent by Mr. Gilder for him to
read, he replied concerning one of them:

Evidently there is balm in Gilead, and hope in the Young South, if this writer is a type. When he says he is "convinced of the greatness of Lincoln and of the treachery of his cabinet ministers Floyd, Thompson and Cobb" we can see that if he does not read as he runs, he at least runs as he writes. But I suppose we ought to be well satisfied with a "Southerner of Southerners" who can take such a dose as the October *Century* gave him, and say he rather likes it. Pat him on the shoulder by all means.

On the other letter he made the terse comment:

In five years they will be swearing that Lincoln was an original secessionist!

During the years when magazine and book publication were going on simultaneously, proofreading was the main occupation in our home. My father gave it the greatest care, but objected strenuously to the habit, beloved of printers, of sending proof sheets in overwhelming quantities and then allowing long intervals to pass when none came at all. With his poor eyesight, such a system became a real hardship, and he demanded insistently that proof come to him "regularly, not spurtically." It followed us on our vacations, and sometimes the zeal of the New York office combined with the efforts of country telegraph offices, from which messages were relayed by telephone, to produce strange results.

Once this message reached my father at Ogunquit, Maine:

G. Nicholy—New York Sept. 25, 1888
          If possible to pecure Faccemigli of final
Grant emanciation croclanition. Answr Telegran
                    Editor Centy. Maj..

It had us all guessing, until he translated it as an effort on the part of Mr. Gilder to get a copy of the original draft of President Lincoln's Emancipation Proclamation to use as an illustration in the magazine.

On another occasion my father sent back a batch of proof with the message:

Some joking printer made the general heading read *Lincoln as an Anarchist*. This I have struck out and marked in what I sent you the other day—namely, *The Territorial Experiment*, which both Hay and I think a suitable general title for the instalment. But we will be glad if you will personally see to it that the joke doesn't get into the stereotypes by one of those singular fatalities which sometimes beset printing offices.

Serial publication of the Lincoln biography continued from October 1886 to January 1890. The book had developed from my father's early idea of a mere campaign "life" of the presidential candidate into a history of the Civil War as well as a study of Mr. Lincoln's entire political career. The final ten volumes contained seventy-eight whole chapters omitted in the magazine, in addition to seventeen others that were partly new.

At Christmastime, 1890, my father had the satisfaction of sending the ten volumes to good friends of his earliest Pittsfield days, not forgetting David McWilliams, and kind Mrs. Garbutt who had "mothered" him. She was quite old then, and in her letter of thanks expressed her gratitude that the books were printed in large clear type that she could still read. Mr. Hatch wrote humorously from Springfield about the book's size, telling how a truck had backed up to his door as if about to deliver a barrel of flour and had discharged, instead, *Abraham Lincoln: A History*, in ten volumes, royal octavo.

The letters of congratulation received by the authors almost invariably expressed wonder at the magnitude of the task they had completed. Few indeed, even of the most experienced, realized to the full the amount of labor involved in all those years of study. Long as the book was, a major problem, from first to last, had been, as my father said, to decide what they could afford to leave out.

Many of their correspondents asked to be allowed to copy or "adapt" selections of their work into books of their own—even fiction. Other letters were very instructive. One pointed out how marvelously Lincoln's life and death had been foretold in ancient Scripture. Others hinted, more or less politely, that after all Lincoln was little better than a plagiarist. One from Fitz-John Porter threatened reprisal, but nothing came of it.

A review published by William Dean Howells pleased them immensely. John Hay was particularly delighted because Howells had picked out for commendation "precisely those features of the work in which, in our opinion, it's success or failure is involved." My father wrote: "My dear Howells: I send you a thousand thanks . . . and if I were to write you a page for each, I could not better convey my gratitude." To John Russell Young, who combined reminiscences of war days with his praise, he wrote: "Reading over your glowing memory pictures . . . . I feel again the pulse of enthusiasm and faith that will always glorify to me the associations and friendships your heart and pen have so vividly called up."

In recent years, when the "debunking" of historical characters has been in fashion, it has been said from time to time that the life of Abraham Lincoln written by his two secretaries cannot be accepted too seriously, since it was written under the close supervision of Robert Lincoln. These critics assert that the President's son was a snob at heart and rigidly censored material that could in any way be interpreted as being derogatory to the President's

THE BOOK IS PUBLISHED

actions, manners, origin, or family. So far as I have been
able to discover from the correspondence between the secretaries and Robert Lincoln, the charge is entirely without
foundation. It is true that they were "Lincoln men all the
time," but from conviction, not compulsion. Their happy,
cordial, deferential relations with Mr. Lincoln during
their years of service could logically have only an outcome
of respect for the President in the writing of his biography. It is true that John Hay assured Robert Lincoln
that they would show him what they wrote and make any
changes he might suggest. It is hard to imagine that the
authors could be churlish enough not to give him such
assurances when he had turned the President's papers over
to them unreservedly for their use. That indicates full
trust on both sides, but not any want of fairness and honesty in the use of material.

26

"PERSONAL TRAITS"

THE BIOGRAPHY WAS FINISHED, BUT work went on as busily as ever in my father's study. The next task was to prepare a collection of the President's letters, speeches, and official documents. Two volumes of them appeared in 1894, similar in size and binding to the previous ten. They had grown, almost inevitably, out of the study for *Abraham Lincoln: A History*.

One irate collector who bought the *Works* returned them to the publishers, complaining that they were not "complete." The collection never claimed to be complete in the sense of containing every word the President ever wrote. The sheer quantity of routine documents he signed, and the passes he wrote, sometimes scribbled on a card for someone who appealed to him on the street, made this impossible. So only a few characteristic specimens of each were included. In the years that have passed since 1894 a few carefully guarded Lincoln manuscripts have come to light, and several new collections of his works have been printed, but the basic authentic collection remains the one assembled by John Hay and my father.

While *Abraham Lincoln: A History* and *Abraham Lincoln: Complete Works*, were the major tasks they had set

(*left*)

JOHN G. NICOLAY

(*right*)

JOHN HAY

LINCOLN'S BIOGRAPHERS
(c. 1891)

themselves, and the only ones in which Colonel Hay and my father were known as collaborators, they were by no means through with the Lincoln material. My father later undertook a condensation of the ten volumes into one, *A Short Life of Abraham Lincoln*, which was almost finished at the time of his death. Both men also wrote a number of magazine articles about different phases of Lincoln's career.

The editors of *The Century* seemed to regard my father as Consultant-in-Chief when it came to deciding on the value of volunteer contributions—anecdotes, reminiscences, and dark hints of startling disclosures—sent them in the hope of having them printed in the magazine.

He answered such questions in confidence, patiently and fully, in letters of which the following is a fair example:

I do not think you can get anything worth while out of Mr Blank as a "personal friend of Lincoln's." He is perhaps a good talker—no qualifications for a successful writer of reminiscences. Nor have we any desire to negotiate with him for permission to use his "Lost Speech."... Blank pretends he took notes, a statement I feel disposed to doubt, from his treatment of it in his book, in which he said not a word about having taken notes.

Only once in a long while was he able to write "They are very interesting and historically important, and so far as I know, entirely new.... Print them by all means."

About the "stoning Stephen" remark that Lincoln was said to have made during a debate with Douglas, he answered:

There is foundation for this anecdote I think, but this version of it seems to me exaggerated. As I heard it, Mr Lincoln made the remark, not to the audience at large, but in a quiet undertone to a friend sitting near him on the platform—"Hold my hat, while I stone Stephen." It would be very much like Lincoln to make such a remark *sotto voce,* but very unlike him to do so in a theatrical and arrogant manner. So also, whether it was a hat or shawl, or duster or overcoat—"you pays your money and you takes your choice."

When the story was sent my father that Mr. Lincoln received news of Andrew Johnson's nomination for vice president by the Republican National Convention at Baltimore in 1864 before he heard of his own and asked, "Is it not customary to nominate a President first?" he replied, "The anecdote you enquire about is correct. It is mentioned in brief on p. 74, Vol. IX of our *Life.*" The explanation was that Mr. Lincoln had gone over to the War Department and thus had missed the telegraph messenger sent to the White House with news of his nomination.

One admirer was deeply concerned over the size of hat the President wore. The lady librarian of a college in Michigan asked my father's advice on spending a thousand dollars left to the college for the purchase of books about Lincoln. He sent her a careful list of twenty-four. An ardent symbolist wanted to know if oak trees grew in Illinois or Kentucky, because, if they did, he wished to plant an acorn from such a tree on New Haven Green, in soil brought from Gettysburg. Many of the questions were far-fetched, but they all betokened real interest. Not a few of them suggested the need for books dealing with some particular phase of Lincoln's complex nature and extraordinary career.

One such book might well have been called *Abraham Lincoln's Faith in God* and could have been compiled from his own writings on the subject. It was a subject my father had consistently refused to discuss with Lincoln admirers. His own attitude on the matter is amply stated in two notes found among his papers. One, evidently made in anticipation of a talk he had been invited to give, is marked "Not used," and reads:

I need not waste words to point out the moral of his life. His career is a sermon, his example an inspiration. The higher destiny to which he guided his country, the beacon-fires he lighted for humanity, are a new revelation of the mysterious and beneficent workings of that Providence in whom he trusted as a child trusts its father.

The other:

Finally, to sum up the whole matter. In default of sufficient positive or direct testimony—in default of specific professions, of church membership, and the strict observance of church rites—yet in the presence of the unvarying enunciation of faith and reliance in a Supreme Ruler, in the practise of justice, of patriotism, of mercy—in the utter oblivion of self—"with malice toward none and charity for all"—the world can utter no other verdict than this—He was a Christian without a creed.

A book that my father expected, but rather dreaded, to write was to be called *Personal Traits of Abraham Lincoln*. It was to deal with the manners, appearance, jests, and pointed anecdotes that people instinctively couple with Lincoln's name. Originally, the authors had intended to include in their larger work a chapter under this heading. Following their usual custom when gathering material, they prepared a huge manila envelope into which to thrust pertinent references as they came across them. Notes soon filled the first envelope and overflowed into many others, but as their plan developed they could find no place for such a chapter without breaking the continuity. They felt, moreover, that the public services rendered by the President were far more significant, and that if, in recounting these, they did not manage to show what kind of man he was their ten volumes would have been written in vain. The chapter was not even begun.

Naturally enough, Mr. Gilder, being the editor of a magazine designed to please a varied public, was constantly urging them not to neglect this personal side, but to write articles that might first be printed in the magazine and then be gathered into a book.

I'll be fearfully disappointed [he wrote] if you don't get into the Lincoln talk. Why, you're full of it! A day with Lincoln in Springfield; a day with Lincoln in Washington. Showing how he went around the room, talking to each. Hay's little paper is excellent, but very general.

Correspondence on the subject went on for years. In June 1888, when the Century Company was pursuing the idea rather vigorously, my father answered one of Mr. Gilder's letters:

Your letter of the 16th about *Personal Traits* is under consideration; but Hay has gone to the Chicago Convention, and I shall probably not be able to get anything from him on the subject until he gets back and gets his throat healed up. Then there remains the possibility that he may have to go to the blacksmith shop to be shod for the dark race—for who is safe when men are no longer permitted to decline?

A fortnight later he reminded the publishers that as soon as the biography was finished they must turn their attention to editing Mr. Lincoln's letters and papers.

Of how much time this will require we cannot in advance form even an approximate idea. My own opinion and hope is that out of this labor of editing the *Works* the chapters of *Personal Traits* will grow in a measure spontaneously and necessarily. I do not think Colonel Hay feels this at present, and I may be entirely mistaken in my view. It may turn out that the *Personal Traits* will grow into the *Works* instead of out of them....There is also from our standpoint another view of the matter. We must say in all frankness to you that should it finally take shape, the chapters of *Personal Traits* will only be an aftermath, neither the material nor the work can possibly be so good as what we have put into the *Life*. Even if we were to agree to furnish it, it would not be safe for you to depend on using it till after you had read and carefully judged it.

Two years later he again assured Mr. Gilder:

I have all along intended and still intend to write several such papers as I suppose you want—that is, treating more of Mr Lincoln's personal traits than we have done in the book. But the difficulty just now seems to be the time at which I can do it. I have been on a terrible strain for a whole year. . . . When I came home last fall I still had several book chapters unfinished; and what with these, and magazine copy and proof, and watching the division of chapters into volumes, and by way of enlivening the cotillion, a ten volume index to run a race with the book publication, it has been a sort of incessant literary fourth of July ever since.

Just now I am completely fagged out, physically and mentally, and don't see much use in books, anyhow. I must get away to where it is cool and I can take a long breath. I hope and expect that my appetite for writing will come again, and then I will experiment on the line you suggest.

John Hay also was tired. When serial publication neared its end and he sent the final magazine instalment to Robert Lincoln, a note went with it that was almost a groan. "Think of reading carefully and critically (Stopping every five minutes to make sure of a fact or a situation) five thousand pages, four times over. This we have to do, *after* the book is finished!" On another day Mr. Hay wrote, evidently in answer to a suggestion that they make an alteration in a magazine chapter, "I would not write 625 words to save 625 editors' lives!"

A month's vacation in New England revived my father sufficiently to permit him to write Mr. Gilder that he believed he could promise the magazine "a few papers" to be published between November 1890 and November 1891. He did write several magazine articles that might have found a place in a book on Lincoln's personal characteristics. One told about *Lincoln's Literary Experiments;* another was on *Lincoln's Personal Appearance;* a third discussed *The Gettysburg Address.* But he was never able to write about the President's personality in the way Mr. Gilder evidently desired. I never heard them say so, but I have a distinct impression that both my father and Colonel Hay believed this sort of thing to be in the nature of gossip, and that the desire for it had its origin in curiosity rather than in regard. They felt that such writing on their part would be little short of a betrayal. My father never forgot that, almost within hours of Mr. Lincoln's death, he had been plied with questions concerning "any change in the President's religious beliefs," and about "the manner, method, customs and pleasures at the White House."

Abraham Lincoln: Complete Works was no sooner issued than the publishers began urging the authors to make an abridgment of their ten-volume biography. Possibly they hoped that by some miracle it might turn into the "personal" volume they desired. The authors showed little enthusiasm, even after they were told how easily the book could be produced by the mere use of paste and shears. When the matter came up again late in 1896, my father assured Mr. Scott that he and Colonel Hay had already experimented enough to convince them that it could not be done in this way without seriously mutilating their original work. He proposed, instead, that an abridgment of the biography be reprinted exactly as it had appeared in the magazine, using type that would permit its publication in two volumes. "Please consider this matter very seriously," he urged.

Mr. Scott was unwilling to give up his own idea, and my father again explained how impossible it would be to reduce the ten volumes, containing a million and a quarter words, to three or four hundred thousand "by the scissors and blue-pencil process." He added that it would be equally impossible to write a new and strictly "personal" biography within the space of three years, let alone within three months as the publishers suggested. Such a book could only be prepared slowly, with the greatest care, and even then it would be of small historical importance compared to their more extended work. Also, John Hay would be too busy with official duties to give him any help.

Colonel Hay had been recalled from his post of Ambassador to England to become Secretary of State. My father was very proud of his brilliant career, and took good care to let him know how deeply he admired and trusted him.

I suppose I need hardly tell you how much I am gratified at your success abroad, and your deserved promotion at home, [he wrote]. It is more than probable that you will have heavy duties and responsibilities laid upon you; but I know you possess both the ability and the courage to meet them.

27

FORGERIES AND MISQUOTATIONS

O NE BOOK THAT MY FATHER THOUGHT
ought to be written would bear upon misleading and
erroneous statements about President Lincoln, and
spurious quotations attributed to him. Mere anecdotes my
father dismissed lightly with the remark that if the President had actually told them all he would have had time
for little else. He knew that he, personally, had heard him
tell comparatively few of them, and Mr. Lincoln himself
claimed responsibility for only about one-sixth, saying
modestly that he was "only a retail dealer."

My father was more critical of stories about the President. One day he scribbled on a scrap of paper the following list of those he deemed questionable, evidently
intending to add others as they occurred to him.

Scotch cap.	Admiral Porter.
Ind. letter.	Taylor letter.
Howard Proc.	Spiritualism.
Corporations.	Pere Chiriqui
Prohibition	Amos Babcock
Whiskey "tipple."	Watterson
Morse footnote.	"You can fool all of the peo-
Anna Ella Carroll.	ple some of the time."

It begins with the hardy perennial that tells how Lincoln "sneaked into Washington disguised in a long cloak and Scotch cap," and ends with the favorite alleged quotation about fooling all of the people. Some of these stories have died of old age, others return as regularly as the seasons. Many were unimportant. Others, my father thought it his duty to combat. He wished, however, to choose his own time for doing so. In 1887, when Mr. Gilder asked him to put in writing some verbal criticisms he had heard my father make, he replied:

"In good time I shall go at these falsifications of history one or all as the case may be; but as every such exposure subjects me to a shower of newspaper abuse and vilification, I must watch my chance and have my weapons within reach. . . . So, let us study our Longfellow and 'learn to labor and to wait.' "

He was especially annoyed by misinterpretations of the President's own words, and by actual forgeries, of which there were several. One of the former he called the "Admiral Porter distortion." This referred to the informal meeting at City Point in March 1865, on the *River Queen*, the steamer that brought the President down from Washington when he discussed with Generals Grant and Sherman and Admiral Porter, the reconstruction of state governments in the conquered states. Accounts of the meeting as reported by General Sherman and Admiral Porter indicate that the President spoke with a freedom that, to quote from *Abraham Lincoln: A History*, does "not seem compatible with the very guarded language of Mr Lincoln elsewhere used or recorded of him."

My father thought it fair to presume that the enthusiasm of these officers colored their recollection of the President's words, though he did not doubt that Mr. Lincoln expressed his willingness to be liberal to the point of prudence, and that he gave them to understand he would not be sorry to learn that Jefferson Davis and other rebel leaders had escaped from the country.

The allegation that Mr. Lincoln was a hard drinker was destined for a long life. Time and again my father was called upon to verify or deny picturesque tales, such as the one that tells how Mr. Lincoln took the pledge when a tall awkward stripling, and how many years later, meeting old "Uncle John Berry" who had persuaded him to this step he said to him:

I owe more to you than to almost anyone else of whom I can think, for if I had not signed the pledge with you in the days of youthful temptation I might have gone the way that the majority of my old comrades have gone, which ends in a drunkard's life and a drunkard's grave.

The favorite "Lincoln quotation" on the subject of drink, however, is one that anti-prohibitionists have used many times.

Prohibition will work great injury to the cause of temperance. It is a species of intemperance within itself, for it goes beyond the bounds of reason in that it attempts to control men's appetite by legislation, and in making crimes out of things that are not crimes. A prohibition law strikes a blow at the very principles on which our government was founded. I have always been found laboring to protect the weaker classes from the stronger, and I never can give my consent to such a law as you propose to enact. Until my tongue shall be silenced in death I will continue to fight for the rights of man.

Answering an inquiry from Mr. William E. Weld of Boston, my father wrote in February 1889:

In the very careful collection of Lincoln's state papers, letters, reported speeches and conversational remarks which we have been years in making, and which we believe is substantially complete, there is nowhere as far as I know, any expression whatever on the subject of prohibition. I am satisfied that the pretended quotation of which you enclose a printed copy is spurious.

Yet it was being circulated as late as 1914!

Among my father's papers are penciled notes, written in the broad lines and odd handwriting he used late in life when trying to substitute touch for sight. They give his explanation of how this and similar false statements probably came into being. He laid it to Lincoln's increasing fame as shown in the growing popularity of his birthday, when every leading newspaper prints pages of eulogies and poems and anecdotes.

It is not surprising that in this mass of discussion and comment there has been forming and growing an element of legend, fiction and downright untruth, which, if allowed to continue without protest and exposure, would gradually harden into tradition, if not into final acceptance as true history, and at least pass into the class of controverted points which later biographers and historians might admit or reject purely upon personal idiosyncrasy or prejudice. Mr Lincoln's authorized biographers therefore feel it to be a duty to the public and to true history, to notice and point out some of the assertions which they know to be incorrect, but which during the past few years have been repeated to such an extent that ordinary readers may begin to regard them as having some foundation in fact.

Such things usually begin in a story or rumor, or reminiscence, or a suggestion or possibility, and in such shape and wording that they may serve equally well either as a plausible fact or a stupendous hoax. In their earlier shape they generally carry their apocryphal earmarks in plain sight. The short paragrapher of some other journal scissors them from their explanatory connection and sets them afloat to drift on the illimitable ocean of newspaper clippings, where they dance like a cork on the billows, and where, after a lapse of time they can neither be traced, directed, suppressed nor verified.

Here, for instance, is a sample of an outright fabrication. A respectable clergyman recently informed us that some correspondent had written the following to one of the Chicago dailies:

"Lincoln was not what might be called a heavy drinker, but he could usually hold his own with all he chanced to meet in private life. His favorite tipple was whiskey. I have seen him down four fingers of the red liquor that would have made a Texan shudder, without so much as the flutter of an eyelash. I have seen President Lincoln swallow drink after drink, and have watched him with intense interest to mark the effect it would have on him, but it was like so much water...."

Of course this is simply a bold reckless lie, as we so replied to the clergyman who made the inquiry. It is cited here not as being either a plausible or dangerous lie, but to call the attention of thinking people to the fact that misrepresentations of Mr Lincoln are occasionally found in the newspapers, ranging all the way from such reckless extremes set afloat by unknown scribblers, to insinuating exaggerations and innuendos from prominent writers and orators who desire merely to round up a period in picturesque diction; or by former acquaintances of the President who strive by printing a startling "reminiscence" to lift themselves into momentary attention from the reading public.

When my father was questioned by the Reverend Mr. Melner of the Armour Mission of Chicago about "Lincoln's drinking habits," he answered on July 11, 1894:

In reply to your inquiry whether Mr Lincoln was "in the habit of drinking whiskey", I answer that during all the nearly five years of my service as his private secretary

I never saw him take a drink of whiskey, and never knew or heard of his taking one. The story of his being "in the habit of drinking whiskey, and somewhat accomplished in that line", is a pure fabrication.

Allow me also to refer you to Mr Lincoln's Address before the Springfield Washingtonian Society, Feb. 22, 1842, printed in full on pp. 57-64 in Vol. I of our *Abraham Lincoln: Complete Works.*

In April 1900, he wrote to James Grant Wilson:

You can truthfully say that Mr Lincoln was absolutely truthful in thought, word and inference; that he never smoked or was profane; and generally that he never drank. The only qualification that could possibly be made on this last point is that he did sometimes at his own dinner-table, and especially at state dinners, sip a little wine; but even that in a merely perfunctory way, as complying with a social custom and not as doing it from any desire or initiative or habit of his own.

More than once I have heard him say that Mr. Lincoln cared nothing for the pleasures of the table; that he ate sparingly, and scarcely seemed to know what he ate. One of the frequently quoted stories tells of Lincoln's answer to a caller, who apologized for troubling him at mealtime: "Oh, that is all right, when Mrs Lincoln is away, I just browse around."

For a time persistent efforts were made to define Mr. Lincoln's attitude on woman suffrage, his support being desired for propaganda equally by opposing parties. On this subject my father wrote:

I know of no allusion or reference by Mr Lincoln to the question or female suffrage except that made in the card printed in the *Sangamo Journal* under the date of June 13, 1836 (which is reprinted in *Abraham Lincoln: Complete*

Works, Vol. I, p. 7) in which he says "I go for all sharing the privileges of the government who assist in bearing its burdens. Consequently I go for admitting all whites to the right of suffrage who pay taxes or bear arms—by no means excluding females."

A statement made by the Spiritualists, who claimed Lincoln as their own, to the effect that he issued the Emancipation Proclamation on the advice of spirits received through the mediums he often consulted at the White House, seemed to my father and John Hay almost too fantastic to deserve serious notice. So, too, did the charge mentioned in the following letter:

Washington, D. C. Dec. 3, 1891.—My dear Sir: I have not heretofore answered your letter of Oct. 30, because I wished first to consult my colleague Colonel Hay who has been absent from the city until within a few days.

To your first question, whether in our studies on the life of Lincoln, we came upon the charge that "the assasination of President Lincoln was the work of the Jesuits", we answer that we have read such a charge in a lengthy newspaper publication.

To your second question, *viz*, "If you did come across it, did the accusation seem to you to be entirely groundless?" We answer—Yes. It seemed to us so entirely groundless as not to merit attention on our part.

Yours truly,

John G. Nicolay

Benedict Guldner
St Francis Xavier College, New York.

"The Dick Taylor story" had to do with a claim made by Colonel Edmond D. Taylor that he had originated the idea of the greenback, offering in proof a letter alleged to have been written by the President in 1864. The letter stated, in very un-Lincolnesque language, that, being in great perplexity, "I said in my extremity 'I will send for Colonel Taylor. He will know what to do.'" Taylor answered the summons and gave his advice, which Secretary Chase thought extremely hazardous to follow. "But we finally accomplished it," continued the alleged quotation, "and gave to the people of the Republic the greatest blessing they ever had—their own paper to pay their own debts. It is due to you, the father of the present greenback, that the public should know it."

This, my father pronounced "an unblushing forgery." He had no better opinion of another version of the same canard, about which Mr. Paul Selby made inquiries in February 1895. According to this story, the corroborating letter had been received through a spiritualist medium after the President's death.

Not quite so pretentious, although it made great claims, was the assertion of a certain Colonel Amos Babcock that it was really he who put down the rebellion. My father said of this story that it looked to him "like the international perpetration of a huge joke."

He also disbelieved that the President, when discussing Pickett's charge at Gettysburg, ever said, "I am proud to be the countryman of the man who made that charge!" Nor did he think genuine a long letter alleged to have been written by Mr. Lincoln from Springfield on December 11, 1860, to the Hon. Thomas Ewing, in which occurs the sentence: "A strong effort should be made to persuade fanatical misguided persons from celebrating the anniversary of the execution of that worst of all murderers, John Brown."

Answering Mr. Gilder's question about another alleged quotation that has had a very long life, appearing at intervals even to this day, he wrote:

In reference to the "prophecy" attributed to Lincoln which was sent the rounds of the newspapers in the late campaign, I have already answered several correspondents as follows:

"I am as confident as I can be without actual examination that the paragraph quoted by you is not in any of President Lincoln's messages nor in any other writing of his of which I have knowledge."

It is easy, however, to see why this was and still is highly prized in certain quarters, for it reads:

Yes, we may all congratulate ourselves that the cruel war is nearing a close. It has cost a vast amount of treasure and blood. The blood of the flower of American youth has been freely offered upon our country's altar that the nation might live. It has indeed been a trying hour for the Republic, but I see in the near future a crisis arriving that unnerves me and causes me to tremble for the safety of my country. As the result of the war, corporations have been enthroned, an era of corruption in high places will follow, and the money power of the country will endeavor to prolong its reign by working upon the prejudices of the people until all wealth is aggregated in a few hands and the Republic destroyed. I feel at this moment more anxiety for the safety of my country than ever before, even in the midst of war. God grant my suspicions may prove groundless.

In September 1894, my father emphatically assured Perry S. Heath that Mr. Lincoln

Never said or wrote anything that by the utmost license could be distorted to resemble it. Any one who critically scans the language will at once discover intrinsic evidence of its falsity in that the phrases employed bear the stamp of having been invented or of having come into popular use fifteen or twenty years after Lincoln's death. Its origin seems to date back to 1888, as it first obtained circulation in a little pamphlet printed by an agitator in Iowa, copyrighted on May 10th of that year. It appears there, as now, without explanation or credit. My attention was first called to it in 1890, and though at the time I made an effort to trace it to its source I could obtain no respectable or responsible clue. Since then my colleague Colonel Hay and I have written dozens of letters, in answer to private inquiries, denouncing the forgery. It deserves exposure and reprobation from all fair-minded journals.

This alleged quotation brought about an exchange of letters between my father and the sponsor of the pamphlet, George C. Hackstaff of the Caldwell Remedy Co. whose Chicago store sold "The highest grade of scientific medicine." Mr. Hackstaff questioned my father's right to pronounce the alleged quotation a forgery and demanded proof, while Mr. Lincoln's biographer maintained that when a man prints an alleged quotation he assumes responsibility for it, and that therefore the obligation to present proof rested with Mr. Hackstaff.

One amazing lie, not to be overlooked, since it found lodgment in so respectable a publication as the *Encyclopaedia Britannica*, concerned, not Mr. Lincoln himself, but an eccentric and not altogether moral Swedish author, born in Stockholm in 1793, who, according to this statement, spent part of his varied career as novelist, forger, and possible murderer under an assumed name in the United States, and during that time served as private secretary to President Lincoln. My father first read this story in a clipping cut from the Chicago *Inter-Ocean*. He then found it also in the *Encyclopaedia Britannica* under the heading "Almquist, C. J. Ludwig," and wrote this emphatic denial, which was given to the press:

I have examined the *Encyclopaedia Britannica* in the Library of Congress here and find the statement printed therein as alleged. I cannot imagine how the editors of that standard work could have been imposed upon by such a story. President Lincoln never had such a secretary, and no person ever stood in any relation to him, who, by the wildest stretch of imagination could be held to answer such a description. Upon inspection you will see that the allegation substantially confutes itself. "Almquist" is said to have been born in 1793, and was therefore when Lincoln became President already burdened with sixty-eight years. The assertion that Mr Lincoln employed an alien, a fugitive, a criminal and almost a septuagenarian as a secretary in war times is not only utterly untrue, but in the light of the President's characteristics and of American customs and habits, palpably untrue.

A statement printed in the *Philadelphia Times* by its editor, A. K. McClure, when former Vice President Hamlin died in 1891, attracted wide attention. According to this item, Hamlin's name had been withdrawn as vice-presidential candidate in the Republican Convention of 1864, and the name of Andrew Johnson substituted at the express request of President Lincoln. Colonel McClure was an ardent admirer of the President, and, as he grew older, liked to think he had been instrumental in changing the course of history, even though events showed the change to have been a mistake. He had been a member of the nominating convention, and, according to this story, was summoned to Washington by President Lincoln, who told him of his desire. "Whereupon," wrote Colonel McClure, "I returned to Baltimore to work and vote for Johnson, although against all my personal predilections to do so."

My father felt that even had this been true, the moment of Mr. Hamlin's death was a cruelly inopportune time to make it public; and, since he possessed proof that it was not true, he "could not stand by in silence and see Hamlin's fame humiliated and Lincoln's character traduced."

His proof was in Lincoln's own handwriting, indorsed upon the letter my father had sent to John Hay from Baltimore forwarding a question asked by B. C. Cook, chairman of the Illinois delegation. Mr. Cook wished to know whether Lincoln's friend Leonard Swett was "all right" in urging Joseph Holt for vice president, or whether the President did not wish to interfere in the choice of a vice president, even to the extent of giving a confidential hint.

My father's letter was shown to the President, who wrote across it:

Swett is unquestionably all right. Mr. Holt is a good man, but I had not heard or thought of him for V. P. Wish not to interfere about V. P. Cannot interfere about platform. Convention must judge for itself.

This exactly bore out my father's memory of a conversation he had with the President just before starting for Baltimore, in which Mr. Lincoln told him that all the candidates for vice president were his friends, and that he did not wish to interfere in any way with the Convention's choice. At the same time however, he had given him to understand that, personally, he would be glad to see the old ticket of Lincoln and Hamlin renominated.

On reading Colonel McClure's editorial in the *Philadelphia Times* in 1891, my father at once telegraphed Mrs. Hamlin a message of condolence on the death of her husband, and a denial of Colonel McClure's statement. Another editorial speedily appeared in the *Philadelphia Times* questioning my father's right to an opinion, on the ground that Mr. Lincoln had never given him his confidence, regarding him merely in the light of an upper servant.

The personal nature of this attack troubled him little. He had been a newspaperman too long, he said, to be disturbed by "journalistic mosquito-bites"; but the accusation that Mr. Lincoln indulged in double-dealing did disturb him. He could not believe that Mr. Lincoln could have sent him such a message and, on the same day, have called Colonel McClure to Washington and instructed him to work for Mr. Hamlin's defeat. "Open Letters" followed on both sides, and the entire correspondence, including Colonel McClure's original statement and my father's telegram to Mrs. Hamlin, was reprinted in leading newspapers.

My father had been entirely courteous, saying at the outset "I concede to Colonel McClure perfect honesty of conviction and sincerity of assertion. I simply believe that his memory is at fault. It is now twenty-seven years since these events transpired, and my historical investigations have shown me that personal memory for these long periods is not to be relied on without some sort of contemporary record proof."

Charles Hamlin, the Vice President's son, sent him a warm letter of thanks for what he had done. That would have ended the matter had not Colonel McClure chosen a year later to print in his book *Abraham Lincoln and Men of War Time* all the arguments favorable to him, while paying little heed to the others. Since Mr. McClure had, as my father said, "appealed from the hot air of ephemeral journalism to the cooler air of history," he felt he had the right to be heard again and impartially printed the evidence on both sides. He had written to O. M. Hatch: "Any one who wants to believe McClure's preposterous assertion rather than Lincoln's written word will of course do so, even if Lincoln were to rise from the dead. I maintain that Lincoln did not write a falsehood, McClure insists that he did. That is the controversy in a nutshell."

John Hay's comment was that my father ought to be well satisfied with the result. Then he added, rather contemptuously, "The whole thing is growing very ridiculous. Every dead-beat politican in the country is coming forward to protest that he was the depository of Lincoln's inmost secrets and the engineer of his campaign. And every one of them whom we have not mentioned is thirsting for our gore."

A paragraph in the original draft of a letter which my father wrote Charles Hamlin, but crossed out and did not send, is interesting, for it shows the combination of forces he thought responsible for Johnson's unexpected nomination.

The three things that in my judgment coöperated to bring about a different result, were, first, the Sumner movement among the New England delegates which you speak of; second, the movement in the New York delegation to prevent the nomination of Dickinson and thereby secure the retention of Seward in the Cabinet; and last, the sudden sympathy excited in the Convention at the moment by a powerful appeal from Horace Maynard depicting the trials and sufferings which East Tennessee had undergone in behalf of the Union cause. I believe when the Convention met that morning everybody felt quite sure that your father would be nominated.

28

OTHER LITERARY ACTIVITIES

M Y FATHER RESIGNED HIS OFFICE OF
Marshal of the Supreme Court in December 1887.
Thereafter he lived on quietly in the house on Capitol
Hill, making little change in the daily routine established
during the fifteen years of his marshalship. The main
difference was that it was not necessary to go so often to
the Capitol, and that he was "no longer under the strain of
trying to please all nine of the judges at once." His personal relations remained pleasant with all of them.

From October till June or July he worked among his
papers whenever strength permitted, and rested when
necessary to gain strength for more work. The remainder
of the year he spent in leisurely travel, or in still more
leisurely vacations.

His writing continued to be in the realm of history—
most of it, but not all, in the Lincoln period. His condensation of the ten-volume biography into a one-volume Life
of Lincoln was practically completed at the time he died
and was published in the following year, 1902. I think the
happening in which he took greatest pleasure, as proof of
the standing he had attained as an historian, was the invitation that came to him to write four chapters on the

American Civil War for the monumental *Cambridge Modern History*. Its editor, Lord Acton, sent him a two-page letter asking him to do this "since you are the highest authority on the War."

"I wrote him that I would deem it an honor to assist," he told John Hay. But as he did not believe Lord Acton had correctly grasped the scope and import of the subject, he added, "I shall therefore go on and fill his order according to my best judgment." Lord Acton was glad to accept my father's judgment, and he wrote the chapters entitled, respectively, *Campaigns in Virginia, War in the West, Defense of Richmond,* and *Abolition of Slavery.*

He was also asked to write the article on Lincoln for the ninth edition of the *Encyclopaedia Britannica*. His satisfaction in this request and his belief in the *Encyclopaedia* as a standard book of reference must have been considerably lessened when he discovered in the same edition the article on "Almquist." This was altered after he made his protest.

My father's familiarity with the White House and its history inspired him to write about some of the earlier scenes there enacted in *The White House from John Adams to James Madison* and *From James Madison to Abraham Lincoln.* He made notes, also, for articles on later times in the White House, some of them relating especially to the Lincoln administration.

He wrote a series of articles about pre-Revolutionary battles for the *Chautauquan* and began collecting material for a *Dictionary of American Politics.* He did not live to carry out this project, but it was done later by others who saw the same need.

While living in France, he wrote several chapters of what promised to be an interesting book on Parisian newspapers and editorial customs.

One historical scheme, which advanced no farther than a brief penciled outline, envisaged a series of little paper-covered booklets, about one hundred pages long, to be sold for twenty-five cents each. The series was to be called *Brief Biographies of Famous Men of the New World*. Beginning with *Columbus*, it was to be followed by *Men of the Mayflower, La Salle, Heroes of Bunker Hill, Washington, Lafayette, Franklin, Jefferson, Fulton, Webster, Jackson, Clay*, and so on down to men of his own day. Still another project was for a *Young Persons' History of the United States*, in six sections to be called *Early Navigators to America, Early Spanish Adventurers and Conquerors, Early Explorers of the United States and First Settlers, The American Colonies, The American Revolution*, and *The War of Independence*.

Jefferson and Franklin, of all the Revolutionary personalities, interested my father most, not only for their great achievements in American history, but because, like himself, they were curious about a variety of things. Although they lived in an age when statemanship was considered too serious a calling to allow straying from its own dignified path, they had courage to pursue other paths for their own pleasure. With Franklin, my father felt the bond of fellow-craftsmanship in the printing trade. With Jefferson, who passionately loved his mountaintop, he shared a deep feeling for nature.

His article on Monticello, printed in *The Century* about ten years after it was written, brought to light another of my father's characteristics—an unwillingness to be too much in the public view. At that time the Lincoln biography was running in the magazine. He suggested to Mr. Gilder that the Jefferson article had better be postponed, or at least printed anonymously, for two reasons:

My first is the danger that the public will think one set
of writers is absorbing too much space; the other, that as
we seem to have a very sure hold on the attention of the
reading public in the Lincoln chapters, it is unwise to give
any room for supposing that that special subject leaves the
authors time to stray into other historical fields. The interest
of the reader would flag quite as quickly as the effort of
the author.

Although forty years of his life were spent in historical research and writing, he continued to regard himself,
until well into middle life, as first of all a newspaperman.
He looked upon the American daily newspaper, with all
its faults, as "the greatest literary achievement of the
New World":

We cannot have everything [he wrote]. We cannot have
the Great American Novel, Drama, and Epic, and also have
the Great American Newspaper. You remember that an
American prophet once said the time would come when the
lion and the lamb would lie down together—"but," he added
in lucid explanation, "the lamb will be inside the lion"....
It is the newspaper which absorbs and devours the literary
energy of the nation.

Already, he said, its mere bulk "would drive us out of
our houses if we did not constantly fight it by fire."
Discussing a newspaper's function and the equipment an
editor needs, he asked:

After all, does the journalist absolutely need a high
education? Does not the weight of facts hamper him—the
contradiction of authorities bewilder him?...For him is
neither the thinker's closet nor the chemist's laboratory.
The journalist is a *popular teacher* whose true mission is to
disseminate leading ideas, clear principles, prominent facts.
To do this successfully strength is better than subtlety ...

wit worth a thousand times more than profundity. The
writer of books is like a rifleman; he fires at long range
with steady aim; the journalist resembles the sportsman
who shoots his bird on the wing. The former bags the
heaviest game, but the latter counts the most scalps.

Throughout life he continued to look upon the editor
of a "live" county newspaper as the most independent and
useful man in America. In 1881, when a friend asked his
help and "influence" in securing a government appointment in Washington, my father wrote him a letter of advice. It was never sent—a more conventional answer being
substituted—but it expressed his honest conviction:

I have yours of the 30th ult. I regret that I cannot en-
courage you about its inquiries, but in all frankness I cannot. I have no vacancies under me; my two deputies have
grown up in the Court and are likely to remain in it all
their lives. The Clerk of the Court of Claims is a young man,
and I suppose will remain there all his life. A man of your
tastes with a family to support would be miserable here in
any petty place with a petty salary. The mere necessaries
of life are expensive here, the comforts and special demands
eat into a man's resources in a way that is a riddle capable
of stumping the Sphinx if you gave him all the guesses. . . .
With your knowledge of the world, of politics, and experience of newspaper work, why don't you look about you,
choose a good location for a *County paper* and build up
a permanent independent business, in a village where living
is cheap, where you can acquire land enough to make a comfortable roomy country home, and where you can build up
local influence and consideration, instead of coming to this
or any other city to be one smart fellow among ten thousand
other smart fellows, caged up in an 18 x 35 brick box,
climbing up and down stairs like Sisyphus, breathing coal-
gas by day and sewer-gas by night? Why toil to pay
monthly rent bills . . . and pass up fares for the bobtail

horse-car proprietor, when you might swing your hammock under your own tree and milk a real cow instead of a pump? ... There is more health, morality, prosperity, enjoyment, true comfort of life, and a better field of usefulness and opportunity for easy distinction in any flourishing country village in America having three to five thousand inhabitants than is possible in any great city.

Consider my suggestion of a County paper.

His love of music led my father to make a few attempts at composition, and the same sensitivity to the cadences of sound made it inevitable that he should take an early interest in poetry. Almost from the time of his entrance into the *Free Press* office he exercised his talents upon the Carriers' Addresses that were sent out to subscribers at the beginning of each New Year. It was only a step to attempts at original verse, or at translations of old German poems that had been favorites in his mother's home. As he worked up through the various grades in the printing office, bits of prose or rhyme from his pen appeared more and more often in the paper, signed by some modest *nom de plume* like "Truth" or "Silva." He continued to write verse all his life, and one of his poems gained a place in an American Anthology (Putnam's *Lyrics of Loyalty*) as early as 1864. But he was never oppressed by the idea that he was an accomplished poet. I imagine he regarded his ability in this direction much as most women regard crocheting—not as work, but as a pleasant diversion.

His feeling for historical writing seems to have developed early, possibly during that period of Bible reading "for relaxation," when his favorites were the tales about the Maccabees, whose deeds of loyalty and heroism were told with measured restraint by writers who never piled up adjectives to gain their points.

The first book he planned to write was an *Early History*

of Illinois. Though never written, it remained long in his mind. In Pittsfield he made careful extracts from library books and in Springfield copied maps from the state records. In Paris, he made his own translations from early manuscripts.

Two tendencies developed in his writing: one, an insistence on accuracy to the last detail; the other, a dramatic conception of history as a mighty stream, sweeping forward through the centuries. His care and thoroughness, partly inborn, and partly learned from his experience with the Lincoln papers, is illustrated in a letter he wrote to Mrs. James A. Garfield, after her husband's tragic death.

My dear Madam.—Seeing in the newspapers a few days ago a letter from yourself to Col. Rockwell, relating to the preservation and care of President Garfield's speeches, letters and papers, emboldens me to offer a few suggestions which are prompted by my own experience in the care and handling of the papers of President Lincoln.

My urgent advice to you is, not only that your husband's papers should be carefully preserved, but that you should, at an early period, institute some methodical and systematic examination and arrangement. In his long and varied public career a great accumulation of original manuscripts, letters, and other material for biography and history must have taken place. Only those who have undertaken similar labors have the remotest conception how painfully tedious and difficult it is to examine and prepare such material for the biographer's or historian's use. Hurry in such a task is utterly impossible, and one mind must practically accomplish the greater part if not the whole, in order that unity of plan may be preserved. Every document, leaf and scrap must be deliberately scrutinized to ascertain its date, relation and historical value; and a convenient method of handling and reference must be devised. Not only this, but concurrently, newspapers and public documents must be searched, persons must be written to to find explanations and supply omissions.

For greatest success and most perfect gleaning the present and contemporary period is in my judgment the most favorable. Much will be lost by delay, while everything the mere lapse of time may disclose, can be all the more readily utilized if such preparation is well advanced. All this does not touch the matter of writing the General's biography. You can choose your own time for that. I speak merely of the preliminary work of preserving, collecting and arranging the biographical and historical material.

My high admiration of your husband's character and career, and my appreciation of the value of his words and acts as a historical legacy to his country, lead me to urge upon you an early beginning of the work I have mentioned above. I have no personal ends to subserve, and no one to recommend to you for the task. You are yourself best competent to select someone of the General's confidential friends who is intelligent, discriminating and thoroughly loyal to your husband's memory. In addition he ought to be familiar with his personal history, his temper, and habits of thought, his methods of labor and study, and if possible, familiar with the papers and materials themselves. In such a task personal knowledge is of infinitely more value that mere literary ability or experience.

Excuse the freedom with which I have written. In closing I beg to assure you of my own and Mrs Nicolay's profound sorrow and sympathy in your great loss.

The record of discovery and colonization of the New World greatly interested my father: Spaniards swashbuckling through Florida and Mexico and farther south; the British claiming practically all the territory on the Atlantic Coast between Florida and Canada; the French advancing from Newfoundland's fishing banks up the St. Lawrence to the Great Lakes, and from the Great Lakes down the Mississippi to the warm Gulf of Mexico, "from where it never thaws to where it never freezes."

Details of the flowing panorama were as impressive to him as was the grand sweep. Of Lincoln's first inauguration, he wrote:

Then there intervenes the half-military pageant of an inauguration, and citizen Buchanan, relieved as if from the terrors of a waking nightmare, escorts President Lincoln to the Executive Mansion, gives him a parting grasp of the hand, and wishes him a successful administration; heartfelt, no doubt, but across what an abyss of incredulity!

A project, never carried out, which evidently had its origin in his studies for the Illinois history, envisaged a romance based on the Mormon trek westward. Like the Illinois history, it remained long in his mind. From the preface, which he did write, we see that to him this also was a detail of the stream of history:

It has been a peculiarity of all civilizations of which History has preserved the record, that in the lapse of time— perhaps in the decay of governments ... there has been accumulated a class of every people who, either by the weight of their own sins, or by the oppression of the collective sins of their fellow men, have sunk down into a pit of degradation and misery from which it has been beyond their strength to lift themselves while remaining in contact with their more favored neighbors. They lived, or rather died—for their life was but one long death—in filth, ignorance, crime and pain— until some man, bearing the commission of Divine Providence, called them to follow him, and, recognizing the authority, they left the graves of their "fathers", went out into a foreign land, and on a new soil—with a new government, religion, system, or philosophy—these dwarfed and stunted and broken seedlings of humanity took new root—began a new growth—and flourished and bore the fairest fruits of civilization. Such was the exodus led by Moses—by our Puritan forefathers—and in our day in a small way, by Brigham Young. These events differ in times and places, but among them all is a remarkable parallel in the fact that the lepers and pariahs of society break the bonds of their literal, political, moral or material slavery under the call of some impulse overshadowing all thought of danger or risk, and again grow into the stature and powers of that supreme effort of the soul and body which in a rude way we denominate aspiration and self-sacrifice.

Much space writing on subjects as diverse as mailbox frauds and mountains; a considerable amount of verse; perhaps half a hundred magazine articles and stories, all of which, taken together, may be considered as little more than exercises and preparation for his serious tasks with the Lincoln material, certainly make up a goodly output for a man hampered, as my father was, by ill health and failing sight.

29

CONCLUSION

FEW MEN HAVE ENJOYED THEIR HOMES and families more thoroughly than did my father. He was too reserved to make friends easily, but to those to whom he gave his affection he did so unreservedly. He fell in love with my mother the day he first entered Pittsfield and saw her there. He formed a lifetime comradeship with John Hay soon after, when the "new boy" came to live with his uncle while preparing for college. David McWilliams, who shared with him the tiny bedroom over the printing office, and who later became a successful banker, was another with whom my father kept in touch all his life. For John Hodgen, the St. Louis physician, and Delphina, his wife, and good Mrs. Garbutt he felt a deep affection. There were others, also, throughout life, whom he cherished in varying degrees. Yet, in spite of knowing everyone in Pittsfield during his editorial days, and being on speaking terms in Washington during the Civil War with everybody of prominence north of the Mason and Dixon Line, he had few intimates.

After *Abraham Lincoln: Complete Works* was published, John Russell Young, who had been employed in the office of the Clerk of the Senate in wartime, wrote of him:

I have not seen Nicolay in years. . . . Hay I see once in an era—exchange a signal with him as ships that meet and part at sea. In the Lincoln days they were close to the President. Nicolay, a German by birth, had the close, methodical, silent German way about him. Scrupulous, polite, calm, obliging, with the gift of hearing other people talk, coming and going about the Capitol like a shadow; with the soft sad smile that seemed to come only from the eyes; prompt as lightning to take a hint or an idea; one upon whom a suggestion was never lost, and if it meant a personal service, sure of the prompt spontaneous return. He had, as I infer, great powers of application [with] the endurance so often seen with the thin frail body upon which disease seems to be doing its work. A man without excitements or emotions . . . absorbed in the President, and seeing that the Executive business was well done. Much of that work, the clerical part at least came . . . within my observation. It was the criticism of some of the old clerks, some of whom had seen service as far back as Quincy Adams, and could enact the Webster reply to Hayne as they saw it, that since Quincy Adams no Executive papers came from the White House in better shape. The credit for this must revert to Mr Nicolay, as in the honors given to Mr Lincoln I have seen none that would award him prominence as a master of clerical detail.

Few people realized the fund of kindly humor that lay just under the quiet surface, or the natural nervousness that he had disciplined into the exterior calm that so impressed people. He could thoroughly enjoy an amusing situation; more so, if it involved himself than if it embarrassed one he loved.

Both he and John Hay were free from the spell of alcohol. Once John Hay wrote him from New York:

Terrible power of drink! Last night I met ———— at the T———— door. You know him, the wittiest journalist of our time. He was covered with mud and plastering. Had been rolling in the gutter.—Was crying like a child—Said they had kicked him out of the last place he was in—Begged for twenty cents and sobbed with joy when I gave him fifty. Some night he will die in the street. You and I have kept drinking company all our lives, and yet have never felt for an instant the claws of the temptation. Let us thank God.

During my father's last years, he rarely went into society. Even when he felt fairly well otherwise, his eye trouble made it torture for him to sit in a room facing a light, even the light from a shaded lamp. He had to pay heavily for an evening at the theater or at a lecture hall. A very few dinner parties, two or three official functions, and a dozen evenings in the homes of friends, where he could choose his own seat, were all he allowed himself.

Like yourself [he wrote Robert Lincoln] I note with some apprehension the shadows of advancing years; but it seems to me that I could still look the future pretty squarely in the face if I were free from this malady which deprives me not alone of the power to work, but the enjoyable pastime of reading and writing.

We had several happy trips abroad. We did not try to see all of Europe at a glance, or even one country. We were willing to change plans quickly to take advantage of unexpected opportunities. Strongly American though he was, my father seemed to feel he was coming home when we were in Germany. In Dresden, when we lingered long over a display of medieval ironwork, the guards became suspicious and followed us, shaking each locked case to make sure we had not pilfered some precious object. In Antwerp, we climbed to the very top of the Musée Plantin to enter the attics where the printing offices had been. My father reveled in the tools of his own trade, and his interest was so great that the guard became sympathetic and unlocked the ancient fonts of type, inviting him to handle the precious bits of metal. This he did delicately, his old skill returning to fingers that had not touched type for half a century.

In other years there were less strenuous vacations. We spent most of them in New England, but we made three or four stays in Colorado, whose dramatic scenery, invigorating air, and opportunities for roughing it were tempered with ameliorations made necessary by his state of health. His favorite spot in Colorado was Crystal Park, not far from Colorado Springs. I believe it was in the summer of 1883 that my father, learning that John Hay was ill, carried him off almost by force to this paradise. They spent happy weeks together, exploring the heights as far as horseflesh and inclination permitted, and lay on sunny slopes of disintegrating granite, lazily hunting the smoky topaz crystals from which the park derived its name.

A legend grew up in Colorado that John Hay and my father "wrote the Lincoln biography in Crystal Park"—a manifest impossibility considering the length of time devoted to the task. My father did write in November 1894 that "a small part of Colonel Hay's portion of the work was written in Cleveland, Ohio, but the larger part in Washington, D.C. All of my portion was written in Washington, except a few fragments of chapters when off on summer vacations." In 1904 John Hay answered a query with these words: "It is true that Mr Nicolay and I spent several summers in Crystal Park, and while there did some work on the life of Lincoln."

They liked Crystal Park so much that they dreamed of making it their summer retreat. Colonel Hay bought several quarter sections of land there, but the plan came to nothing. The railroad journey seemed long to all of us, and Mrs. Hay could scarcely have been comfortable in that wild country. Eventually, both families established homes in the lake region of New Hampshire.

One of my father's favorite amusements when visiting a new place was to select some building site and draw plans for the kind of house he would build there if he owned the land. We found it a delightful game, and one year, quite unexpectedly, the game came true. My father agreed with John Hay that "only cats and congressmen" could stand the temperature of Washington in August. We had been kept in the city very late with proofreading and index-making, and he was very tired when at last we packed our luggage and started for the station, literally without having a definite destination in mind. We only knew that we must seek a cooler spot. Two weeks later my father wrote to Mr. Gilder from Holderness, New Hampshire:

We went to the Shenandoah Valley, where it was too hot. Then to the Isles of Shoals, where we couldn't get in. Next to Plymouth, where we didn't like it; and finally landed here on top of a hill between a trio of charming lakes, and in the midst of a complete circle of beautiful mountain scenery.

We had intended to spend a week end. Instead we stayed six weeks. Throughout the remainder of my father's life we went there practically every summer, and in time build a cottage according to one of my father's plans. A friend described its architecture as "Early dog-kennel," but it suited our needs perfectly.

In the autumn of 1900, after the *History* and the *Works* were both published, my father fulfilled a dream he had carried with him since boyhood when he had pored over the big German Bible. He had been disappointed in his hope for a "boat-ride up the Nile" with John Hay when both were abroad just after the Civil War, but finally we were able, with a minimum of luggage and a very simple schedule, to set out for Egypt. On the ship in which we sailed from New York were Mr. S. S. McClure, editor of *McClure's Magazine*, and his family, also bound for a winter in Egypt. In Cairo we were all at the same hotel together, and when the McClures hired a dahabeah to take them to the First Cataract, we were invited to join them. Thus my father was able to make the trip in the most restful and enjoyable manner possible. The dahabeah was the most luxurious on the Nile that winter—and the slowest. Indeed, it was the only one left that relied entirely on sails for motive power. It took two months to cover five hundred miles. As we sailed between Old Testament scenes on the riverbank or visited the wonders of temples and tombs, we dropped completely out of the present, while centuries long ago became real and vital to us.

I do not know which of these experiences appealed most to my father. Perhaps none of them satisfied him more fully than our visit to the Pyramids, made a few days before we started up the river. He was able to climb Cheops, despite a lameness he had developed. From its top we could look down on the wounded Sphinx and over endless miles of undulating sand. My father's eyes shone as he turned to me and said that that moment, when we seemed to be looking back over a thousand years of history, repaid him for all the weariness of a journey half around the world.

The Egyptian holiday was the last really happy time he knew. He contracted a cold in Genoa and reached home sadly out of health. The cold passed, but he grew less well, losing strength and tormented by increasing pain until his death on September 26, 1901. Four months after his return, he had written to Colonel Hay:

I am very little better than when I saw you, and the outcome is very uncertain, judging from all I can make of it, and all the Doctor's explanations.... Medicine is a farce, or nearly so ... and so the days go by.... Meanwhile every day leaves me a large over-balance of pain.

As far as possible the household routine went on as before, normally and even cheerfully. On days when my father felt a little better, he tried to work on the closing pages of his one-volume abridgment of the biography.

On September 6th, President McKinley was shot while he was making a speech in Buffalo. My father was still well enough to ask for the details. He inquired about the location of the wound, and when he was told said quickly, "Then there is no hope." His memories of Civil War fatalities seemed to make him sure of this. The President died on the 14th. Theodore Roosevelt succeeded him and asked John Hay to continue as Secretary of State.

Shortly after this, Colonel Hay came to see my father, who had grown much weaker. I told Colonel Hay I had not thought it best to let my father know of the President's death. Colonel Hay's hand flew to the band of crape he wore on his arm. "I must take this off before I go up to him!" he exclaimed and would have torn it from his sleeve. I had to tell him that my father would not see it— that he was already more in the other world than in this. He mounted the stairs slowly. I stayed below. He came down more slowly still, his face stricken with grief. He never saw his old friend again, for, before my father died, Colonel Hay had left town, and it was impossible for him to return in time for the funeral.

Mr. Gilder and David McWilliams, who were both in Washington, stepped into the place Colonel Hay would otherwise have taken and did all the kind things people do for those in sorrow.

At the funeral, there were flowers from the White House, from the Century Company, and from many others. Expressions of sympathy came to me from friends in all walks of life. I was amazed at the number of young people who remembered with gratitude his kindliness and understanding. The next day a letter came from John Hay:

I shall not try to comfort you by any conventional words. ... But after a while you will take consolation in reflecting what an inheritance of pleasant memories is yours. You have never seen a man purer in heart and in life, of higher principles and nobler thoughts than your father.

In his philosophy of life, as in his conception of history, my father followed two lines of thought. One, almost cynically practical, was always tempered by the other, which was quick to recognize forces unseen by the eye and only dimly recognized by the ear as the voice of conscience. On the practical side he wrote:

Beware of the politician who promises that if elected he will make the sun rise at noonday.

Beware still more of the politician who declares that the world can be conquered by an inkstand.

Commenting on the power of the pen, he reminded us that

Bulwer's assertion that the pen is mightier than the sword must be read with the qualification placed before the famous sentence, which is *"In the hands of the truly great."*

Yet, he said again:

America, where the pen finds the readiest recognition, is most cowardly of all in the utterance of sentiment.

In America it is the rule to shun abstractions. We do only

the momentary, the needful—that which pays. The best service the pen can do us is to receipt a bill.

To do unto others is beautiful in theory, but impractical in universal application, and can only be approximated.

Every increase of personal relations increases the difficulty of fulfilling Christ's law of personal duty.

In our dealings with semi-civilized nations we are as yet compelled to invoke the Mosaic law as our standard of reason and punishment; but we must not forget that if we insist upon its rigors for the savage, we cannot claim the charity and compassion of the Golden Rule for ourselves.

Discussing "greatness among men," he wrote:

We can no more compare Napoleon with Newton than we can compare the mountains with the sea. Even when we descend to classes, and compare soldiers with soldiers and orators with orators, the infinite modifications of times and circumstances upon the gifts and labors of men change the proportions of their works. Each historical character stands, as it were, by himself.... True greatness does not consist in special or technical acquirements,—not even in their wider application. A warrior, a statesman, an artist, an orator, a poet, may be great, but after all, *merely as such*. Their greatness is limited to their specialty. To be truly great, the man in his specialty must also be great in those universal qualities of manhood, honesty, fidelity, unselfishness, benevolence, patriotism, philanthropy.

It was his belief that Lincoln measured up in every requirement to this highest standard.

It is an interesting point in the career of Abraham Lincoln [he wrote] that his sudden elevation to the presidency had no deteriorating effect upon his personal qualities; that his mental equipoise remained undisturbed, his moral sensitiveness unblunted, his simplicity of manner unchanged, his strong individuality untouched. That on the contrary his new responsibilities served to clear his vision, steady his judgement, confirm his courage, and broaden and deepen his humanity.

He held that no man should be judged by a single act, good or bad:

The career of a man is not fixed by the inspiration of a single moment—the strained exertion of a single hour—the effort of a single day. . . . Only those limited by physical or mental incapacity are debarred from building up a record for some virtue or excellence.

He held to an optimistic belief that, despite stupidity and sin and many backslidings, mankind was slowly growing better—but that the mills of God grind very slowly, Omnipotence having all eternity to work in. Mortals were in too much of a hurry.

Did you ever see a crowbar? [he asked]. It is a long iron rod, strong enough to bear tons and tons of weight, yet it is shaped and beveled to a thin edge so as to enter a crevice that would not more than give space to a darning needle. Now you must first slip in the thin edge of your reformatory crowbar before you can begin to lift.

I believe the sum of good outmeasures the sum of evil. I believe that in life there is more pleasure than pain, more happiness than sorrow. In man more truth than falsehood, more courage than cowardice; in woman more constancy than deceit, more love than hate—yes, a thousand times more. Perhaps you will call this German sentimentalism. If so, I again confess my belief that all that is best in man, and most precious in woman, and strongest in nations—is sentiment.

Recognizing the audacity of human beings who "appropriate bits of divinity out of which to build their human records . . . taking God's stones to build their rude cairns," he also recognized the sublimity of it; saying it was only to be excused by their inner conviction that every man has in him elements of the divine, "and that in combining these lies humanity's only hope for a more glorious and better future."

Like Mr. Lincoln, he never joined any church; but, again like him, he carried in his heart and practiced in his daily life an undeviating code of uprightness and good citizenship. He believed that, while observing a strict moral rule of life, it was man's privilege to get all possible enjoyment out of his contact with this beautiful world; that one ought to accept physical handicaps graciously, adjust oneself to them, and carry on to the best of one's ability. Work, he said, was one of life's greatest blessings.

My father was called upon to play many parts in the course of nearly seventy years, and he observed many sharp contrasts in his travels. In America, he saw life from Indian tepees to the White House, and from peasant homes to kings' palaces abroad. Yet, every change in his environment and duties came about quietly and naturally, and through every change he was an efficient, constructive force.

To those who really knew him, he left the most precious of heritages, a heart full of loving and inspiring memories. To the world, he left a great book about the greatest man of his age.

INDEX

Kellogg, Hon. William, 56
Kennedy, James C., 223-24
Kentucky, 123, 125
Know-Nothing party, 41
Koerner, Governor, 124

Lamon, Captain Ward H., 62, 70, 284
Lamon and Black, *Life of Abraham Lincoln...*, 269, 276
Landau, 3
Lane, Jim, 96
Lee, General Robert E., 169-71, 180, 222, 297; Grant's campaign against, 205-6; surrender, 231
Library of Congress, 268, 286, 321
Life of Abraham Lincoln (Howells), 35, 36
Lincoln, Abraham, 5, 10, 168-69, 171, 184-85; schooling, 14; patent, 17; first meeting with Nicolay, Pittsfield, 19, 23; in Springfield, 25, 27; Lincoln-Douglas debates, 27-28, 305-6; first nomination, at Wigwam, Chicago, v, 29-32; 1860 campaign, 33-45; elected President, 44-45; appoints Nicolay private secretary, 34-35, 74-88; anxiety for safety of, 41; visitors, in Springfield, 48-55; interview with Edward Bates, 50-54; reply to Pennsylvania militia, 56-57; Springfield, headquarters in, 58, departure from, 59-62,

offer of mail shirt, 59-60; farewell speech, 61-62; journey to Washington, 59-76, loss of inaugural address, 63-65, description of train, 65, crowds en route, 66-70, change of plans at Baltimore, 68-70, flag-raising, Philadelphia, 69-70, arrival in Washington, 70-71; first inauguration, 71-73, 334; beginning of war, 91-94; call for volunteers, 90, 112; Cabinet, 49-54, 155, 158-61, 200, 277, 300, crisis, 158-61, signatures to pledge, 214, 218; character, 100-2, 105, 299, 300, laughter as outlet, 100, 102, unconsciousness of self, 101, depths of feeling, 101-2, benevolence, 118-19, clemency in court-martial cases, 119-20, 217, personal courage, 120, dignity of office, 144, 161, lack of ceremony, 160-62, faith in God, 306-7, evaluation, 83, 85-86, 114, 344-45; effects of war on, 88, 95-96, 102, 105, 114; visitors, 82-86, 88, 117-18, "public opinion baths," 118, letters, 84, 86-87; varioloid attack, 83; governor's committee, interview with, 104-5; "Garibaldi Guards," review of, 107-8; Bull Run, battle, 110, 111; war duties, signatures, desk work, 113, 119, responsibility, 113; danger of assassination, 120-21;